THE PARVENU PRINCESSES

By the same author
The French Exiles, 1789–1815

THE PARVENU PRINCESSES

The Lives and Loves of Napoleon's Sisters

Margery Weiner

WILLIAM MORROW & COMPANY
New York

 Library of Congress Catalog Card Number 64-22208.

For my sister, Joyce,
this story of sisters
with my love

FOREWORD

It gives me very real pleasure to thank most warmly those people who have so generously given me help in writing this book. To Sir Compton Mackenzie I am particularly indebted for his meticulous reading of the manuscript and much wise advice. My gratitude is also due to Dr. Harold Avery, who untiringly pursued French medical sources concerning Pauline Bonaparte's health, and to him, to Dr. Dick Alexander, Dr. C. S. Cane and Mr. J. R. Armstrong for their assistance in considering her illnesses; to Mr. H. D. Ziman, whose kindly gift of a rare work, *The Revolutionary Plutarch*, opened up unsuspected avenues of research; to my good friend, Raymond Clavreuil, of Paris, always ready to produce the right book at the right moment; to Miss Lois Dwight Cole of William Morrow, Inc., of New York, for editorial advice and tracing for me a recondite source; to Miss Jane Boulenger of John Murray for her indefatigable care in preparing the manuscript for printing; to Professor Giulio Cirri, Director of the Museo Stibbert of Florence, for very kind permission to reproduce the painting by Benvenuti of Felix Baciocchi; to the Earl of Ilchester for kind permission to quote from the *Journal of Henry Fox*, afterwards Lord Holland; to the Vicomte Fleuriot de Langle for his kind permission to quote from letters in private collections of Elisa and Pauline Bonaparte; to Count Gian Battista Spalletti for allowing me to quote from the memoirs of his great-grandmother, Comtesse Rasponi; and finally to Signorina Camilla Roatta of Florence for scholarly and unstinting zeal in finding books, tracing obscure paintings and photographs and much valuable local information.

Very few of the foreign sources I have used exist in an English translation. I have, therefore, made my own translations for which I am willing to accept full responsibility!

CONTENTS

Part One

Part Two

Part Three

ILLUSTRATIONS

between pages 84 and 85

PART ONE

CHAPTER ONE

ELISA, PAULINE AND CAROLINE

' My sister, Elisa, has a masculine mind, a forceful character, noble qualities and outstanding intelligence; she will endure adversity with fortitude. Caroline has been formed by events. As a child we considered her the dunce and Cinderella of the family, but she developed into a very pretty woman and schooled herself to be a clever one; there is good stuff in her, vitiated by a vaulting ambition. Pauline was always probably the most beautiful woman of her time and will, to her end, be the best creature in the world.'

Thus, at St. Helena, Napoleon Bonaparte assessed his three sisters. He had changed his earlier opinion of Elisa and Caroline but about Pauline his feelings had remained constant. Reluctantly her elder and her younger sister would have been obliged to concede that ' he always loved our sister most '. How far does the verdict of posterity agree with Napoleon's?

Virtues and vices alike can be concealed from the world but never from one's family; to no one are strength and weakness laid so bare as to brothers and sisters.

They were born Maria-Anna, Maria-Paola and Maria-Annunziata in Corsica, where their family, Italian in origin, had been settled for several hundred years. Their birth was gentle but their fortune was small, so that they seemed destined for uneventful lives; to marry young, rear large families, perform their religious duties with at least outward piety, and finally to lie peacefully in the churchyard at Ajaccio, leaving no other memorial. Because towards the end of the eighteenth century Corsica had passed from Genoa to France and their surname was Buonaparte their lines fell in other places.

Carlo, their handsome father, was indolent and extravagant. Dress and display absorbed too much of his time and substance for him to have much of either left for the care and maintenance of his family. In spite of her punctual pregnancies it therefore fell to his beautiful wife, Letizia Ramolino, to supplement her husband's deficiencies as head of the household. His energies were expended solely in wringing from his French patrons the maximum benefits for himself and his family, and he was absolved by his success in this direction from making further efforts of his own.

The Buonapartes had thirteen children, of whom only eight survived infancy. Little is recorded of their childhood beyond the normal anecdotes of childish exploits. Few of these stories concern the sisters; in Corsica women were important only for the dowries they brought to a marriage, their fertility, and the number of their male relatives to support the eternal Corsican vendettas, the chief activity of the turbulent island.

Except that it involved him in no expense it was, therefore, unusual that Carlo Buonaparte had sought a nomination for his eldest daughter, Maria-Anna, to the Royal Academy at St. Cyr near Paris. His three eldest sons had already been sent to France to be educated; Joseph to Autun, Napoleon to the military academy at Brienne, and Lucien to Aix. No doubt it was his intention that the two younger boys should follow their example; the future of the two younger girls was, as yet, undecided.

In 1785 Carlo Buonaparte himself took Maria-Anna to Paris but, on his way back to Corsica, he died at Montpellier of a cancer of the stomach, having exhausted himself and his efforts on his children's behalf. There was nothing more he could do for his family. Since he left little fortune the elder children would now have to make their own way in life, while the younger ones would be their responsibility; particularly it would fall to his sons to find the dowries essential if their sisters were to marry suitably.

Maria-Anna was barely eight when she left home, and the

abrupt transition from its happy-go-lucky atmosphere to the semi-military, semi-religious school at St. Cyr was a severe shock to the little girl.

The Royal Academy was still dominated by the stern shade of its foundress, Madame de Maintenon, the morganatic wife of Louis XIV. Her portrait frowned down from every wall on the pupils, all daughters of aristocratic French families. According to Horace Walpole, who had visited St. Cyr in 1769, she was 'not only their foundress, but their saint, and their adoration of her memory quite eclipsed the Virgin Mary'. In the years which elapsed since his visit and Maria-Anna's arrival the school had changed not at all.

At St. Cyr the preservation of the seventeenth-century curriculum, manners and modes had become a superstitious fixation, and the girls were encouraged in stiffness and arrogance rather than in grace and humility. Even the piety inculcated at St. Cyr was exaggerated and, in the event, superficial; once released from its tutelage religion fell away from its pupils like the dropping of a veil. Most prized were regimentation and outward conformity, an arid routine including interminable church services in which the whole school played its part.

Walpole had watched them march 'two by two, each band headed by a nun, orderly to their seats in the chapel, to sing the whole service'. He thought their dress very pretty,

> . . . black, with short aprons of the same, the latter and their stays bound with blue, yellow, red or green, to distinguish the classes, with hair curled and powdered, their coiffure a sort of French round-eared caps, with white tippets, a sort of ruff and a large tucker.

If Marianne de Buonaparté, as she figured on the roster, the daughter of a barely noble Corsican and a 'foreigner', was privileged to form one of the select company of aristocratic young girls, she enjoyed less the unenviable distinction of being the poorest and loneliest among them. Her sole defence against the isolation and inferiority of her position was to exaggerate her hauteur, the better to cloak the wounding knowledge of how little consideration attached to a girl without fortune and family influence. It was her poverty that she felt most keenly.

When her brother, Napoleon, paid one of his rare visits to St. Cyr in company with Madame Permon, a Corsican friend of the family, Marianne came into the parlour, sad and dispirited, and when asked what was amiss burst into tears. At last Madame Permon cajoled the truth from her ; she did not possess the small sum necessary to contribute to a farewell celebration for one of her schoolfellows.

Napoleon's hand went immediately to his pocket but, as he drew it away empty, he reddened with anger and wounded pride. Both sister and brother were stung by their humiliation although Madame Permon kindly gave Marianne the few francs she needed.

By 1792 the Revolution in France had reached a pitch of violence which made it unsafe for Marianne to stay any longer in a royal convent and risk being cut off from Corsica, so her schooldays ended abruptly when she was sixteen. In the autumn of that year Napoleon, now a captain in the army, escorted his sister back to Ajaccio, to a home dimly remembered and to a family virtually strangers.

While Marianne knew only too well that the family was poor, the actual modesty of their means affronted her aristocratic pretensions. She was pleased to be reunited with her family but, after so long a period of institutional life, adjustment to home was difficult ; she felt out of place and missed the ordered regulation of her days, nor was there any outlet for the accomplishments she had so assiduously acquired.

Marianne would have been lonely but for Lucien, the budding poet, dramatist and present firebrand, who had flung himself ardently into the most violent Revolutionary politics. With Lucien, in spite of his Jacobinism, she felt an immediate intellectual affinity. For the rest of the family she had little sympathy. It was a waste of time to try to dazzle her little sisters with her grand air and superior education; neither then, nor ever afterwards, were they interested in book learning. Jerome was a mere child, Louis, a year older than herself, the faithful satellite of Napoleon. She did not feel drawn to Joseph, also absorbed in politics, nor to Napoleon, with whom she already had her differences of opinion. Neither of them paid her much attention and no doubt Napoleon's disparagement of her looks in favour of Maria-Paola's was a secret source of mortification to her.

'She was the one of our three sisters,' said Joseph, 'who in character and appearance most resembled Napoleon.'

The similarity in appearance did not flatter Marianne. She was not plain, but in comparison with her sisters she could not be considered good-looking; her figure was angular and her body badly made. Her brilliant, black eyes flashed expressively but her heavy, rather masculine features and rigidity of bearing made her the least physically attractive of a handsome family; a smile would have softened the severity of her expression, but Marianne felt she had little cause to smile.

Marriage was her object, an ambition which was not forwarded by her mother's continual lament about the impossibility of finding dowries for her daughters, nor by Napoleon's project of going to India to return a rich nabob, bringing back good dowries for them. The years were passing and Marianne was disinclined to wait indefinitely for a husband.

Although the family exerted itself to find her a *parti*, the task was difficult, both on account of the uncertainty of the future and the smallness of her portion. One or two half-hearted suitors made advances in her direction but did not linger; one, an admiral, Truguet, tacked towards her but soon set full sail and sheered off into the blue.

In 1793 revolt against its French rulers flared up in the island, led by Paoli, the great Corsican patriot whom Lucien denounced as a traitor. This excess of Revolutionary zeal reacted unfortunately on his family. Their situation at home became untenable and the Buonapartes were forced to flee from their native *maquis*, to enter on a period of poverty and privation as refugees in France, driven from one pillar to another post, often with little enough to eat, no moment for arranging a marriage for Marianne.

The family went first to Marseilles, where they may briefly have earned their living as milliners and dressmakers, but so many glosses have been imposed on this period of their lives that it is wiser to discount them all.

About this time the Buonapartes, following Napoleon's example, Frenchified their surname to Bonaparte while the girls adopted less parochial Christian names. Marianne became Elisa, Maria-Paola Pauline, or Paulette in the family circle, and Maria-Annunziata Caroline, but as they moved from place to place along the southern shores of France little else changed for them.

When (for his part in defeating the English at the siege of Toulon in 1793) Napoleon was promoted brigadier-general, and Joseph married a Marseillais heiress, Julie Clary, the family's social and financial position improved without, however, any immediate matrimonial benefit to Elisa, still condemned to wilt under a virginity increasingly onerous. Her anxiety and malaise were increased by the fact that the younger girls were growing up fast, Pauline's loveliness in particular attracting a swarm of admirers, few of them eligible, but suitors nevertheless.

It was unlikely that her younger sister would be allowed to damage Elisa's consequence by marrying first, but she viewed with particular alarm the heady and precocious love affair into which Pauline plunged with Stanislas Fréron, an accomplished charmer of unsavoury reputation, who held an important post in the south of France as emissary of the Convention, the Revolutionary government.

While in her formative years Elisa was subjected to the strict discipline of St. Cyr, Pauline and Caroline were running wild at home with a minimum of education and maternal correction.

In her early childhood Pauline was pure tomboy, noisy, intractable and wilful, fonder of long excursions into the country with an eye to someone's apple orchards than of her lessons. Only one regularity could be counted on with her, that she would return from her escapade dirty, dishevelled and with her dresses torn from tree-climbing. Madame Letizia did little to curb Pauline's waywardness, which was thus allowed to continue unchecked, her impetuous behaviour frequently landing her in situations as awkward to her family as to herself.

Pauline was a loving child who, failing to find in her mother the demonstrative affection she craved, sought it from her brother, Napoleon, who flitted in and out of her childhood during his periods of leave in Corsica. Since they shared the same boisterous sense of fun his gaiety responded to hers, while her naughtiness merely amused him. He was charmed by her beauty and grace, which belied her tomboyish behaviour, and was touched by her affection. To him she gave some of the love due to a father, coupled with a shy hero-worship for the shabby young officer whom even Madame Letizia treated with respect.

Napoleon managed to combine the rôles of indulgent and loving brother and stern moralist, exercising a parental control over his little sister. Since her father's death when she was five he had represented the only masculine authority Pauline could remember; she submitted to his discipline, but to his alone.

Because of the attention she received Pauline's consciousness of her beauty and powers of attraction developed precociously, even before she was wholly aware of them herself. By the time she was sixteen she was a finished flirt; dress and the cultivation of her looks was now of greater importance to her than forbidden apples.

Her youth and beauty titillated Fréron; it was a piquant obligation for him to awaken the passions of a young girl in whom an ardent temperament was, as yet, in germ. He was soon caught in his own net, the flirtation entered on so lightly maturing on both sides into a serious determination to marry, for Pauline had become intoxicated by her subjugation of a man of so much power and sinister prestige.

Either from want of occupation or because it gave her a vicarious satisfaction Elisa helped Pauline to write her love letters since she found composition tiresome, but if Elisa's elegant seventeenth-century prose came oddly as from her pen, the Italian superlatives Pauline used so lavishly were all her own.

'*Ti amo, sempre, et passionnatissimamente, per sempre ti amo, ti amo, amo, amo, amo, amo, si amatissime amante,*' she wrote, a form of expression which evidently pleased her, because it became a recurring feature of all her love letters, compensating by its ardour for lack of style.

Then suddenly Elisa tired of acting as love's amanuensis, resentful, perhaps, that lovers' meetings and passionate kisses were reserved for Pauline while she was left alone in the chillier company of Racine and Corneille.

In any event her aid was now superfluous ; Pauline and Fréron had seemed to be assured of final family approval of their marriage when, without warning, Napoleon withdrew his consent. Was it because he had at last woken up to the gross immorality of Fréron's private life or because his own political importance was increasing while Fréron's was diminishing ?

Pauline, drowned in love, was indifferent to Fréron's morals ; grand passions take no consideration of age or eligibility. Yet it is hazardous to cut the gossamer thread of first love with an axe since passion, suppressed in one direction, may burst out in another ; the damage done to the tender tissues of the heart may be irreparable, the wound apparently healed forever carrying its scars. In dismissing this passion as calf love the Bonaparte family failed to realise its psychological significance in Pauline's life, nor guessed that hereafter she perpetually chased the elusive shadow of a perfect love.

In spite of her near heartbreak Pauline submitted to her brother's will in a pathetic letter, written without assistance from Elisa.

As for me I would rather be unhappy all my life than marry without your consent and bring your curses down on me. If, my dear Napoleon, you, for whom I have always had the most tender affection, could see the tears that your letter has caused me to shed, I believe that even you would be touched.

Napoleon *was* touched. As a man now deeply in love himself he realised what his veto meant to Pauline so, to distract her from her grief, he invited her to visit him, chaperoned on her journey by their uncle, Madame Letizia's half-brother and man-of-all-work to the family, the Abbé Fesch.

After Toulon young General Bonaparte's career had hovered between success and disaster, from which he was saved by the fortunate circumstance of being on the spot when a soldier was needed by the government to suppress unrest in Paris. His readiness to use his guns in the *coup d'état* of 13 Vendémiaire (October 5th), 1795, had not gone unrewarded by the Directory, the new government of France. It was to join the Commander-in-Chief of the Army of Italy that Pauline embarked for Italy.

With a potential rival out of the way Elisa's prospects of marriage improved. Lucien, once again playing the *deus ex machina* in Bonaparte affairs, had made the acquaintance of a fellow-Corsican, Felix Baciocchi, who lodged in the same house in Marseilles where the family, thanks to subsidies from Napoleon, were now settled in some comfort.

Baciocchi belonged to a family allied by marriage to the Bonapartes. His appearance was pleasing, his manner amiable, his insignificance complete, his only sign of individuality a passion for playing the violin. His other disadvantages were his opposition in Corsican politics to the Bonapartes, the fact that, by the age of thirty-five, he had risen to no higher rank in the army than captain, and the modesty of his fortune. His willingness to accept the proposition put to him by Lucien outweighed them all.

It is difficult to determine precisely what attracted him about the marriage or Elisa unless it was that, lacking forcefulness himself, he was drawn to it in her, or perhaps he was so splendidly null that he was flattered that anyone wanted to marry him.

Elisa accepted Baciocchi's offer of marriage thankfully; even if not a brilliant match it was at last an offer. Beneath her arrogant veneer she was essentially shrewd and sensible, as well as highly conscious of the fact that her twentieth birthday had already passed and it was now or perhaps never. It was of vital importance to her to be married, to whom was not of such consequence.

Napoleon seemed determined to put a brake on his sisters' plans. He was already displeased with his mother for allowing the Fréron affair to go so far, disregarding his own share in it, and his displeasure was intensified by her choice for Elisa. Madame Letizia should not have encouraged so unacceptable a suitor; he deplored the opinion she shared with Elisa that any husband was better than no husband.

His attitude seemed to the rest of the family to be that of a dog in a manger. Why should he stand in the way of his sister's marriage when he himself had been unable to bring forward a candidate, and more particularly since he had lately married without informing his mother or seeking her consent?

Madame Letizia was not only affronted by her son's failure to seek her consent to his marriage; she strongly disapproved of his choice.

Napoleon had married a widow with no fortune, who admitted to being five years older than he, which meant that she was probably more. She also had two children, a boy, Eugène, now nearly fifteen, and a girl, Hortense, of thirteen. Not much mathematical ability was needed on Madame Letizia's part to work out that it was highly unlikely that her son's wife would produce the large family so essentially part of Corsican tradition.

Marie-Josèphe-Rose Tascher de la Pagerie was a Creole from Martinique in the West Indies who, on her arrival in France, had married the Vicomte Alexandre de Beauharnais. Since his execution during the Terror and her own release from prison she had supported herself and her children in a way which could not recommend itself to her austere mother-in-law. Conduct above reproach meant more to Madame Letizia than beauty, charm and unrivalled powers of seduction ; also a dowry rather than debts would have made her more welcome as a daughter-in-law.

Had Josephine (as she was called) de Beauharnais possessed any fortune it is unlikely that she would have married young General Bonaparte for whom her feelings were tepid, but he represented security in the life of shifts and uncertainties of which she was tiring. Unfortunately for Josephine, Napoleon's passion for her was too ardent to allow her to remain in Paris, as she had intended while he went campaigning. Reluctantly she was obliged to follow her new husband to the war.

Since Napoleon had presented the family with a *fait accompli* in the matter of his own marriage then they would do the same with Elisa's. Conspiratorially Madame Letizia, Elisa and Lucien, himself lately married to Christine Boyer, decided to ignore him ; the marriage was hurried forward to take place on May 1st, 1797. Yet it was not without some apprehension as to their reception that Madame Letizia, Elisa, Caroline and Jerome set out to join Napoleon in Italy, with the uninvited supercargo, Baciocchi.

The war in which France had been engaged since 1792 was drawing to a close. One by one the states, with the exception of Great Britain and Austria, had sued for peace ; now Austria, too, was entering on peace preliminaries. After a year's brilliant campaign in Italy General Bonaparte had assured France of the rich Austrian provinces in Italy which she coveted to fill the depleted French treasury.

He felt entitled, after his glittering victories at Arcola and Rivoli, to pause and ask the Directory for some rest, 'having acquired more glory than is necessary for happiness'.

The opportunity to relax and invite his family to share in his triumphs was the more welcome to Napoleon because the Bonapartes had dispersed from their home so early that their chances of getting to know one another well had been slight; this gathering was the first occasion in some years of their all being together. Joseph and his wife had joined the party, Louis was serving as aide-de-camp to his brother; only Lucien, always odd man out of the clan, was missing, away in the north on his new duties in the War Department.

For the reunion Napoleon had chosen an ideal setting in the Villa Crivelli at Mombello, a few miles out of Milan along the Como road. The Villa looked out from a hill-top over the green Lombardy plain, whose flatness was broken only by the campaniles of neighbouring villages. Its bell-tower and white marble colonnades guarded by dark, sentinel cypresses, its magnolias, fountains and rockeries, ilex groves and statuary, with a wide, double drive for mounting and descending carriages, made it a luxurious and magnificent country home.

> What memories are evoked by the mention of Mombello, what activity, what grandeur, what hopes and what gaiety! At that time in our lives ambition played a secondary rôle; we thought only of duty and of pleasure. Complete and cordial harmony reigned amongst us all; we were a closely knit fraternity, united against external attack or influence.

So Marmont, Marshal of France, Duc de Raguse, recalled the eager young officer he had been, one among many in the suite of the General little older than themselves, all exhilarated by their youth and success, and panting for fresh opportunities to cover themselves with glory. But these young officers, and the rest of the jostling company which crowded out to Mombello, knew themselves to be mere walkers-on in the drama in which all the spotlights were directed full on the spare, small figure of General Bonaparte, confidently holding the centre of the stage.

Already General Bonaparte knew that a great man must not only be great, but must be seen to be great, and that a ruler—and he was in effect the ruler of northern Italy—must assume visible signs of his power, so at the Palazzo Serbelloni in Milan and at the Villa Crivelli at Mombello he had established what was virtually a court, where already a strict etiquette prevailed, casting long shadows of the future over sunlit days, '*Déjà Napoléon perçait sous Bonaparte!*'

Madame Letizia found on arrival at Mombello that her anxiety was exaggerated. Napoleon was less displeased with Elisa's marriage itself than with the flouting of his authority, because his feelings towards her were cool. 'There was never any intimacy between us,' he recalled much later, 'our characters were too opposed.' Clearly he did not share Joseph's opinion of Elisa.

Here at Mombello Elisa's haughtiness stood out in contrast with Josephine's graciousness, a fault of which Elisa herself was unconscious, insulated from criticism by her satisfaction with her marriage. She strutted through the gaieties of Mombello, the balls, receptions and excursions to the lakes, with all her natural self-consequence.

Elisa, in fact, cared little for her brother's approbation, anxious only about her dowry nor, when she saw the evidence of his power, did she appear to regret not waiting for him to propose a more brilliant match. In Baciocchi she had found a husband who would not overshadow her, and who showed a dutiful respect for her attainments.

With Elisa's problems settled Madame Letizia relaxed, giving herself over to the enjoyment of her maternal satisfaction in her son's achievement, which was regarded more subjectively by the rest of the family. They were ready to applaud and profit by his good fortune so long as he did not consider himself their superior; in a family even its most brilliant member is merely a brother or sister to the rest, and it was inherent in the Corsican tradition that the individual exists for the good of the clan. It is possible that at this time Napoleon still shared this conviction, valuing his success less on his own account than for the opportunity it gave him of establishing his family and making provision for their future.

Nevertheless, an atmosphere of tension had been created as soon as Madame Letizia's contingent arrived because of Josephine, whom they were meeting for the first time. The aura of a court and the habits of society were familiar to her, a milieu in which the proud, unbending but provincial Bonapartes were at a disadvantage. They disliked Josephine's intrusion into the clan and had been predisposed to dislike her but, when faced with her cool elegance, their resentment increased because she made them conscious of their social insufficiency.

Even though Madame Letizia stiffly arrogated to herself an equal share in doing the honours the family could make no apparent inroad into Josephine's exquisite social façade while she, who had been languidly ready to accept the Bonapartes, was dismayed by the actuality of the pack. Mutual antipathy soon deepened into real hatred and here at the Villa Crivelli at Mombello began the feud between Bonaparte and Beauharnais, which developed into a bitter Corsician vendetta so decisively influencing the destinies of them all.

Pauline's particular animosity, which sprang from her belief that Josephine's intervention had made Napoleon veto her marriage to Fréron, had already had six months to mature, with jealousy added to enmity. In spite of her superior beauty Pauline envied Josephine's finished manners, social graces and elegant wardrobe, while on her side Josephine, already sensitive about her age and her growing children, found it hard to forgive Pauline's youth. She thought her self-will abominable, and particularly disliked Napoleon's indulgence towards his sister when, at some hoydenish trick, the gleam in his eye belied his words of reproof.

As she flirted her way through her brother's entourage Pauline seemed to have forgotten Fréron, but her brother, more concerned with her future than he had been with Elisa's, was thinking seriously of marriage for her, although it was not always easy to reconcile her preferences with a suitable alliance.

Andoche Junot, Napoleon's earliest and most faithful brother-in-arms, madly in love with Pauline, had been kindly but firmly rejected because of his lack of fortune; Madame Permon had laughed away Napoleon's offer of *la jolie Paulette* for her son;

and there had been other offers besides Fréron's. Undeterred by past failures Napoleon pursued his plans.

> While we were at Mombello, [wrote Marmont] General Bonaparte was concerned with marrying off his second sister, Paulette. He offered her to me through his brother, Joseph. She was charming and the beauty of her face and figure almost ideal in their perfection yet, in spite of all the attractions and advantages such an alliance presented, I refused it, giving up a marriage which would have had an immense influence on my career.

Clearly marriage with Pauline offered Marmont no prospect of realising the kind of warm, domestic felicity of which he dreamed ; it was one thing to flirt with General Bonaparte's delightful sister and quite another to marry her.

Napoleon's next choice was happier, or perhaps it would be more accurate to say that Victor Emmanuel Leclerc had already chosen himself, because he had fallen passionately in love with Pauline a few years earlier.

Leclerc was a better financial proposition than Pauline's other suitors as his family were rich millers from Pontoise. Since he came from northern France it might be expected that his cooler blood would temper Pauline's hot southern temperament. Leclerc was good-looking although small in stature, bearing, apart from his fairness, a strong resemblance to Bonaparte. His military ability was not outstanding but he was a good subordinate and, moreover, accounted one of the most cultivated generals in the French army—a distinction which, if unimportant to Pauline, was valued by her brother.

Pauline shared Napoleon's anxiety about marriage and, since love was vital to her nature, she promptly fell in love with Leclerc.

Napoleon was now prepared to barter his formal consent to Elisa's marriage, which in practical terms meant settling the amount of her dowry, against his mother's approval of his choice for Pauline. When Pauline and Leclerc received the Church's blessing on their civil wedding in the domed chapel of the Villa Crivelli, Elisa and Baciocchi were allowed to receive it at the same time.

A silent but by no means passive spectator of all this matrimonial activity was Caroline Bonaparte who, as the youngest sister, had inevitably been regarded as ' the dunce and Cinderella ' of the family, although her growing prettiness and the firmness and determination of her character were fast proving the family's assessment wrong.

Caroline had gained a precocious maturity from watching Pauline's flirtations ; if the family still discounted her as a child she was sufficiently adult by the time she arrived in Italy to have made up her mind about many things, and primarily that her future was to be a brilliant one to compensate for the lean years.

More perspicacious than the rest of her family, she saw how Josephine could serve her ends since, young though she was, she already knew what those ends were. Caroline liked Josephine no more than her family did, but at sixteen she knew she would have to exercise much patience before she was old and experienced enough to meet her sister-in-law on her own ground ; in the meantime, by showing attention to his wife, she would bring herself to her brother's notice and earn his gratitude.

From her lowly place at the tail end of the family Caroline was not in the least dazzled by her elder brother's success ; he was to her merely the brother who had as yet taken no interest in her. She would have needed singular prescience to see even in the General Bonaparte of 1797, regarded by the world at large as the conqueror of Italy, the saviour of the Republic and the bright star rising on the French horizon, the master of Europe and Emperor of the French.

Caroline did not believe that her brother's achievements need be unique nor that they could not be equalled or even surpassed by someone in his entourage, so coolly she assessed the potentialities of his staff ; she had no intention of making Pauline's mistake of attaching herself to a Fréron. It did not take her long to find what she was seeking. Joachim Murat was not easily overlooked.

Over six feet tall, Murat's lithe body showed off to advantage in the eccentric uniforms he affected and he was always distinguishable, on or off the field, by the white heron's plume topping the extravagant feathers in his hat, the *panache blanc* which he wore like that other redoubtable Gascon, Henri IV.

Murat was not handsome. His features, though strong, were coarse, while his cleft chin and sensual mouth gave clear indication of self-indulgence, but his smile had great charm and the blue eyes lighting up his dark complexion and luxuriant mop and whiskers of jet-black curls combined to make him an arresting figure.

He came from the Quercy, that enchanting country of wooded limestone hills and deep valleys between the rivers Lot and Dordogne. His father kept an inn in the village of La Bastide-Fortunière (now La Bastide-Murat) near the ancient city of Cahors.

Intended for the Church, Joachim Murat was too turbulent to settle down in a seminary and on impulse he ran away to join the Army where, because of his plebeian origins, his rapid progress would have been blocked at non-commissioned rank but for the Revolution.

Murat was not slow to profess the most violent Revolutionary principles in the interests of his career; political opportunism, coupled with his very real genius as a cavalryman, soon gave effect to his boast, 'at my age and with my courage and military talents I can go further'. Now, at thirty, he was a general in the Army of Italy and aide-de-camp to the Commander-in-Chief.

His facile Gascon tongue, his effervescent personality, his dash and impudence, all combined to dazzle, and he prided himself on his successes in the boudoir no less than on his victories in the field although, strangely enough, it was to Caroline's reason as the man most likely to outstrip her brother that he appealed first. Then, quite simply, she fell in love with him.

Murat was flattered and then seduced by the decided preference shown him by the rose-pink and white sister of the general for whom he professed so much love and admiration, but no doubt even he was surprised when the charming flirtation matured on both sides into a serious passion, and he fell deeply in love with Caroline.

The association was viewed with displeasure by Napoleon, his disapproval not entirely due to the fact that Murat had boasted too loudly of Josephine's kindness to him, which had exceeded the limits of what one of her husband's staff might reasonably expect. Murat was known as an intriguer and Napoleon despised him as a womaniser.

'How many mistakes Murat has made,' he exclaimed scornfully, 'in order to establish his quarters where there are women!'

So the nascent romance was coldly forbidden although Caroline and Murat considered themselves betrothed. Repeatedly Napoleon told her that she would regret it if she insisted on marrying Murat, pointing out his deficiencies in education which stood out in sharper relief against Leclerc's culture. In time, he warned her, she would come to realise what Murat's lack of behaviour and standards of conduct meant in a ménage, but to all these arguments Caroline remained impervious, while his final shot, inexcusable in so brilliant an artilleryman, fell wide of the mark.

The evident coarseness and sensuality of Murat's temperament repelled Napoleon, himself fundamentally prudish. His ultimate deterrent advice to Caroline was that she would be nauseated when Murat brought cavalry tactics into the bedroom for he was 'a man prodigious in love'.

'One day you will find what it is to sleep with a man who has no notion of behaviour when, without your chemise, you find yourself alone with him and the man will be there in all his nakedness.'

Rather than frightening Caroline this prospect titillated the imagination of an ardent adolescent, whose sexual curiosity had been awakened by Pauline's confidences and more strongly aroused by Murat's courtship. His physical attraction and her determination to marry him were only thereby strengthened; while it was obvious that his military capacity was far superior to that of Elisa's stupid Baciocchi or Pauline's plodding Leclerc.

The argument was cut short when Napoleon decided that Caroline must be sent to school but, since he was gratified by the success of his remedy to cure Pauline of her infatuation, he was convinced that a change of scene for Caroline also would bring about a change of heart. He therefore allowed her to accompany Joseph to Rome before going to school in Paris.

The interlude was over; the Villa Crivelli had played its decisive part in the lives of Pauline and Caroline. They never returned to Mombello.

For over a hundred years now its patrician owners have abandoned the Villa. The great salons are peeled of their magnificence, the shaded walks and orangery deserted; the strident city of Milan has encroached on its solitude and the Villa Crivelli, hemmed in within its suburbs, now houses the city's insane.

Is it fanciful to imagine that the new occupants, with the hyper-sensitive perception of the deranged, at times glimpse white dresses floating through the ilexes, hear the silvery laugh of the woman who once presided over the gaieties of the Villa, and see a beautiful girl poke out her irreverent tongue at the great ones of the earth behind their backs?

Do they catch echoes still hanging on the air of passionate vows exchanged by a pretty pink-and-white child and her dashing cavalier? Do they hear the clank of ghostly swords and sharp words of command as a little man, dressed in the dark blue uniform laced with gold of a general in the Army of the French Republic, dismounts from his charger, his eyes roving beyond the confines of Mombello to vaster horizons?

Perhaps they see the shades of a family at the beginning of its pride and good fortune, those Corsicans who here began their wild adventure. Even madmen would not see a future overstepping the bounds of reason.

CHAPTER TWO

MADEMOISELLE CAROLINE BONAPARTE, MADAME LECLERC

Joseph Bonaparte's nomination as French Ambassador in Rome had been secured by Napoleon's influence, not his own merits. Although the eldest he had abrogated his rights as head of the family to his younger brother, but he was still able to enjoy the privileges of seniority without its obligations. He could thus indulge Caroline, of whom he was fond, without having to control her.

It was pleasanter by far for Caroline to be with Joseph than to return with her mother and Elisa to Corsica, or to stay with Pauline in Milan, where Leclerc now held the post of Deputy Chief of Staff to the Army of Italy; it was infinitely better than remaining with Josephine and Napoleon, who had been recalled to France after the signature of peace with Austria at Campo Formio in October, 1797. Going to Paris with him would have meant instant school.

In Rome Caroline made the most of her liberty, her social success the greater because no sisters shared the limelight, nor did Joseph's wife, Julie, a gentle creature who effaced herself throughout life, interfere with her pleasures.

Even though Caroline was enjoying her new triumphs Napoleon's complacency about the efficacy of his cure was ill-founded; he judged her by Pauline, who always yielded to his wishes if she found she could not shake his will. He had yet to discover that Caroline, still very much an unknown quantity, was cast in a different mould. She clung tenaciously to the idea of marrying Murat although he, still with the Army in northern Italy, and with a couple of mistresses in tow, was not noticeably sighing for her, seeming content to let time and *her* determination work out their joint future.

Six months after the Bonapartes arrived in Rome the French Embassy party was increased by the arrival of Julie's mother, Madame Clary, and her younger daughter, Désirée, who had once hoped to marry Napoleon, who now destined her for General Duphot. The two girls were not together long enough for Caroline to find a rival in Désirée. Only a few weeks after Désirée's coming Duphot was killed on the steps of the French Embassy by the Roman mob, rioting at French inspiration against Papal rule.

For both young girls it was a terrifying experience; in the blood which spattered Désirée's gown was written Caroline's first adult lesson in the realities of politics.

Next day Joseph, never distinguished for his physical courage, scooped up bag and baggage, sister and sister-in-law, and hastily left Rome to return to Paris.

It was a melancholy satisfaction to Caroline to go to Paris at last as she was immediately taken by her brother, Lucien, to Madame Campan's school at St. Germain, although taking a girl to school does not mean that she will learn.

In her old age Madame Campan talked about the strange quirks of fate which brought some of her pupils to undreamed-of eminence.

'I must admit that it was very good for us all that we had no suspicion of what was to come, thus their education was the same as that of the other pupils and all were treated alike. They left my school very accomplished, except for one who was extremely intelligent, but whom I was never able to teach anything.'

Was Madame Campan speaking of Caroline, whose eyes were always more firmly fixed on Murat's mental image than on her books? If she was not thinking of him then she was sighing for the happy days of freedom in Rome and its brilliant assemblies, where the plumed troop of young officers deferentially bent their heads to her blonde curls.

How dreary, instead of delicious flirtations and charming compliments, to listen to Madame Campan's endless homilies on the whole duty of woman, of how she should avoid, as being in the worst possible taste, talking in her drawing-room about the details of her fortune and domestic arrangements ! Let women who had not been well brought up talk about carriages and servants, laundry and cookery ! Those who had received a good education should know how things ought to be done and order them so, but that should be all.

Caroline was more concerned with catching the faintest echo of news of Murat than with heeding this excellent advice, but little enough news came her way and soon he was removed far from her orbit.

Bonaparte had been recalled from Italy to take part in the Directory's plan for invading England, but it was a project about which he was unenthusiastic.

'The real moment for preparing this invasion,' he said, 'has passed, perhaps for ever.'

It was the East to which he looked, perhaps recalling his talks with his mother when he had toyed with the idea of going to India to bring back a fortune. Always fascinated by the Orient, Bonaparte persuaded the Directory to change its plan and send an expeditionary force to Egypt. Thence he would push on to India, there defeat the enemy, England, and realise his dream of a French empire in the East.

'I will rouse and arm the whole of Syria. I will march on Damascus and Aleppo, reach Constantinople and overthrow the Turkish Empire. In the Orient I will found a new and great empire which will secure my place in posterity. It may be that I shall return to Paris via Adrianople or Vienna, having there destroyed the House of Austria.'

More even than England, Austria was the arch-enemy; no one believed that the peace signed at Campo Formio would be lasting.

Just before he left Paris in May, 1798, Bonaparte attended a performance of *Macbeth*. Could he, even with his intuitions of his destiny, have conceived any analogy between himself and the Scottish thane, or entertained the wild idea that his sisters might ever play a part in his life comparable with that played by the three weird sisters in that of Macbeth?

Bonaparte would have preferred to relegate Murat to some obscure post with an army of the reserve, but his genius as a cavalry general could not be overlooked, so Murat accompanied him to Egypt. His personal estimate of Murat's character was confirmed when Joachim brought back with him to Paris 'his heroine from Brescia', the Contessa Gerardi, whose eyes Stendhal praised as being the most beautiful in that city. Napoleon may have been reassured about Murat's intentions towards his sister by judging that little Caroline was no rival to the ox-eyed Contessa and that, by keeping Murat with him, he risked no matrimonial *coup d'état* behind his back.

Such a possibility seemed remote to Caroline, drearily waiting at Madame Campan's school to grow up, for time passed slowly. Already Désirée Clary was married to Bernadotte, one of the most able generals of the Republic, while Caroline yawned on the hard benches at St. Germain, wholly indifferent to lessons on how to make her own clothes and mend her lace, convinced that she would never require such skills. She did give her languid attention to lessons in drawing, music and dancing because these accomplishments belonged to the world in which she burned to figure, but she was less interested in instruction on how to administer a household or draw up a budget.

It was gratifying to act the Lady Bountiful and accept the thanks of the poor for the nourishing dishes she had to make and take to them, but these sorties from school were less exciting than the visits she was allowed to pay to her family and friends in Paris where she might glean news of Murat. Her most useful line of communication was obviously Josephine so she cultivated her and her daughter, Hortense, her schoolfellow.

In Egypt Bonaparte pursued his private campaign against Murat, watchful not to encourage his matrimonial ambitions. He could not, however, overlook or abstain from admiring Murat's brilliant exploits in the field, particularly his great success at the battle of Aboukir, which re-established him in Bonaparte's favour—as a cavalry commander if not as a potential brother-in-law.

It is highly unlikely that Murat remained faithful in deed as well as in thought to Caroline, but every victory won by Bonaparte increased Joachim's satisfaction at the prospect of allying himself with the general's family. If there was any correspondence between him and Caroline at this time none has come to light, but he may have chosen an oblique method of sending news which he hoped would somehow percolate to Paris; the letter he wrote home after he had been wounded in the face at Aboukir was scarcely calculated to interest a father.

> 'If in Europe there is some beauty who, after a year's absence, keeps a soft spot for me (the Contessa Gerardi or Caroline ?), the nature of my wound will make terrible inroads on her constancy', he wrote gloomily; then the natural ebullient Murat reasserted himself. 'They assure me I shan't be disfigured in any way, so you can tell these beauties, if there are any, that although Murat will no longer be as handsome as he was, he won't for all that be less valiant in love !'

When Bonaparte's successes on land were nullified by Nelson's victory at the battle of the Nile, and the French Army was virtually cut off in Egypt, even less news got through to France so, as the summer of 1799 wore on, Caroline was fortunate that most of her family had gravitated to Paris.

From Mombello Elisa returned to Corsica with her mother and Baciocchi, for whom Bonaparte had obtained the command of the citadel at Ajaccio, a minor appointment but far superior to any Felix had ever achieved for himself.

While her mother was putting in order the Casa Buonaparte, which had been severely damaged in the Revolutionary troubles, Elisa, her senses gratified and her sensibility soothed, rustled about Ajaccio, kindly condescending to former friends and benefactors. Baciocchi's transfer to Marseilles offered her further opportunities for showing off her married state and prosperity, particularly pleasing in a city where the Bonapartes had once lived on the ration bread of charity.

Soon pregnancy brought her more real satisfaction destined, however, to be short-lived as her son, Felix-Napoleon, born in June, 1798, survived only for six months. Elisa consoled herself for his loss because children were apt to die in infancy. She herself was the third Maria-Anna Bonaparte, although only the first to live. With a complaisant and obliging husband like Baciocchi there would be other children.

After the baby's death Elisa felt she would benefit by a change of scene so, leaving her husband in Marseilles, she went to Paris, where for her the greatest attraction was the presence of Lucien, now playing an active part in politics as deputy for Corsica in the Council of Five Hundred. In the summer of 1799 she was joined by Pauline and soon followed by Madame Letizia so that the whole family, with the exception of Napoleon, was now in Paris.

Pauline's honeymoon months in Italy had been clouded only by Josephine's continued presence. When Napoleon returned to France she regretted his going the less because his wife went with him, leaving Pauline undisputed ' queen ' of Milan. Before they left she whispered to her brother that he might investigate the conduct of one Hippolyte Charles, a charming young dandy for whose society Pauline showed a decided preference and resented the fact that Josephine did too. Charles taught Pauline many valuable social lessons yet she could not but see that the perfection of Josephine's manner, elegance and *ton* still eluded her.

Josephine was forgotten when Pauline became pregnant and her pregnancy did not go well; she was barely eighteen and her frame was not robust. Leclerc, an admirable and adoring husband, was most solicitous and under his anxious eye she spent much of her time lying on a couch, a posture which became habitual when she found how much it suited her. In love with love Pauline may have been but she was also unquestionably in love with her 'little Leclerc', who concentrated all his thoughts and ambitions, his desire for glory and fortune to the sole end of making her happy.

When, in April, 1798, her son was born she was pleased with the accomplishment but, like many young mothers, she did not show much maternal feeling. The child was named Dermide, in compliment to her brother's love of Ossian, a choice undoubtedly made by Leclerc since Pauline was acquainted only with a few stanzas of Petrarch and her knowledge of any other literature was hazy.

Pauline was probably too young for maternity. From the time of Dermide's birth, she was bedevilled with poor health. A difficult confinement left her debilitated and probably with some minor disorder easily rectified nowadays but, without proper treatment, a constant source of malaise and lassitude. It is likely that she suffered from a post-natal inflammation for which contemporary medicine could prescribe only a round of therapeutic waters and baths, recommending in desperate cases baths of beef tea, surely more efficacious to swallow than to wallow in.

Already in these early days of their married life Leclerc was hard put to it to find enough money to gratify Pauline's increasing desire for jewels and dresses so, after certain financial disagreements with his chiefs, he resigned his post in Italy and the young couple went to Paris.

Leclerc had had some success in curbing his wife's exuberance but her lack of the most elementary education rebuked his own culture. Pauline's delight at finding herself in Paris turned to dismay when she discovered that, married woman and mother of a child though she was, she had to join Caroline at Madame Campan's school. During her six months at the school she made rapid progress, which is not surprising since none of the Bonapartes lacked native intelligence, but she showed no signs of becoming a blue stocking.

The military appointments obtained by Leclerc were respectable but not brilliant and none of them offered him the opportunity of making money. From the Army of England, still gathered in Boulogne, he moved to the Army of the West, quartered at Rennes in Brittany. When Pauline could tear herself away from the charms of Paris she followed the drum.

Much of the charm of Parisian society was found by the Bonapartes in the house of Madame Permon; together the Permons and the Bonapartes formed the heart of the Corsican colony in Paris, living virtually in each other's pockets with daily visits on one side or the other.

It is the celebrated memoirs of Laure Permon, who became Madame Andoche Junot and Duchesse d'Abrantès, which tell much about the early Parisian life of the Bonapartes. Elisa she detested and lost no opportunity of making her the target of her satirical pen. She thought Elisa the most disagreeable and touchy person she had ever known, while her literary ambitions and eccentricities laid her open to easy ridicule.

Laure and Caroline, who were of an age, soon became fast friends as Caroline frequently visited the Permons on her exeats from St. Germain. It is pleasing that Laure, who later had small cause to love her, tells us how pretty, how fresh and how good-natured she was at this time, always bubbling over with pleasure at being allowed out of school. Although Madame Permon had not wanted Pauline as a daughter-in-law she was charmed by the pretty creature, spoiling her and indulging her manifold whims, which naturally made her a favourite with Pauline.

To her Madame d'Abrantès is much kinder than to Elisa, although there is always a point of malice in what she writes, understandable when one remembers that Junot, her husband, had been so much in love with Pauline. She piles anecdote on anecdote to show how inconsequential and egocentric Pauline's behaviour and conversation were, not perceiving that Pauline, who was lacking neither in shrewdness nor in common sense, followed a logic of her own, being both generous-hearted and kindly when it did not involve her in too much exertion. To her beauty Madame d'Abrantès always does full justice.

'She really lit up the salon when she came in,' she recollected many years later, Pauline's dazzling appearance at a ball dressed as a faithful copy of a bacchante, her golden ornaments repeating the golden glints in her brown eyes, still fresh in her memory. The occasion was a particularly exciting one for Pauline, who was confident that the dress she wore would immortalise her, not dreaming that her immortality springs from her statue by Canova in which she dispensed with almost all clothing.

This year of 1799 was perhaps the happiest Pauline had yet known as, when she began to test her powers in the crucible of society, she found them to be of high carat value. Some of her success she owed to Josephine since from her she had learnt that one must put oneself out to please and, when she forgot her languishing airs, she did indeed charm.

Other Parisian ladies were less generous in their praise than Madame d'Abrantès. They murmured indignantly about the shameless luxury of a woman who only three years before had not a penny to her name. The Bonapartes already had many enemies and detractors in Parisian society who resented their sudden elevation.

Nothing women said or did interested Pauline, who soon found an excitement greater than arousing their envy. While Leclerc was away she plunged into a triple love affair with three sworn friends and eminent soldiers, Generals Moreau, Macdonald and Beurnonville. Her object was not solely to gratify her desire to be adored but also, while concealing from each that she was having an affair with the other two, naughtily to undermine their mutual regard. Her triumph was deservedly short-lived since, discovering what was afoot, the three decided that their friendship was more precious than the charms of Madame Pauline, so they doffed their plumed hats to her and left her to her own devices. Thereafter, somewhat chastened, Pauline limited herself to one adorer at a time, at least temporarily.

Why did Pauline, loving and beloved, embark on this adventure?

The immediate causes were almost certainly idleness, pure mischief and the piquancy of the enterprise, but the fundamental reason must be sought elsewhere.

Pauline had no natural moral sense and her mother had clearly failed to inculcate in her those principles of conduct or religion which were lacking; without Elisa's intellectual interests or Caroline's ambition, her only standards were those of her own whims. In addition, her father's death when she was a child, and the subsequent vicissitudes of her family, had deprived her of a sense of security. The only constant in her shifting world was her own beauty, but of that constant she needed continual reassurance, whether she found it in narcissistic admiration or in the eyes of men.

Unfortunately Pauline's ignorance of society and its cruelty made her unaware of the vulnerability of a lovely woman to gossip, or of the necessity for circumspection in her conduct; the affair of the three generals was soon whispered about in Paris and the whispers eagerly taken up by scandal sheets on both sides of the Channel.

According to these slimy publications Pauline was merely walking along a well-trodden path, having lived from early youth as a courtesan given over to prostitution in the brothel kept by her mother—and much more nauseous matter of the same kind. It was not long before all the Bonapartes were the victims of an unremitting campaign of vilification, which increased in ferocity and scurrility, although harping always on the same monotonous theme of the viciousness and immorality of the Bonaparte brothers and the corruption and licentiousness of their sisters.

Pauline neither realised nor cared that her amusing pastime did not appear as such to others. Had Napoleon been in Paris it would certainly not have gone so far, but he was still in Egypt and more nearly affected by the news that Josephine had completely lost her head and was living openly at Malmaison with Hippolyte Charles. To flaunt such an association would at any time have been ill-advised; with the Bonaparte vultures eager to pick her bones it was pure folly.

Napoleon's mind was now seriously bent on divorce, although it was as much the precarious situation of the government as of his marriage which inspired him to return to France with the determination of saving his country's as well as his personal honour. His failure to achieve his grandiose project of founding an empire in the East induced the belief that he had missed his destiny, although the situation in France now suggested that, after all, that destiny might be in Europe.

Nelson's victory at the Nile had raised the hopes of France's enemies that her final annihilation was in sight. In 1799 war broke out again in Europe which lasted, as these hopes were continually dashed, until 1815, with only temporary periods of peace.

The new campaign opened badly for France with reverses at the hands of the Austrians and the Russians. At home threats of a royalist rising, combined with a resurgence of extremism, rendered the Directory's position increasingly insecure. For the liberty, equality and fraternity of the vernal Republic the Directory had substituted corruption, confusion and chaos, surviving chiefly because of military success; when success turned to defeat the Directory was left with no credit on which to draw, bankrupt morally as well as financially. France, which longed for stability at home and peace abroad, saw Bonaparte as its only hope; no other public figure could approach him in prestige. On his return he and the country entered into a liaison which he, at least, had every intention of regularising at the earliest possible opportunity.

Napoleon's political projects were of less immediate concern to his brothers and sisters than the future of their family life as they plotted their first concerted attack on Josephine. Familiarity with their sister-in-law had made them only more determined to secure her expulsion from the clan. Their sustained malevolence is hard to understand except that they saw her and her children as a threat to their exclusive possession of their brother's affections and patronage.

When Napoleon succumbed to the superior force of Josephine's seduction the amateur strategists retired, the battle lost almost before it was joined. It was, however, a retirement not a rout and they re-grouped their forces to await a more favourable tactical occasion.

Once his domestic affairs were settled Bonaparte was ready to act again as his country's saviour, his opportunity arising from the well-known fact that the policy of pursuing war abroad to divert attention from deteriorating conditions at home inevitably leads to the generals, and not the politicians, becoming the decisive factor in a country's fortunes.

For three weeks after Bonaparte's landing in France in October, 1799, there was hurried plotting to counter an alleged terrorist conspiracy, which was to be the cause of the projected *coup d'état.* On 18 Brumaire (November 9th) the conspirators decided to act.

Supported by troops, Bonaparte went to the legislature and denounced the mismanagement of the country's affairs but, faced with a body of civilians, he lost his head. It was only with the aid of Lucien, who presided over the Assembly, and of the grenadiers, that the day was won.

Bonaparte's fellow-plotters were cruelly deceived; far from using his shoulders on which to climb to power they found themselves used as a ladder to support his elevation. The Directory had been overthrown, but in the Consulate, which succeeded it, it was Napoleon Bonaparte as First Consul who became the ruler of France.

Both in the conspiracy and its consummation it was Lucien who played the decisive rôle, a part for which his brother never entirely forgave him. Napoleon did not share his family's view that he was first among equals and, fond though he might be, he was not fond enough to bear a brother near the throne, still less a brother-in-law.

Although Murat, supported by Leclerc and even Baciocchi, gave signal service in chasing the opposition into oblivion with his grenadiers, Bonaparte was still unwilling to give him his sister as a wife, but he was fighting a rearguard action against her insistence.

Caroline learned of the *coup d'état* by a thunderous knocking on Madame Campan's door late at night, which scandalized the whole household. It was to announce a message from Murat which said with more dramatics than truth,

'Bonaparte and Murat have saved France!'

Caroline believed her lover's braggadocio. Having chosen him as being capable of rising to the greatest heights here was confirmation of her judgment—the names of Bonaparte and Murat linked in an enterprise of great hazard which had been successful. It was not impossible that one day the rubric might read 'Murat and Bonaparte!' Nothing now was to stand in the way of her marriage to him.

Napoleon was still not ready to cry for quarter, and he lamented to Madame Campan Caroline's determination to have her own way. He believed firmly in *mariages de convenance*, where fortune, family approval and compatibility were of greater importance than inclination; he distrusted what he called 'passing fancies'. His hand was being forced and Caroline was throwing herself away on a man unworthy of the brilliant future he now foresaw even more clearly for himself.

Bitterly he told Madame Campan that he had had other plans.

'Who knows what kind of marriage I might not have arranged for her? She is a silly goose and does not appreciate my position.'

If Napoleon had been able to read the heart and mind of a teenage girl he would have found worse still, a latent disloyalty to himself and the clan which would have shocked profoundly his intense family feeling.

Desperately he tried to retrieve the position, even going so far as to inspire the announcement of Caroline's engagement to General Moreau, one of his leading rivals, but when Moreau, singed by his third of the affair with Pauline, politely rejected the oblique offer of another Bonaparte sister, and Lannes, his other candidate, withdrew, Napoleon had to concede victory to Caroline. She was indebted to his wife for having brought her influence to bear on her husband. Gratified that one member of the formidable family showed her some deference and affection, Josephine insisted that Caroline, 'the child whom my heart has adopted', should be allowed to marry Murat.

Napoleon consoled himself that she was marrying a brave soldier.

'Although where I now stand that is not enough. Destiny must be served.'

It was Caroline's destiny which was served.

Napoleon was present at the signature of the contract but showed his displeasure by absenting himself from the ceremony, which took place in the presence of the rest of the family at Joseph's country home at Mortefontaine near Paris. Murat's own family was not there; in fact he only informed them about the wedding on the day before it took place. As a subtle reminder to his new brother-in-law that there were other generals of merit in France he chose Bernadotte as one of his witnesses.

Murat's part in the *coup d'état* was rewarded with the command of the Consular Guard. He was married in its blue coat faced with white, white kerseymere waistcoat and breeches, a uniform markedly sober when contrasted with the elaborate carnival uniforms he normally affected, which caused Napoleon to dub him scathingly 'the ring-master of the Army'.

Louise Murat, one of Caroline's daughters, has left a description of her mother, based on a portrait painted at the time of her marriage, in which she appeared even younger than her eighteen years.

> She was small rather than tall, a little plump and of a complexion so dazzlingly white that, in evening dress, her shoulders looked as if they were covered in white satin.
>
> My mother's features were not as regular, nor did they have the purity of line which distinguished her elder sister, Pauline, with whom she has often been compared. Pauline looked like a Greek statue in all its perfection but my mother, although she was less perfect, pleased as much and perhaps more than Pauline by her natural grace, her amiability and her elegance. Her eyes were almond-shaped and velvety and her look was soft and sweet. Her hands and feet were tiny and

of a rare perfection and were the things about her most truly beautiful.*

(It was apparently a family saying that the Bonapartes were notable for their tiny and beautiful hands and feet, their bad handwriting and their lack of musical talent.)

Everyone who knew Caroline emphasised the quality of her complexion. Her great defect was that her head was too large, and her neck too short, for her body and as she got older she looked top-heavy. Now she was wholly fresh and charming so that when, after an absence of two years, Murat saw her again he was delighted that he had remained faithful to his idea of marrying her; Caroline was a bride any man might desire even if her brother was not master of France.

When it became obvious just how powerful Bonaparte had become his family gave themselves over to self-congratulation. It was natural, since they identified themselves as a unit with his achievement, to regard themselves as shareholders in their brother's take-over bid for France, even if they held their holdings on collateral, for the Bonapartes considered that first and foremost they were a family.

His sisters were slower to seize the tremendous scope of the new deal; women tend in general to have a highly personal view of political events, seeing them mainly as they affect themselves, their families and their own aspirations. Although quite indifferent to the issues involved only Pauline was concerned during the actual operation of the *coup d'état* because she was anxious about the safety of her beloved brother.

When news of his triumph was brought to the waiting women of the family Pauline celebrated it by lying on her favourite divan, complacently looking at herself in a mirror and disposing the folds of her dress and cashmere shawl more gracefully. She and her brother had touched a pinnacle of glory—if he was the most powerful man in France she was unquestionably its most beautiful woman.

* *Souvenirs d'Enfance de la Comtesse Rasponi.*

CHAPTER THREE

MADAME BACIOCCHI, MADAME MURAT

It is a commonplace that large families often constitute a closed circle, into which even husbands and wives are admitted only grudgingly; the alliances formed in childhood and youth between brother and sister or brother and brother may persist into maturity, the ties of blood proving stronger than those of marriage.

Elisa's affection for her brother, Lucien, was unquestionably much stronger than her feelings for her husband, nor was Baciocchi able to give her the sympathy and support in her intellectual aspirations that she found in Lucien. She would have preferred that he, rather than Napoleon, had first place in France and shared his disappointment that the vital part he played in 18 Brumaire was rewarded only with the Ministry of the Interior. For herself, to be near him, to participate in his interests, ambitions and distractions, was satisfaction enough.

While Baciocchi alternated between Corsica and Marseilles Elisa settled down with Lucien at his house in the Grande Rue Verte (now the Rue du Faubourg St. Honoré), able to dominate his household since his wife, Christine, was ill and spent much of her time at their country home at Plessis-Chamant.

'My sister, Elisa, I then loved tenderly', wrote Lucien in his memoirs, an affection she deserved for the loving care she gave Christine during her last illness and, after her death, for the motherly way in which she looked after his two little girls.

Rousseau temporarily supplanted the seventeenth century as Elisa's guiding literary influence when brother and sister sentimentally mingled their tears over Christine's imposing tomb, set in an elaborate funerary garden at Plessis, although the romantic scene was somewhat marred by the spectacles Lucien's short sight obliged him to wear.

An Englishman, who met him two years later, described Lucien as ' having in every respect the manners and address of a gentleman, with the countenance of an Italian Jew.' The ex-Jacobin, self-styled Brutus Bonaparte, was young and brash enough to dare to address his august elder brother as ' Jupiter '. Office had not brought him a greater sense of responsibility; he was still opportunist enough to use his political position for his own advantage. His patronage was particularly extended to his preferred intimates, the leading literary figures of Paris, who were gratified by the interest of so powerful a personage as the First Consul's brother.

Lucien as a writer and Elisa as patroness of the arts ran in harness. She was convinced that presiding over a literary salon was the only activity worthy of a woman of education and sensibility. In spite of her delicate health (she was already suffering from stomach disorders and rheumatism), she showed conspicuous physical energy running about Paris to create a reputation as a *salonnière*.

Alas, the nineteenth-century Marquise de Rambouillet came perilously near degenerating into Mrs. Leo Hunter, as she never hesitated to convey directly, or indirectly, to those people whose acquaintance she wished to cultivate, that they should visit her salon. She pushed hard enough to earn Lucien's reproaches for the catholicity of her invitations, which endangered the exclusiveness of their circle, since his own preference was for small gatherings of intimates rather than the large receptions favoured by Elisa, where quantity ousted quality. Finally he persuaded her into his own way of thinking. This inner circle was made up chiefly of elderly men of letters. Although Elisa, and later Caroline, were both very friendly with Madame Récamier, the beauty whose own salon was a centre of opposition to the new régime, Elisa did not care for women, only for men of superior intelligence. Many of them had associations with the *ancien régime*, which gratified the snob in her. The youngest, most gifted and vital among them was the Vicomte René de Chateaubriand, but the guiding spirit of the coterie of poets and dramatists was Louis de Fontanes, who had shared Chateaubriand's exile in England.

The twenty-two-year-old Elisa presided over all the sessions of this mutual admiration society, talking about everything with great force from a sofa, where she lay fanning herself coquettishly while they read their works aloud. For Chateaubriand it must have been a piquant experience to read in the house of the brother of the First Consul those passages from *Atala* and the *Génie du Christianisme* which he had first read to a circle of émigrés in his London garret. Lucien's house was more elegant and the food superior to the starvation fare in London, but there he was not obliged to pay polite attention to his host's theatrical declamation of his own bad verse, undeterred by the presence of his literary betters.

To Elisa Chateaubriand was obliged for a signal service, about which he is strangely silent in the *Mémoires d'Outre-Tombe.* It is Bourrienne, Napoleon's former school-fellow and sometime secretary, who recalls a visit paid by Madame Baciocchi to Bonaparte, when she asked him to read the small volume she carried.

At first he brushed it aside but, hearing that the author was Chateaubriand, agreed to read it and, when Elisa solicited the erasure of his name from the list of émigrés, he said immediately to Bourrienne,

'Write to Fouché to erase his name from the list.'

Elisa may have wished to pursue her friendship further with Chateaubriand, whose wild good looks and romantic melancholy were most attractive to women, but his affections were always bespoken. It was with Fontanes that a relationship developed so ardent that for the rest of their lives he was always 'full of admiration and in a state of adoration'.

Laure Permon could not understand why Fontanes with his wit, charm and elegant social graces attached himself to Madame Baciocchi. Perhaps her youth, her vitality and her dynamic personality attracted him, or he may have found her asperity stimulating. It might be cynical to recall the advantages to a returned émigré, whose position was by no means assured, of a close connection with Bonaparte's sister.

Neither Pauline nor Caroline shared Elisa's lofty pursuits, Pauline because she was passionately absorbed in her own cult, the perfection of her person and its adornments, Caroline because her marriage took her into her husband's world of action. Where Elisa led Baciocchi trailed behind but, as a young bride, Caroline was content to follow Murat's lead; all her dreams were realised in marriage and her happiness made nonsense of her brother's forebodings.

Caroline must, after all, have paid some heed to Madame Campan's teaching because the dinners she gave at her new home, the ci-devant Hotel de Brionne in the Cour des Tuileries, were notable enough to win the approval of the Second Consul, Cambacérès, the arch-gourmet who ate his way through his period of office. The handsome Murats were much admired in the new Consular society, especially Caroline, who shone at the many balls held that winter when General Murat, who did not dance, watched her tenderly, proud to hold her fan and tiny gloves.

Caroline herself was a proud observer when Murat deposited the flags won by the Army of Egypt at the Invalides at the same time as a solemn ceremony was held in honour of George Washington. The First Consul had just issued an order of the day to the Consular Guard and to all the troops of the Republic.

> Washington is dead. This great man combated tyranny. He consolidated his country's liberty. His memory will always be dear to the French people, as well as to all the free men in the two hemispheres, and especially to the French soldiers who, like him and his American troops, are fighting for liberty and equality.
>
> The First Consul, therefore, decrees that, for a period of ten days, black crêpe will be draped over all the flags and guidons of the Republic.

Caroline was also present when Murat reviewed the Consular

Guard in the gardens of the Tuileries and at the superb review by her brother of the whole of the Paris garrison at the Champ de Mars, but her honeymoon period ended when Bonaparte left for Italy to redress the parlous military situation and took Murat with him to command the cavalry.

Even had she wished to do so Caroline would not have been allowed to accompany her husband. To ladies petitioning to be permitted to follow their husbands to the war Bonaparte returned the stern answer :

'Example to be followed : Citizeness Bonaparte has remained in Paris.'

In fact a more potent reason than her brother's order kept Caroline in Paris.

'Caroline will shortly make me the happiest of fathers as she has made me the happiest of husbands,' wrote Murat to his 'adorable' mother in his deplorable style.

Wives did not always have such valid reasons for staying at home when their husbands went off to the wars, nor did they always rush to join them when they settled down in winter quarters or with an army of occupation. They were often loath to leave Paris, which had an irresistible fascination for them, and distractions not always innocent.

Pauline showed no inclination to join Leclerc serving with the Army of the Rhine under General Moreau, whose brilliant successes equalled those of Bonaparte. She found ample consolation for her husband's absence in one Lafon, an actor from the Comédie Française. Like other members of her family she was fascinated by the theatre and spent more time in the company of actors and actresses than with her brother's entourage.

Caroline's time was spent more profitably in attendance on Josephine and in studying the reports of Murat's success. It was between the ranks of his cavalry that Bonaparte entered the sullen city of Milan, while for her the victory at Marengo on June 14th, which regained Lombardy for the French, was less a victory for France than for her husband, whose brilliant handling of the cavalry during the battle earned him a sword of honour. As Byron wrote in an astonishingly bad piece of verse:

> While the broken line enlarging,
> Fell or fled along the plain,
> There be sure was MURAT charging . . .

Even Bonaparte, who considered Murat to be a fool off the field, was obliged to recognise his courage and *élan* on it. On his return to Paris at the end of the campaign Murat was given the command of the reserve Army of Dijon, an appointment which he nevertheless considered too minor for a general of his consequence. He sought to wheedle a more important command by flattery, writing, 'My happiness dates only from my marriage and it is to you I owe it,' not the most tactful line to take since he knew of Bonaparte's strong opposition.

Murat's importunities wearied Bonaparte, nor did Joachim understand his brother-in-law's ambivalence: that he blew hot when he needed his genius as a cavalry general, icy when Murat's servility disgusted him. From Dijon Murat was sent early in 1801 to Italy, which took him even farther away from his beloved Caroline, but he was still luckier than Leclerc, bogged down in Germany, and failing to make the progress in the army for which he had hoped.

Uncle Fesch, who constituted himself the family chronicler, wrote to Murat:

> Leclerc would like to follow you: he wants to go to the Army of Italy. He loves glory. But I hope you will force the house of Austria to make peace, that you will come back and that Leclerc will accept the command of Corsica.
>
> Then I should have a nephew at both points of the globe where I should like to spend my days, the winter in Corsica, the summer in Paris, and I should thus always be with my nieces.

Fesch's hopes were not fulfilled; both his nephews by marriage remained where they were, although Murat continued to bombard the First Consul with letters, in which he begged to be allowed to return to Paris, be it for a day or an hour, to see Caroline, only to meet a cold refusal.

While her husband was fretting in Italy Caroline continued to enjoy the round of entertainments which were still so fresh to her, particularly the balls. The Bonapartes were present in full force at the ball given by Madame Permon to celebrate Laure's marriage to General Junot, Pauline as always *la belle des belles* while Caroline concealed her ' rotundity ' in black velvet.

There were days spent at Mortefontaine with Joseph and, on a special occasion there, in October, with all the family to celebrate the signature of that treaty with the United States, still in force today, of which the preamble runs :

> There shall be a firm, inviolable and universal peace and a true and sincere friendship between the French Republic and the United States of America as well as between their two countries, territories, cities and towns, and between their citizens and inhabitants without exception of persons or places.

The fête was brilliant, the *décor* emphasising the friendship between the two countries. The three rooms in which the dinner for 180 guests took place, among them, naturally, Lafayette, were named for the occasion the Union, the Washington and the Franklin, their walls hung with shields and flags, commemorating Lexington, Saratoga and Yorktown. Bonaparte proposed a toast to the shades of the Frenchman and Americans killed on the battlefield for the independence of the new world, while Cambacérès proposed a toast to Washington's successor. Fireworks with set pieces representing the union of France and the United States, a concert and theatrical performances followed the dinner but, in spite of all the lavishness, it was whispered that everything was done very awkwardly and that the Bonapartes had not learned the art of receiving.

Delightful though this round of gaiety was, pleasure was subordinated to Caroline's primary duty of furthering Murat's career and of demonstrating to her brother how worthy they both were of his confidence. Fate sometimes played into her hands.

In December, 1800, Caroline, eight months pregnant, was driving with the other Bonaparte ladies to the opera when a bomb, intended for Bonaparte, who had preceded them, exploded in the Rue St. Nicaise. Caroline, whose condition might have excused hysterics, alone maintained her sangfroid, showing a coolness which earned her brother's approbation. He always warmed to a display of courage and now began to suspect qualities in 'the ugly duckling' which he did not know she possessed.

The dangers Bonaparte and Caroline had escaped stirred Murat to fresh appeals to be recalled to Paris but his letters remained unanswered. Bonaparte was preoccupied with the difficulties caused him by other members of the family. Lucien's literary circus had been meddling in politics; his younger brother's participation in their intrigues precipitated a revulsion of feeling in Bonaparte against his family and a mood now far removed from that of Mombello.

One day he burst out to Roederer, the counsellor of state who received many Bonaparte confidences,

'I have no child, nor do I feel the need or advantage of having one. I have no family feeling.' (An extraordinary statement from one who had all too much.) 'The thing I feared most at Marengo was that one of my brothers might succeed me if I were killed.'

When scandal about money enabled Napoleon to dismiss Lucien from the Ministry of the Interior he was not, therefore, wholly sorry, although he immediately softened the blow by appointing him as ambassador to Spain. Baciocchi, whose sole merit in Napoleon's eyes was that he caused him no trouble except in so far as the mediocrity of his talents frustrated Bonaparte's conscientious efforts to promote him, accompanied Lucien as secretary of embassy.

It was Lucien's departure that Elisa regretted, her grief at losing his company so acute that, even in Josephine's presence at the Tuileries, she was unable to restrain her tears. Furiously she wrote to Joseph, who was one of the French delegates negotiating peace with the Austrians at Lunéville,

> Bonaparte blinds himself. He reads and sees only through his police, his wife and his secretary. That's the pass we're in now! It is up to you to find a remedy.

The year Elisa had spent in Lucien's orbit had been profitable and pleasurable. It had established her as an important literary hostess and through him she had met Fontanes, whose companionship and admiration she valued greatly. She was fortunate in having attached him as death was shrinking her elderly circle, although her restless energy found fresh outlets, one of them the founding of a female literary circle, for whose meetings she devised a fearsome costume which aroused Laure Permon's mirth.

Elisa was quite unconscious that anyone could think her ridiculous, going serenely on her way content with her reincarnation as a seventeenth-century *salonnière* with a noted literary celebrity in her train. If to Laure Permon she was a *précieuse ridicule* Elisa had no doubts that she was a *femme savante.*

Although Elisa missed Lucien greatly there was nevertheless a secret point of satisfaction that he could no longer criticise her. She wrote to him constantly, leaving to her mother the task of writing to Baciocchi. Madame Letizia herself wrote to Lucien that Elisa was the only one of the family who visited her daily, which helped to assuage her anxiety about the family now they were all scattered again. Elisa's own letter is more revealing.

> I don't need to be advised to spend time with my family as I don't let a day go by without seeing Mamma and I've even succeeded in getting her to be very fond of me. I think that after you it is I whom she loves most. You'll agree that I've really made great efforts to reach this point.

But it was in Lucien's heart that Elisa wanted to occupy first place, after his children of course. As for Baciocchi, she wrote airily:

> Do what you like with him. If you think it would be more advantageous for him to go with the Prince of Peace* I am quite agreeable so long as he gets advancement and, what is more important, that he does you credit. You know how anxious I am that he should be noticed.

Then, with an access of compunction, she insisted more strongly on what might be done for him.

> I do wish if there is war that he will distinguish himself and make himself noticed. I don't know what demon of glory agitates me, but I can assure you that all my ambition is limited to his getting himself known.

Still, for Baciocchi there was only a cool embrace while to Lucien Elisa sent a thousand and thousand kisses.

When she was not writing letters or receiving her friends Elisa rode a good deal for she was a fine horsewoman. She was a constant visitor to the theatre in which she took a passionate interest; one of her chief distractions was to act in the amateur theatricals of which all the Bonapartes were so fond. Her views had undergone a great change since Napoleon insisted, in spite of her shocked refusal to go with him, on taking her to the opera for the first time when she was at St. Cyr.

'First of all she closed her eyes then, when she was induced to open them, she was very disconcerted to see so many people. This was by no means the work of the devil or whatever other nonsense she had imagined.'

Elisa also spent much of her time with Caroline whose confinement was drawing near.

From Lunéville Joseph wrote Caroline a charming note:

> It is my hope and desire that we shall all be together again in the spring, when I hope you will be running about as you did when you were thirteen. They say that a young mother reverts to being a child again until she must at last leave

* Manuel Godoy, Spanish statesman and lover of the Queen of Spain.

> childhood to her children—but you are a long way from that sad state. You know, when you have deposited on the grass the *petit paquet* you have been carrying in front of you for nine months, you'll think you've gone back to Madame Campan's and have had a very strange dream for one of your age.
>
> What is no dream, my dear Caroline, is the very lively tenderness I have for you and your baby. Tell him to kiss his mamma and I embrace her also.

When Caroline received this letter she had already deposited her *petit paquet*, for her son, Achille, was born on January 21, 1801. From the moment of his birth he was destined by his parents to fill the empty place in Napoleon's nursery and he was always referred to by Murat in his letters to his brother-in-law as ' your Achille '.

Murat's joy and excitement at becoming a father led to renewed appeals to Bonaparte to be allowed to return to Paris to see his son, appeals which produced the unvarying answer that conjugal and paternal affections took second place to duty. Not only was Murat to remain where he was but he was rebuked for not sending enough money from Italy to the French treasury.

Murat's facile pen covered pages to explain that the country was completely ruined and that he could squeeze no more out of it. Perhaps he was constrained by a sense of guilt that he had done some squeezing on his own account as he cringed,

> Have more confidence in me. Don't treat me like a child. I am sure and I assure you that I am no longer one. It is you who make me timid. Believe me that there is no one who is more attached to you than I am.

Letters in this vein were rarely answered but, when Murat became increasingly exasperated that Caroline lingered in Paris instead of joining him with the child, he wrote again to Bonaparte, begging him to scold Caroline: with all her running about to balls and other gaieties she would fall ill and he would lose his dear, sweet Caroline and Achille his little mother.

It was Fesch who replied, reproving Murat for doubting Caroline's pleasure in seeing him again, but she trembled at her brother's voice and he became impatient when his orders were resisted or anticipated. Murat's letter had distressed her very much: she would already have left for Italy only Achille had just been vaccinated.

'Keep calm, my dear Murat' was Fesch's counsel of perfection to one whose temperament was the reverse of calm. 'I know Caroline's nature and her conduct. She is worthy of your affection and nothing, not even calumny, could have any influence over her.' What was the calumny of which Fesch wrote? Was it connected with Murat or with Caroline herself? It is unlikely that Murat was leading a celibate life in Italy. As Bonaparte said of him with contempt,

'Apparently Murat has to sleep with a woman every night but any woman does for him. Nothing stops him whether she has the pox or not. When one is so easy to please one finds what one needs anywhere, which is indeed, fortunate!'

Since her brother had been at such pains to acquaint her with Murat's nature this in itself must not have unduly troubled Caroline, who by now had some personal acquaintance of his temperament, nor should his amassing a fortune for himself have been the subject of scandal because it was common practice in the army.

On the other hand the scurrilous accusations against Bonaparte and his family were gaining momentum and Maria Edgeworth's testimony proves that many of them were fabricated in England: 'In England many are the tales of scandal that have been related of the Consul and his family.'

Mere immorality was now discarded for the more titillating accusations of incest between brothers and sisters:

> Who shames a scribbler? Break one cobweb through,
> He spins the slight, self-pleasing thread anew;
> Destroy his fib or sophistry in vain,
> The creature's at his dirty work again . . .

These stories, originating or circulating in a country with which France was at war, were no doubt regarded as legitimate political warfare, while in France the First Consul had enough enemies to welcome the noxious odours wafted across the Channel.

An Englishman, who called himself 'The Revolutionary Plutarch', was among the most virulent of the pamphleteers. Ignoring Elisa, whose close association with Lucien might conceivably give rise to slander, he concentrated his venom on Caroline, aiming at her his most deadly arrows. She was '. . . a despot in her house, a tyrant over her lovers and vanity and affectation itself. Liberty is in her mouth, equality in her heart and fraternity in her garters'.

With a fine confusion as to dates and probabilities 'Plutarch' decided that it was during Bonaparte's campaign in Egypt that Caroline (then, of course, safely at school at Madame Campan's), cohabited with her brother, Lucien, and had a child by him.

> When Murat returned to Paris from the Army of Dijon he found the scandalous boasting of his brother-in-law, Lucien, concerning an incestuous intrigue carried on with Madame Murat, the common topic of conversation. Three duels during two months were the alleged consequence and Lucien's removal from the Ministry of the Interior was due, not to his pecuniary misdemeanours, but to Murat's righteous indignation.

Poor, pretty, pink-and-white Caroline, bending adoringly over her child's cot, with no other thought in her head but dress and balls and enjoying all the fun and frolic her eighteen years demanded, had done nothing to merit this vicious attack.

Fesch made no further reference to calumny but reminded Murat that Caroline was young and naturally wanted to join in all the festivities in honour of the peace with Austria which had now been signed at Lunéville.

> Anyway she is by herself all day while the others are enjoying themselves, and nurses her child the whole time.

> Surely you don't expect her to spend the whole night looking at him while he is asleep? Write to her at once and restore her peace of mind and tranquillity.

At last Caroline set off with her son to join Murat in Florence, and Pauline wrote to him an affectionate letter, telling him how sorry she was to see her sister go, but consoling herself with the reflection that it was after all a very natural thing for her to want to join her husband! Although Pauline and Murat had a strong affection for each other, each no doubt recognising a similar temperament in the other, no breath of scandal ever touched them. As an admirer of women Murat had a tenderness for his beautiful sister-in-law, who in her turn appreciated his panache and superabundant masculinity, in such contrast to her quiet and studious Leclerc.

When Caroline arrived at Florence in May Florentine society made much of her and sought her out to hear the latest news and see the latest fashions from Paris. It was a happy time for her except that, as Napoleon had foretold, incompatibilities in temperament between her and Murat were developing after a year and a half of marriage, made more evident by their frequent enforced separations. They still adored each other but Caroline was becoming increasingly aware of the violence of Murat's temper, which he was quite incapable of controlling, and of his faults. It was more than ever necessary for her to pay court to Josephine, to ensure an ally for the *ménage*, as she now began to realise how much those faults irritated her brother.

Josephine, still unsuspecting any ulterior motive, responded with genuine affection to Caroline's advances.

> My dear little sister, I found your sweet letter awaiting me on my return from Plombières, together with the pretty parure of shells.
>
> I was delighted to have this proof that you are thinking of me and to know that you realise, my charming little sister, my tender love for you, for your kind and excellent husband and for dear little Achille. Remember that you will never have a

truer friend nor one who is more attached to you than your sister Josephine.

When Murat at last obtained his desire and was appointed Commander-in-Chief of the Army of Italy it was due to Caroline's tactics rather than his own; his preferment reinforced her conviction that it was she who directed their affairs best.

Soon after the Murats reached Milan, the headquarters of the Army, Caroline found herself again pregnant. She used her pregnancy as an excuse for returning to Paris, feeling the advantage of ascertaining her brother's state of mind with regard to her husband. Yet once again the comedy repeated itself, Murat begging to return to Paris with Caroline and Napoleon again refusing to agree.

Murat had to be content with Fesch's assurances that Caroline was not over-exerting herself and that, although she went to balls, she did not dare to dance, and was keeping well and gay.

In Paris Caroline found that Pauline had once again been ill, with a tertiary fever from which she had now recovered, although she continued to complain about the health which was also of great concern to her family, for they never wrote a letter to one another in which they did not refer to it.

In addition to his own anxiety about Pauline Leclerc was consumed with the desire to emulate the success of his brothers-in-law, always excepting Baciocchi, and to make for himself the fortunes they were amassing. He cast desperately about in every direction for opportunities to enrich himself, ever more febrile since his marriage had presented him with the insoluble problem of keeping abreast of Pauline's demands for the luxury she felt to be due to her beauty.

Disappointed in his attempt to go to Italy, Leclerc wrote to Lucien in Madrid to seek his help. 'If you can find any way of increasing my fortune in Madrid I shall be greatly indebted to you.'

Although Lucien was enriching himself to millionaire point he had nothing to spare for Leclerc, who had perforce to be content with command of the Observation Corps of the Gironde and of the Army of Portugal, from which he returned no richer than when he went; he clearly did not have Murat's talent for squeezing the orange.

During his absence Pauline occupied her restlessness with moving houses, for which she had a mania, in admiring herself and in being seen everywhere but at the Tuileries; if the memory of Fréron had faded, her rancour against Josephine had not.

With Elisa she made common cause as both hoped for some post of real importance for their husbands; Elisa because she wanted Baciocchi to be worthy of her by distinguishing himself, Pauline moved by the desire that Leclerc would make more money for her to spend.

The imminent conclusion of peace with England meant nothing more to Pauline than a renewal of the gaieties which had followed the Peace of Lunéville. She had most probably never heard of San Domingo, France's richest colony over which control had been lost during the Revolution, nor did her brother take her into his confidence about his plan to win it back. If she heard anything of his intention she may have thought vaguely that anything which increased wealth was a good idea, and was very gratified when she learned that Leclerc had been nominated as Captain-General of the island and Commander-in-Chief of the expeditionary force to be sent there.

She was looking forward happily to spending the rich rewards he would obtain when, to her awful consternation, she found that her brother, whose ideal of marital duty for others was very high, intended her to accompany her husband. Was Napoleon really serious in insisting that she leave Paris, her modiste and her milliner and her beloved gewgaws just because he considered a wife's place was with her husband?

Pauline felt herself bitterly ill-used when she found that Napoleon stood firm, and that she must embark on a long and hazardous sea-journey with a small child to go to an island inhabited by Negroes and in a state of insurrection. And what of her health? Caroline had been allowed to return to Paris merely because she was pregnant which was a normal state, while her own health was abnormally and chronically bad. And of what use was it for Napoleon to give her a house if she was not to live in it?

All argument was fruitless. As in the *affaire Fréron* the last word was Napoleon's.

CHAPTER FOUR

SAN DOMINGO

Even if its inspiration was very different, Victor Leclerc's consternation at the order to proceed to San Domingo equalled Pauline's. He appreciated to the full the hazards and difficulties to be overcome and he was unprepared and unwilling to assume the responsibility of restoring French authority in the island where the Negro general, Toussaint l'Ouverture, was in full command. In spite of his pleas, he was not allowed to relinquish the command. It was finally the opportunities dangled in front of him of winning glory and of making money which reconciled him to the inevitable, the hope of renown appealing to him most since, like every other soldier in the French armies, he thirsted for glory.

Pauline, too, responded in the end to a mirage of glory. When it was pointed out to her that, as queen of the island, her position would rival Josephine's, she consented to go after much coaxing and cajoling, which took the practical form of loads and trunkloads of clothes.

At Brest she found a harbour so storm-tossed that, after a week on board ship, the weather was still so bad that the ships could not sail and she disembarked. It was an ominous start to the enterprise. Real heroism on her part was demanded to re-embark and watch the coast recede, knowing that she would not see France again for an indefinite period or land at all for two months.

Pauline was unaware, for he chivalrously kept out of her way, that in another ship of the convoy Stanislas Fréron sailed to take up the miserable appointment of Vice-Consul at San Domingo, a position vastly different from what might have been had he married her.

From the beginning Leclerc's forebodings were justified; he was faced with a task beyond his powers. He had never given proof of outstanding capacity, yet this operation demanded both administrative and military ability of a high order and a faculty for ruse which he did not possess. The immediate arrest and deportation to France of Toussaint roused the blacks to ferocious resistance, in which the advantage ding-donged from one side to the other.

Leclerc's letters and despatches to Napoleon and to the Minister of Marine, who was responsible for the Colonies, tell of initial success soon turning to failure, then of the disease which virtually annihilated his army and doomed the expedition.

Repeatedly he called for men to fill the gaps, for doctors to tend the sick, for food, for clothing for the army and for money, while daily the situation grew more uncontrollable. The government seemed to have abandoned him completely, sending him neither reinforcements nor money, or if flour and medicaments came they were already rotten and had to be thrown into the sea.

Leclerc continued to implore help for himself and for his army. Worse even than neglect by the people at home, and a far greater menace than the Negroes, was the creeping disease.

> I ordered a report on this illness, [he wrote with controlled calm] and it seems that it is what is called yellow fever or the Siamese illness. It begins either with a slight headache or with internal pains and shivering, or it can strike suddenly, but not a fifth of those stricken escape death.

The illness was not contagious; it had no need to be as it struck a great swathe through the white population of San Domingo. Soon 160 men a day were dying and Leclerc had lost half his general officers, but there was worse to come.

> In addition to the illness known as Siamese we have the American yellow fever, which began here two months before its normal time, and we shall still be suffering its ravages for three months.

There was nothing to do but wait and the army waited with Leclerc, every man looking fearfully over his shoulder to see if the scourge was behind him.

Napoleon made up lavishly in words what he did not give in material aid, seeking always to strike the chord which he knew would evoke the greatest response.

> Great national recompense will be accorded to you and to your principal generals, and to the officers and soldiers who have distinguished themselves. Carry out with integrity the business of the Republic which will be grateful to you and will take care of your interests . . .

Hollow words to a man two months away by sail from France, to whom every day brought morning states of the sick and dying. No promises of handfuls of silver and ribbons to stick on their coats could arrest the disease. Only doctors might perhaps have done that, or at least alleviated the suffering of those stricken down, but they would have had to be doctors of experience and courage, doctors whose morale was strong enough to withstand the painful daily sight of so many dying. But the doctors were not sent.

On the edge of despair but still with dignity and moderation, without the bombast and hyperbole Murat would have used, Leclerc continued to plead,

> I know that the French Government cannot make the same financial sacrifice that the English made when they occupied San Domingo, but there is a mean between parsimony and prodigality, without which a general is always helpless.

Occasionally, when he was a little more hopeful, Leclerc wrote cheerfully—he was pleased with Jerome, who had accompanied the flotilla and was now on his way to the United States; he had everything required to make an excellent naval officer. And there were other moments when his pride asserted itself and he begged Bonaparte not to consider him as overwhelmed by events. He would always rise to the occasion, however unpropitious it might be. For Pauline he had nothing but praise.

> 'Madame Leclerc and my child are well. Considering how cruel it is for her to remain in a country where she has before her eyes only the sight of the dead and dying, I urged her to return to France, but under no circumstances would she consent to do so, telling me that she must follow my fortunes, good or ill.' (And he concluded, rather shyly) 'Her presence here is very pleasant for me.'

Not surprisingly, Pauline had fallen ill on her arrival but she overcame her weakness and rallied her courage, rising magnificently to the rigours of life in San Domingo for which no previous experience had prepared her. In spite of all the dangers and difficulties and the handicap of her own temperament, she tried to follow her brother's impeccable advice.

> Remember that fatigue and difficulties are nothing when one shares them with one's husband, and is useful to one's country. Make yourself loved by your thoughtfulness, your affability and by conduct which is irreproachable and never frivolous. We have had some trunks of fashions made up for you and the captain of the *Syrene* will bring them to you. I love you very much. Behave in such a way that everyone about you will be happy and always be worthy of your position.*

Pauline obeyed to the best of her ability, trying to maintain the outward forms of normal life by giving balls and concerts and creating something of a Parisian atmosphere for the forgotten soldiers and their wives. She sent home little gifts but wrote sadly that she received few letters, although every letter she did get from Napoleon strengthened her courage and determination to earn that praise which was of paramount importance to her.

Her brother certainly encouraged her, he loved her, he admired her stoicism but, being Napoleon writing to Pauline, he did not fail to chide nor to remind her that anyone as harassed as Leclerc needed all the kindness and comfort his wife could give him.

* Quoted by Fleuriot de Langle in *La Paolina.*

When Leclerc himself fell ill from exhaustion and misery and wrote to Napoleon, as he had been charged to do, about Pauline's health, it may be that the First Consul's conscience smote him a little because he reiterated his promises of a brilliant future.

> You are on the right road to gaining great glory. The Republic will put you in the way of enjoying a suitable fortune and the friendship I have for you is unalterable.

And by way of home news he added that the island of Elba had been reunited with France and that the French were in possession of Porto Ferraio. An island in the Mediterranean was of small interest to the man on the island in the Caribbean helplessly watching the progress of yellow fever. Leclerc began to feel that he could not hold out much longer. Soon he was dominated by longing to leave San Domingo but not until he could do so with honour. He was no longer influenced by dreams of glory and of fortune, only by the will to survive the dreadful summer at San Domingo. When he wrote home he made his viewpoint clear.

> If the man you send here (to take my place) is not experienced as a soldier and administrator, if he is not a man of character, who desires glory more than fortune, our possession of the colony will be compromised.

His prophetic words were not heeded.

In August, 1801, he reported that Citizen Fréron was dead of the yellow fever, and he recommended his widow and children to the doubtful gratitude of the French government, saying,

> He died a poor man and, although much that is bad has been said about him, I venture to remind you that, as the people's representative with the Army of Italy, he always showed himself good and kindly. He went out of his way in the days of his power to be useful to me, and I should regard as a personal favour the consideration that the government shows his family.

Leclerc expressed himself like a man of honour and a gentleman; he could not have been unaware of the relations between Fréron and Pauline, but Fréron was dead and he himself was still tenuously alive. He rallied himself from his illness to take personal direction of the defence of Cap Haïtien, besieged by the blacks, and this time he sent an order that Pauline and Dermide should withdraw to the ships.

At once Pauline was surrounded by ladies chattering with terror and begging her to leave, but they got from her only the disdainful answer,

'You may go if you wish. You are not the sister of Bonaparte.'

Pauline might wave aside Leclerc's orders, but his soldiers could not do so. Without further ado four grenadiers picked her up in her chair and a small procession set out for the beaches, Dermide perched on the shoulders of a tall soldier and playing with the plumes in his helmet.

As the ladies peered fearfully into the shadows the shrill cries of maddened Negroes were heard in the distance while the blaze of burning buildings lit up the sky, but Pauline remained unconcerned, chatting about her next concert. When, still in her chair, she had been lowered into a boat, an officer rushed up to say that the blacks had been thrown back, she yawned gracefully and asked to be taken home, saying rather smugly,

'I knew very well that I should not go aboard ship.'

Her courage was amply rewarded by her brother's praise:

> I am greatly pleased by the way in which Paulette has conducted herself. She should not fear death since, by dying at her husband's side in the midst of the army, she would die with glory. Everything earthly is evanescent except the impression we make on history.

Pauline's concern with history was small but historians and memorialists have concerned themselves very much with her and with this period of her life. Many of them ask us to believe that, with a sick and overwrought husband, who was strained to the utmost to maintain a semblance of normality, her sole thought was of her own amusement and of a kind of amusement which did her little credit. They reported, they knew for an undeniable fact that Pauline was gaily betraying Leclerc on all sides, not least with Negro generals whom she exhausted in erotic orgies on beds of roses. She revelled in every kind of sensual excitement to match the ardours of the tropical sun and her depravity had no limits:

> She often enjoyed, and even commanded as an amusement, the disgusting sight of mutilated blacks roasted alive, or devoured alive by her husband's faithful allies, the Spanish bloodhounds.

Sense gives the reply.

> Legends have been woven round the life of Leclerc and Pauline Bonaparte, which ring falsely with the situation of the army and the spectacles of death always before their eyes. It is impossible to believe that they spent their lives in gaiety when everyone around them was dying. Were they not too young to be insensible? And by what unexplained phenomenon were they exempt from the devouring fear the epidemic inspired, the fear which claimed as many victims as the fever itself? Why should they alone not have been subject to the influence of the climate, of their isolation from home, of the war and of the dangers they and their child were running?
>
> Pauline gave parties, she received guests, she kept, if one insists on the word, a sort of court at San Domingo, but, in so doing, she was only carrying out her duty as the wife of the commanding general. If she tried to drown herself in gaiety she was at the same time fulfilling her task which was to keep up the morale of the army and of the population. She was not even allowed to appear frightened.*

If the French in San Domingo grasped at such opportunities as

* Paul Roussier: *Lettres du Général Leclerc.*

they found for a moment's oblivion they knew almost for a certainty that tomorrow they would die. With the fever already mounting in them they snatched feverishly at ghostly straws of better times and happier thoughts, but for thousands of them it was only the grim reality they found in their hands.

And now, with the blacks gaining the upper hand, the French government committed the criminal folly of re-establishing slavery in their West Indian possessions, which cut the ground from under Leclerc's feet.

> I have no false step with which to reproach myself here, Citizen Consul, and, if very early on my position deteriorated, the only culprits are the illness which has destroyed my army, the premature re-establishment of slavery in Guadeloupe and newspapers and letters which talk of nothing else.

Then he set down his personal apologia and final testament.

> As for me, I have always served you with devotion. I shall continue to do so and will execute your orders to the letter. I will justify the good opinion you have of me, but I cannot resign myself to staying here another year. Since my arrival I have seen nothing but fires, insurrections, assassinations, the dead and the dying, and nothing can expunge these hideous images from my mind and heart.
>
> I am fighting here against the blacks, against the whites, against poverty and lack of means, even against my army which has lost its courage. When another six months like this have passed I ought to be able to demand some rest.
>
> Madame Leclerc is ill, but she is a model of courage and truly worthy to be your sister.

Five days after Leclerc wrote this letter to Bonaparte, Dr. Peyre, the chief medical officer to the army, diagnosed a slow nervous fever. Pauline and his staff urged him to take some rest but he refused to spare himself so that it was inevitable that he took the 'Siamese illness' from which, in his exhausted state, he had no chance of recovery.

Careless of infection, Pauline sat beside him in a darkened room where the sun penetrated cruelly through the slatted blinds, casting corrugated shadows on the floor. Perhaps they talked of Italy and the cool groves of Mombello and longed for the snow-clad Alps towering over Lake Como where they spent their brief honeymoon.

Pauline was Leclerc's last thought as for so long she had been his first. He sent for his second-in-command to whisper his final orders that Pauline and Dermide were to return to France. Then, his last service to his wife done, on Brumaire 11th, 1802, almost two years after he had helped to bring Bonaparte to power, Victor Emmanuel Leclerc died in San Domingo. Soon afterwards it was lost to France.

He was not buried in the island. When, a week later, Pauline and Dermide embarked for France in the *Swiftsure*, the coffin containing his body was hoisted aboard with them and within it lay Pauline's long, lustrous dark hair which, with a magnificent gesture, she had cut off and laid at his feet.

During her voyage back to France she remained in her cabin, weak, ill and overcome with grief and, when she landed in January, 1803, she was still too ill to accompany the body to Montgobert, their country home, where Leclerc was to be buried.

Leclerc had been promised glory. The promise was fulfilled as he made his last journey with great pomp on a catafalque painted in black and white to simulate marble, festooned with white silk tied up with black ribbons, and drawn by six white horses with black trappings. The laurels were there but they were mingled with cypress and he wore them not on his brow but on his coffin.

Pauline crept into Joseph's new house, the Hôtel Marbeuf in the Rue du Faubourg St. Honoré, there to recover from her illness, her journey and her grief.

'My sister,' said Joseph in his memoirs, 'arrived in Paris with the germs of the illness she contracted at San Domingo,' and round this illness a huge fabric of conjecture has been built on the shifting foundations of rumour and innuendo.

Men like Fouché, the malevolent Minister of Police, who thought he knew everyone's secrets, and Lewis Goldsmith, the arch-traducer of the Bonapartes, did not hesitate to attribute Pauline's illness to her excesses in San Domingo and during her return journey to France.

The story goes that, as soon as San Domingo was left on the horizon, Pauline resumed her association with one General Humbert, who was being repatriated because Leclerc had discovered that he was her lover. Humbert was certainly a womaniser of the worst type but he was, in fact, sent home not on account of his private conduct but because of peculation and extortion, and it has been found that he did not even travel on the same ship as Pauline; but the rumour gained credence.

The sign on which contemporaries seized was the deep and nasty sore which marbled one of her hands, which Fouché, with more spite than medical knowledge, declared 'revealed her incontinence', and the pains she took to conceal it were held to be irrefutable proof that she was aware of its source. Yet it seems unlikely that Pauline, however frivolous and amoral, was unfaithful to Leclerc at San Domingo, indulging selfishly in love affairs which were no more than mere gratification of the senses. His letters are proof enough of her good behaviour and, on the small island, it would have been difficult, if not impossible, to conceal any liaison from him. On her own admission the sore, which made its first appearance on her return voyage, came and went whenever her will was opposed or she was in any way frustrated; her efforts to hide it were due to her distaste for any blemish on her beauty rather than to guilt as to its origin.

Nevertheless Pauline was dogged by whispers about her 'inadmissible illness', although if she were in truth suffering from a social disease it is hard to understand why her brother, Joseph, should have pin-pointed the date of its commencement or why her mother and the rest of her family should have shown such constant and public concern about her poor health.

In recent years a French doctor has made an analysis of

Pauline's illness, reaching virtually the same conclusions as Fouché and Goldsmith. Other doctors, working under the same handicap of no accurate description of the sore, tend to the view that it was hysteric in origin, a nervous eczema which would be a likely complaint for a person of Pauline's temperament.

Another French medical theory which carries some weight is that in San Domingo she may have contracted a tropical fever, an undulant malaria or even a mild form of yellow fever from which she was one of the rare people to recover, although with a system, already impaired by Dermide's birth, considerably undermined. Since she was always thereafter affected by climatic conditions this seems to be a real possibility, while psychologically her obsession with her health may have been intensified by the fear of illness inculcated at San Domingo.

All argument for or against the 'inadmissible illness' is fruitless since there is no absolute evidence one way or the other, nor is there any record of an autopsy after her death which might have provided some proof.

What is certain is that at the age of twenty-two Pauline was a widow with an illness destined to yield to no cure. The security she had gained by her marriage was shattered and her future was in doubt. Lying alone in her bed at the Hôtel Marbeuf Pauline must have been apprehensive as to what her future would be.

CHAPTER FIVE

1802

By 1802 disorder had given way to order, discord to concord, inertia to energy, and a foreign observer remarked that France was invigorated and beyond measure benefited by the Revolution. Stability at home had been strengthened by the series of peace treaties, initiated by the American treaty of 1800, and culminating in the treaty with Great Britain signed at Amiens in March, 1802.

The dove might have superseded the cock as the national emblem in this *annus mirabilis* of peace after ten years of war —peace with France's enemies, peace with the Church effected by the Concordat with the Pope, political peace by the general amnesty of the émigrés and the election of Bonaparte as Consul for life with the right to choose his own successor.

The prevailing spirit of peace was noticeably absent from the family life of the Bonapartes and only Pauline, far away in San Domingo, was not involved in their dissensions. Napoleon's mood of disenchantment with his brothers was revived when Lucien returned from Spain, where he had put his time and talents to good use for his personal advantage, for he brought with him not only a peace treaty and the cession of Louisiana to France but also a large fortune and a mistress, the Marquesa de Santa Cruz.

This liaison particularly annoyed the First Consul, who was making a sustained effort to establish a strong moral tone in society and was determined to suppress the decadence which had succeeded the unbridled licence of the Revolution. He called to his aid, as models of social behaviour to be imitated by the uncouth new hierarchy, the aristocrats of the *ancien régime*, now cautiously emerging into the world again. Although they hated him as an upstart, and maintained a steadfast disdain for his parvenu entourage, they were curious to see for themselves what Consular society was like.

The transition from the old to the new order was made easier for them because Josephine Bonaparte belonged to their world. Her charm and grace of manner were invaluable to her husband in effecting that fusion of the old aristocracy of birth with the new aristocracy of achievement which was the foundation stone of his social policy.

It was inevitably a gradual process because an order to don white satin breeches did not automatically turn the coarse and foul-mouthed soldiers of the Revolution into gentlemen; at assemblies the blue bloods still sniggered at the lack of refinement and elegance shown by the wives of these men.

The Bonaparte sisters were not exempt from the sneers but it was their assumption of almost royal airs which most affronted the aristocrats of the Faubourg St. Germain. If they were contemptuous of Pauline's imprudent behaviour it was Elisa's arrogance which they resented most and she was not popular in Parisian society.

To Elisa Lucien's return brought disappointment; their previous intimate association was not renewed since the Marquesa usurped a large part of the place she had held in his life. Nevertheless, it was painful to her to see Lucien made the butt of Napoleon's displeasure, particularly when she was made to share it.

'I no longer love him as a brother,' Lucien flung at Roederer, 'and Joseph is even more tired than I am of the way in which he treats us. My mother trembles every time she has to go to the Tuileries and whenever Elisa goes she is made the object of sneering remarks and comes away crying. At table we're put anywhere, even shoved pell-mell with the aides-de-camp.'

But Lucien got himself into worse trouble for, when he tired of the Marquesa de Santa Cruz, he fell desperately in love with Alexandrine Jouberthon, whose husband had conveniently been sent to San Domingo with Leclerc's expedition.

The exchange of one mistress for another was not in itself the cause of Napoleon's increased anger, but the birth of a son to the couple in 1802. Alexandrine's husband considerately died shortly afterwards which enabled them to marry, but a child legitimised only by the marriage of his parents after his birth could not be countenanced as heir to France.

> 'I did not wish to recognise Lucien's second marriage which flew in the face of every convention and was most immoral. Her conduct was the subject of much scandal and her first child by Lucien was born during her husband's lifetime.'

Napoleon was prepared to forgive Lucien for the price of his abandoning Alexandrine but this he refused to do and withdrew to a semi-retirement at Plessis-Chamant. His brother continued to woo him by heaping distinctions, but not public office, on him, no doubt with the hope that he might be cajoled into a divorce, but he remained impervious as well as to all the family's efforts to promote a reconciliation between the two brothers.

After a year spent in the country Lucien decided to go into voluntary exile in Italy and was soon followed by his mother, who was more angry with Napoleon for causing this split in the family unity than with Lucien for provoking it. Together with her other children she had not yet come to understand the motives which actuated him, nor that it was essential for his authority to be recognised in the family if it was to be recognised by the nation.

Neither Lucien nor Joseph showed any signs of conciliating Napoleon although Joseph did say,

'He was the friend of my childhood and I never wanted him to have cause to complain of me at any time.'

If Parisian society was irritated by the airs of consequence his sisters gave themselves Napoleon was equally annoyed by Joseph's pretensions and his ridiculous attempts to make of Mortefontaine another Versailles.

'*I* was bred in poverty,' he said irritably, 'and like me he was born into very humble circumstances.'

The younger members of the family were more submissive. Leclerc's encouraging reports about Jerome's progress in the Navy pleased his brother while Louis was marrying the woman chosen for him, Josephine's daughter, Hortense. Neither his brother nor her mother appeared to care that bride and bridegroom were equally reluctant, the face of one overcast as he thought of the girl he had been prevented from marrying and the other openly weeping for another man.

Possibly the happiest thing about this thoroughly unhappy occasion was that, at the termination of the ceremony, Murat, who had at last been allowed to return to Paris, surprisingly led Caroline up to the celebrant and asked him to give them the Church's blessing on their civil marriage, a request somewhat inopportunely timed since Caroline was noticeably pregnant with her second child.

In spite of her advanced pregnancy Caroline attended the Te Deum sung to celebrate the promulgation of the Concordat at which she looked charming in a dress to match her complexion made of India muslin, beautifully worked in *broderie anglaise*, over an underdress of rose-coloured satin, and wearing a hat trimmed with tufts of rose-pink feathers.

This ceremony was one of the most splendid and imposing that had taken place since the Revolution and was breathlessly reported for English readers by the *Gentleman's Magazine*.

> The softened light through the painted windows, the grandeur of the vault, the splendour of the tapestry, the waving standards above and the vast assemblage below in rich and diversified costumes, and the two orchestras which provided the solemn music, conducted by Méhul and Cherubini, presented a dazzling spectacle.

An Englishwoman, Anne Plumptre, mingled with the crowd outside Notre Dame and caught the murmurs of admiration as the First Consul's magnificent coach went by, drawn by eight horses, each led by a servant in dark green livery richly embroidered with gold, and escorted by the aides-de-camp on horseback and the Consular Guard. The crowd sighed with satisfaction, 'At last we recognise our own country.'

The day seemed in fact to be what was emphatically termed from the pulpit, 'the day which reconciles France with Europe and France with herself'.

It was perhaps appropriate that the sermon should be preached by the same Archbishop who had preached at Rheims at the coronation of Louis XVI, for it was this splendid occasion which first brought home to people Bonaparte's virtual royalty. His increasing authority was particularly remarked by the numbers of foreigners present in Paris, able to gauge on the spot the advantages for France of reverting to the hereditary principle, the exchange of Bourbons for Bonapartes, of the old for the new order.

Thousands of foreign visitors had flocked to Paris when the peace enabled them to travel abroad again, Russians, Americans, who were much approved as 'good people and natural virtuous republicans', as well as English, eager to see the sights but most of all the man who had so lately been 'the Ogre' and 'the Corsican Tyrant'. Everywhere in Paris the English in particular were treated with marked civility and soon Anglomania was as rampant as in the days of Louis XVI.

The public appearances of Charles James Fox created a furore. At a performance of *Phèdre* he was recognised and the whole audience stood up, shouting 'Fox, Fox!' to the chagrin of the actress who was making her début that evening and was obliged to share the honours with him.

Fox was among those invited to a levée and subsequently to dinner at the Tuileries, where he noticed in the lower apartments busts of himself and Nelson, placed there either by coincidence or diplomacy. Bonaparte entertained a high regard for him:

> I knew his talents by report. I soon recognised his fine character, his good heart, his wide, generous and liberal point of view. He was an ornament to humanity; I loved him.

Fox's considered opinion of Bonaparte was that he was 'a

young man who was a good deal intoxicated with his success and surprising elevation'.

Not all travellers had his opportunities for close contact with the First Consul; they had to content themselves with staring at him from a distance at reviews and parades. The general consensus of opinion was unfavourable for his appearance did not impress. One English visitor went so far as to remark that 'the lineaments of his face bespeak a violent nature, marked with the expression of dark and unruly passions.'

Josephine also came in for her share of disapprobation as her 'drawing-room' was thought by some guests to be cold and insipid, while it was noticed that even her use of rouge failed to conceal the disparity in age between herself and her husband. No one has recorded his opinion of the sisters. Pauline, of course, was not in Paris in 1802, Caroline spent much of the year in Italy and Elisa kept to her own special society.

Fanny Burney, Madame d'Arblay, living modestly at Passy with only one servant, recorded her impressions of Bonaparte whom she saw at a review. She found that he had more the air of a student than of a warrior; that his deeply impressive cast of countenance was marked by a penetrating seriousness and even sadness. She was surprised to observe that he had 'by no means the look to be expected from Bonaparte but rather that of a profoundly studious and contemplative man' and nothing of a commander of enterprising ambition and daring bravery.

When the foreign visitors were not queueing up to gape at the First Consul they went sight-seeing—the Louvre, filled with the spoils of the Italian conquest, being most popular. They went much to theatres, thought poorly of the opera but well of the ballet, admired the gardens of Tivoli and Frascati, found Versailles empty and degraded and the Petit Trianon declined into a tavern, and unanimously condemned the Palais Royal, which Henry Redhead Yorke castigated as:

> A nursery of loathsome vice, that abomination of all virtue and profanation of all religion—infernal sink of iniquity, a

lazar house placed in the middle of a great city, which has reduced the whole of society to degradation and corruption, haunt of pimps, prostitutes, gamblers, licentiousness and cupidity in all its forms.

A more respectable focus of sight-seeing was the Murats' new house, into which they moved that year, the magnificent Hôtel Thélusson, whose furnishing did great credit to Fesch, raised since the Concordat to the dignity of Cardinal, who had supervised it during Caroline's absence in Italy. Money had not been spared to arrange it with elegance and taste, for plenty was forthcoming from Murat's depredations in Italy.

The house itself was superb, particularly the noble grand staircase and a circular room lit by branches of lights held by numbers of white marble statues placed in niches, but it was Caroline's bedroom which was most admired. Extremely elegant and rich, it was hung with green velvet with gold motifs and was large enough to contain four canapés, four armchairs and four chairs, as well as the gilded bed raised on a dais in an alcove. The counterpane of green velvet was embroidered in a design of palm leaves and stars about a great golden cypher. Mirrors lined the walls and doors and reflected the light from great candelabras. All the furniture was made after Egyptian or Grecian models in a combination of mahogany, marble and bronze.

The Murats' villa at Neuilly, which they had lately acquired in addition to their country house at La Motte-Sainte-Héraye, impressed less, the outside being thought ugly and paltry and the surrounding countryside flat and hideous; the inside was not open to view.

Shortly after his second wedding Murat returned to Italy while Caroline remained in Paris to await the birth of her child.

It was Fesch, as usual, who announced the birth of the baby, a daughter, Letizia, who became Murat's idol; she was a big child and Caroline's confinement a very difficult one and she was exhausted after the birth. As for Achille he sulked and would have nothing to do with the new baby, but Caroline had other problems on her mind than the child's tantrums.

Murat's peculations had this time been too flagrant to be overlooked; he was recalled to Paris to be taken to task, although with his habitual adroitness he managed to bluster his way out of the accusations. To complete his rehabilitation Caroline gave a magnificent fête at Neuilly in her brother's honour. Napoleon was very much impressed with her gifts as a hostess and by her powers of organisation, congratulating her warmly on her success, while Murat was allowed to return to Milan completely exonerated of all charges against him.

Before he left he took part in an amusing incident, which might have had dreadful consequences, at Bièvre, the pretty little country estate near Paris which was a wedding gift from Napoleon to Laure Permon and Junot.

Laure, who longed to show her new home to her dear friend, Caroline, arranged a hunting party in honour of the Murats; the ladies were to follow the hunt in a carriage and join the huntsmen at a picnic party in the woods. When the men had left, Laure ordered a young horse, Coco by name, to be harnessed to a tiny buggy and the two young women set off, making a charming picture in their high-waisted muslins and chip hats, Laure's auburn hair and pale skin in delightful contrast to Caroline's blonde curls and rose and white complexion.

Laure flicked a whip about Coco's flanks and shoulders and they went like the wind, but the horse, who had never before been harnessed to a carriage, resented the treatment. As their pace grew wilder Caroline laughed gaily and asked Laure whether she could really drive a horse.

When Laure confessed that she had never yet done so Caroline took the reins herself, but by now Coco was so maddened that he dashed straight for an old sand pit with a sheer drop below with not even a tree to break their fall. As the buggy swayed ever more dangerously it seemed that nothing could save them but they rocked with laughter until, through a cloud of dust, they saw a horseman bent low over the neck of his horse and riding after them as if pursued by all the devils in hell.

'It's Murat!' cried Caroline.

Loath to be deprived for a minute of Caroline's company, Murat had turned back to the house to escort her and had learnt from the distressed servants of their mistress's folly. Waiting only to hear in which direction they had gone he set off in pursuit with all the fire which made him so brilliant a leader of cavalry.

When he at last caught up with the buggy he dashed round it at imminent risk to his own life, wheeled in front of Coco and by consummate courage and force of desperation, stopped him on the very edge of the precipice.

As soon as the carriage was on firm ground General Murat lifted his wife out and smothered her laughing face with kisses then, setting her on her feet, he tenderly drew off her gloves, alternately kissing her fingers and gently slapping her tiny hands.

To Laure he spoke severely; 'I hope Junot will make his displeasure felt with more slaps than kisses!'

This exploit does not figure on Murat's battle honours but it must be counted as one of his greatest equestrian victories.

All too soon serious considerations obtruded into Caroline's life. The news which came after Murat's return to Italy was not reassuring; he was already getting into political difficulties. Caroline felt she must rejoin her husband to prevent his making any more gaffes, although she was reluctant to leave Paris which was at the height of its gaiety. Gayest of all were the gatherings at Malmaison at which the guests formed, although it was not yet so called, the Court of Madame Bonaparte.

> They were like a basket of fresh flowers [wrote Laure d'Abrantès, who herself was one of the young women who formed the group]. All were young, and nearly all pretty, and it was delightful to see this charming band, dressed in white, with garlands on their heads as fresh as their happy

faces, dancing gaily in the salons through which the First Consul strolled with the men with whom he was weighing the destinies of Europe.

Women naturally played an important part in the renaissance of society; it was their demands which were largely instrumental in reviving the moribund luxury trades of France. For the balls, dinners, country excursions and amateur theatricals every woman attended she needed the services of a coiffeur, a shoemaker, a florist, a perfumer and a fan maker. She used up thousands of yards of satin, crêpe, velvet and tulle, and her home had to be embellished with the same luxury as her person so that the craftsmen were hard put to it to meet all the demands on their skills.

Young John Trotter, who had accompanied Charles James Fox to Paris as his secretary, bore witness to the improvements which had taken place since the Revolution.

> The very manners and dress of the inhabitants, recovered from republican rudeness and inelegance, has assumed a better style; not so effeminate and foppish as in the old régime, and not so careless as in the republican period. It is impossible not to feel the general douceur and politeness of manners pervading every class, and everywhere smoothing the path of life.
>
> In society the French are eminently pleasing and the women in point of elegance, vivacity and penetration, seem calculated to render the life of a man a happy dream, in which he discovers flowers at his feet, and a fragrant air continually around him.

Society was enriched not only by a better moral tone and improved manners. As trade revived so did agriculture flourish and, with its revival, the art of good eating, which had almost vanished during the Revolution when the peasants neglected to till the soil, returned. To meet the renewed taste for good food every region of France sent its delicacies to Paris; Périgord its *foie gras* and truffles, Bresse its poultry, nougat came from Montélimar, while the vineyards of Burgundy and Champagne offered their best vintages.

At Cambacérès' table, where the host had to have a hollow carved out of the side of his table to accommodate his paunch, four courses each of sixteen or eighteen dishes were served by fifty or sixty lackeys, dressed in blue frogged with gold. Marvels of the pastry-cook's art graced the tables, harps, lyres, bowers of trellis—work and vines, Venetian gondolas and Athenian ruins and trophies of war, all moulded in delicate white sugar work on tiers of nougat and decorated with garlands of spun sugar or waving palm trees cunningly contrived of green almond paste.

Yet, as social gatherings, Cambacérès' dinners were a failure because conversation was not allowed to interfere with a proper appreciation of the feast. Here all was solemnity in the interests of gastronomy, although in other houses conversation was full of charm and grace. According to Carême, the great chef who presided for ten years over his kitchens, Talleyrand's table was 'graced with wisdom and dressed with grandeur', but the almost perpetual Foreign Minister of France had grown to manhood under the *ancien régime* and was the arch-exponent of the *douceur de vivre*.

A more simple home was that of the American Minister, Robert Livingston, who earned special praise for the plainness and simplicity of his manners and dress and the propriety and dignity with which he represented his Republic. He showed himself to be a very unaffected, natural character and, although he did not keep the style of the great Consular officials, the set who met at his house were considered more sociable than any other in Paris; unfortunately, his own deafness prevented his taking much part in conversation.

In foreign society in Paris much of conversation was concerned with the new régime and, if the women discussed fashions and the latest creations of the great hairdresser, Hippolyte, the men were more interested in talking about the new order and the consequences of Bonaparte's election as Consul for life.

Although this election affected the nation greatly it was not of such immediate interest as to Bonaparte's own family for whom the question of the succession loomed large, giving rise to much speculation as each one considered his own claims paramount.

It was now patent that, even if Josephine drank the therapeutic spas of Europe dry, she would not have any children and, if Napoleon continued his refusal to entertain the idea of divorce, on whom would his choice of a successor fall? It was unthinkable that he would make that choice outside the family but their great fear was that he might select his adopted son, Eugène de Beauharnais.

Given the great importance of seniority in Corsican tradition Joseph was the logical successor, but he had only two daughters and seemed unlikely to have any more children. Moreover he was older and would probably predecease Napoleon.

Lucien had ruled himself out and there remained only Louis and Jerome. For the moment the question officially remained in abeyance but not in the minds of the family. Caroline and Murat continued to press Achille upon Napoleon, certain that his claims could not be overlooked.

CHAPTER SIX

PRINCESS BORGHESE

The problem of the succession was of no personal interest to Pauline; on the contrary it envisaged a time when her beloved brother would no longer be alive, a prospect on which she did not care to dwell. All she wanted on her return to Paris was to rest, to recuperate her forces and drive from her mind the horrors and sorrows through which she had lived.

For several months she remained in Joseph's house, seeing no one and going nowhere, until gradually the memories of despair and desolation faded, her health improved and slowly she began to come back to life. Now once again she began to take an interest in her former preoccupations, her own beauty and its setting. She seems to have made no subsequent reference to the year spent in San Domingo, but plainly, since its consequences remained with her, it never wholly vanished from her consciousness.

According to Laure d'Abrantès Pauline's beauty suffered considerably during her stay in the tropics. She returned faded, even withered; no one who had not known her previously could appreciate just how beautiful she had been.

Fouché, on the other hand, who never hesitated to speak in unflattering terms of his master's sisters, and who roundly described Elisa as haughty, nervous, passionate, dissolute and eaten up with love and ambition, decided that Pauline was even fresher and more brilliant than before!

> This was an unexpected result of the illness from which she was cured by all the treasures of Aesculapius, like those strange flowers which manure causes to grow more beautiful and with brighter colours!

Today it is not easy to seize upon the peculiar quality of Pauline's beauty since none of her portraits justify her reputation as one of the most beautiful women of her time. All of them show the same lissom body, exquisitely moulded mouth and beautiful eyes, but her singular charm, the seduction of her expression and her grace, the bearing, the walk, the way in which she turned her head, which her contemporaries found ravishing, have defied the painters' efforts to communicate to canvas.

In his statue of Pauline as 'Venus Victrix' Canova admittedly exaggerated the classic lines of her features, although around her lips he has allowed to play an earthy smile which recalls the 'strange thoughts, fantastic reveries and exquisite passions' of Mona Lisa.

Nearly all beautiful women are vain of their beauty so that it is carping criticism to reproach Pauline with making such painstaking efforts to preserve hers and to retain the admiration it excited. If she dwelt with beauty there was always the nagging fear that beauty must die. Had Leclerc lived she might, under his influence, have developed more serious interests but he was dead, and now his widow had to take stock of her new position.

She found herself sufficiently well off for he had, after all, amassed enough money to leave her reasonably well provided for and Napoleon made her handsome gifts of money. Characteristically one of the first acts which showed the revival of her interest in life was the purchase of the luxurious carriage of which she had always dreamed, but this in itself was not enough. She could not forever live with Joseph and, when the hôtel neighbouring his, the Hôtel Charost, came into the market, Pauline bought it; the opportunity of setting up house for herself beckoned enticingly.

Possession of a house and carriage cheered her so much that her cure was almost complete. If she was a widow then she would be a merry one; after all life was for living and the living. Continued mourning would not bring back her 'little Leclerc'. Soon she was again deep in the important conferences with the most elegant furnishers in Paris which filled her days, with the brothers Jacob, the cabinet makers, with the porcelain factory at Sèvres and with Biennais, who designed exquisite gold- and silver-ware. And, now she was casting her weeds aside, there were dresses and hats and cobweb lingerie to be commanded from Mesdemoiselles Lolive et de Beuvry, Madame Germond and, of course, from Leroy.

Louis-Hippolyte Leroy played a major part in the lives of French women of the Napoleonic era and long afterwards. He knew all the great ladies' secrets—just for whose benefit they ordered diaphanous négligés trimmed with *point d'Angleterre* lace and whose husbands made scenes when his bills arrived. Pauline now had no husband to protest at her extravagance but she herself had a nice sense of what things ought to cost and often chose Leroy's rivals because they were cheaper.

No one could really replace him, however, for as a dressmaker he was a divinity, drawing his inspiration from Greek statuary of gods and goddesses with the help of David and Debucourt, the painters. From their sketches of classical models he evolved his Empire line which outlasted the Empire, the long, graceful skirt, magnificently embroidered, the small, puffed sleeves, the waist under the armpits and the décolletage so low that much of the bosom which should have been tucked into the tiny bodice escaped.

It was to Josephine that Leroy owed his pre-eminence. At some time when the Vicomtesse de Beauharnais was one of the slightly shady stars of Directoire society her path crossed the erstwhile hairdresser's. Thenceforward they rose in the world together, she to her rather shaky position as wife of the most powerful man in France, he to be absolute and unchallenged dictator of fashion.

When her elder brothers observed that Pauline was once again picking up the threads of her life, and that one of the threads was Lafon, they began to cast about for a husband for her because it was clear that, if left to her own devices, she would commit all sorts of follies.

As usual Pauline had her own ideas and her idea of the moment was called Camillo Borghese. She met him first at Joseph's house, was much taken with him and thereafter saw a great deal of him, but just how well she knew him has always been open to question.

Borghese was twenty-eight, a Roman prince bearing one of the most noble names in Italy, and immensely wealthy. As a very young man he had been an ardent Revolutionary, going so far as to enlist in the French army. In appearance he was very distinguished, tall, with abundant crinkly black hair and whiskers, and his air of aristocracy made him 'a welcome addition in a drawing-room'.

Napoleon was indifferent to Borghese's appearance but he seized on the importance of an alliance which would be an asset in his policy of conciliating the Italians, welcoming the opportunity of being able at last to use one of his sisters in the furtherance of his political aims. The French aristocracy thought Pauline very lucky to have the possibility of allying herself with a blue-blooded family while curiously it was the Italians who felt that Borghese would do very well for himself to marry a Bonaparte.

Borghese was attracted by Pauline but alarmed when the question of marriage was broached to him. However, like Mr. Bingley, 'so easily guided that his worth was invaluable', he had a friend, the Chevalier Angiolini, to play his Darcy. Angiolini was an Italian diplomat who had met Joseph Bonaparte in Italy where they became very friendly, so that it did not take long for them to agree that Borghese would be an ideal match for Pauline. Angiolini soon discovered that the pair were very much in love. He decided that they would be happy together, managing finally to persuade Borghese into making an offer of marriage.

Pauline, as impatient to be married now as she had been before, ignored her brother's decree that a widow must wait ten months before re-marrying. She and Borghese were, therefore, married very quietly at Mortefontaine at the end of August, 1803, without informing Napoleon, although the rest of the family were present at the wedding with the exception of Elisa who was again pregnant. (Her hopes that she would not lose this child proved vain for her son lived only a month.)

To console herself for the loss of Lucien's companionship and also of his home to live in Elisa had bought herself a grand new house, the Hôtel Maurepas, in the heart of the Faubourg St. Germain. She was gratified when Baciocchi was at last promoted to the rank of colonel and, with a generous allowance from Napoleon, she was able to receive old friends and many new ones in a style she thought suitable, while the acquisition of a country home near Caroline's at Neuilly put her on the same level as her sisters.

It is a common misconception that the sisters were jealous of each other, that much of their time was spent in puerile efforts to score at the other's expense although little evidence has been produced to prove this jealousy; there was, of course, some rivalry but no more than was natural. Since the sisters' interests and talents were so diverse and their aims in life so different the genius of one never rebuked the other. They were, in fact, quite attached to one another, Pauline and Caroline more so to each other than either to Elisa. Nearer in age and as pretty women they had more in common.

Pauline was not able to conceal her marriage for long from her brother, who was so displeased with her for flouting his decree, that, immediately after the civil marriage in November, he told her she was to leave at once for Rome, with all the familiar adjurations as to behaviour.

> Make yourself remarked for your gentleness and politeness to everyone. More is expected of you than of anyone else. Above all conform to the customs of the country; never denigrate anything; and don't say, 'We do this better in Paris'. Love your husband, make your household happy and don't be frivolous or capricious. You are twenty-four and it is time you were mature and sensible.

However anxious Pauline may have been to follow Napoleon's advice disillusion set early in for her in Rome. Even the beauty of the city and the glories of the Palazzo and Villa Borghese could not reconcile her to a place which she did find inferior in every way to Paris. She showed herself at rather less than her best and called down on her head reproof, which came to her via her Uncle Fesch, who had evidently been telling tales. Although Napoleon told him that he didn't believe half of what he had said he sent his sister a message:

> Tell her that she is no longer as pretty as she was and that, in a few years' time she will be less so, but all her life long she should be good and held in esteem. She ought to cultivate a social poise worthy of her rank, instead of her present bad manners, which would be looked at askance even in the most unruly circles in Paris.

Pauline must have felt herself ill-used to be thus reprimanded. Clearly her brother did not recognise how difficult life had become for her! Camillo's qualities, his wealth and his nobility, could not compensate for his deficiencies, nor did his presence reconcile her for the loss of her family and Paris and to living in a provincial society under the eye of a severe mother-in-law.

Poor Borghese was categorised for all time by Lamartine as 'one born to enjoy and make others enjoy, but not to govern, an effeminate man, an indulgent husband and a colourless prince'.

In these early months of marriage Borghese was not quite such an indulgent husband. Even before the couple left Paris he was complaining about Pauline to Angiolini, who soothed him with sound advice.

> In my opinion a lot of the trouble arises from the fact that you are still very much in love. Give Paulette a son and you will have gone a long way to being happy with her.

This was the crux of the matter. Borghese's contemporaries contemptuously asserted that he was incapable of following this instruction, but surely Angiolini, his most intimate friend, is a more reliable guide than gossip tinged with spite? As Angiolini over a period of years continued to reiterate this counsel he must have known it was not beyond Borghese's powers to follow, nor would Camillo have had specially inserted into the marriage contract a clause safeguarding the interests of the children of the marriage, if any, nor would he later have congratulated Angiolini on his wife's pregnancy, saying wistfully, 'It is something which can't happen to me seeing how far away we are from each other. I too, would very much like to be called "father".'

Gossip apart, all the evidence tends to show that Borghese may have been inadequate for Pauline but he was not impotent and, in view of her post-natal history after Dermide's birth, it may well have been as much her fault as his if Angiolini's advice as well as the marriage was doomed to sterility.

Undoubtedly, once the first attraction had worn off, Pauline found Camillo physically incompatible and their temperaments were in many ways too similar for them to make the adjustments necessary for living in some sort of harmony. They shared a predilection for luxurious avarice and since 'to follow the fashion, to be noticed, to have his physique continually admired, was Borghese's main preoccupation' they were plainly rivals in securing public attention.

In a few months Pauline was tired of Roman society and impatient with Camillo. She was quick-witted and he was a fool with little education. However scant her own education had been she had lived for five years with Leclerc so that she appreciated the difference between a man of culture and one with none at all. Camillo bored her in the drawing-room and disappointed her in the bedroom. In spite of Angiolini's optimistic reassurances that all their disagreements originated in lovers' quarrels Pauline soon felt that her marriage was a mistake.

Not even the presence of her mother who had come to Rome, nor the kindness of the Pope, nor the eager welcome extended to her by the Romans made any difference. Once again the sore re-appeared on her hands and she complained that the climate of Rome was insupportable, which may have been true if she did indeed bring a malarial germ back from San Domingo. The state of her health and the irritation of her nerves led her to beg Napoleon to allow her to return to Paris, but her pleas met with the same kind of reception as Murat's, He categorically refused to let her leave her husband and her wifely duty. Both required that she should stay in Rome and there for the time being she had perforce to remain.

Caroline was more fortunate. She had returned to Milan shortly before Pauline's marriage and there gave birth on May 16th, 1803 to her third child and second son, whom she called Lucien. To call the boy after her brother, who was in disgrace, was something of a gesture of independence.

It would have been pleasant to be the wife of the Commander-in-Chief of Italy and quartered again in a palace had not Murat been continually quarrelling with the civil authorities. Impetuosity may be a desirable quality on the battlefield but it sits badly on an administrator and the more precipitate Murat's actions the greater were his entanglements. This propensity was becoming ever more obvious to his wife, who felt that only her own presence in Paris near her brother could save Murat from jeopardising their joint future. It was as vital to her to know what was going on in Napoleon's mind and councils as it was to breathe and, by returning to Paris, she would be able to pursue her own methods undisturbed by Murat's faculty for antagonising people and taking the wrong decisions.

So once again she set out on one of those interminable journeys half-way across Europe, made more bearable this time by the almost royal state in which she travelled, in a carriage drawn by six horses, and received in every town where she stayed with almost sovereign honours. It was therefore small wonder if, by the time she reached Paris, her ideas of her own importance, never to be underestimated, had become considerably inflated.

Beneath her exterior of a pretty and frivolous woman Caroline's intelligence was rapidly developing. Marriage had unleashed her latent forces and her mind had been sharpened by contact

Pauline Bonaparte, Princess Borghese, 1806, by Robert Lefèvre

Cliché des Musées Nationaux

Général Victor Emmanuel Leclerc by Kinson

Foto Alinari

Elisa Baciocchi by Stefano Tofanelli

Museo Stibbert, Florence

Felix Baciocchi by Benvenuti

Photo Bulloz

Caroline Bonaparte and her children by Gérard

Caroline Murat   Pauline Borghese   Elisa Baciocchi

Detail of t

[Ho]rtense Bonaparte Julie Bonaparte *Photo Bulloz*
[...] by David

Bibliothèque Nationale

THE IMPERIAL FAMILY

1. Emperor Napoleon Bonaparte; 2. Empress Marie Louise; 3. Empress Josephine; 4. Mme Letizia; 5. Eugène de Beauharnais; 6. Queen Hortense; 7. Joseph Bonaparte; 8. Lucien Bonaparte; 9. Jerome Bonaparte; 10. Louis Bonaparte; 11. Princess Pauline; 12. Princess Elisa; 13. Queen Caroline; 14. Napoleon, Duc de Reichstadt

Cliché des Musées Nationaux

Prince Camillo Borghese by Gérard

Copyright Country Life

Pauline Bonaparte's bedroom in Paris

Photo Bulloz

Joachim Murat by Gros

Bibliothèque Nationale

The Execution of Murat

with the men of high calibre whom she met constantly in society. She was shrewd enough not to assume a culture she did not possess, content to leave the intelligentsia and literati to Elisa, but her memory, which was excellent, enabled her to talk about any subject which she had heard discussed. Her natural judgment was acute and her practical training served her better than the formal education she had disdained.

This growing understanding of her own powers was reinforced by the perception that she could influence her brother and, reasonably secure now that she could get what she desired by force of personality, the scope of her ambitions widened, 'as if increase of appetite had grown by what it fed on'. It may be that she was unconscious of how ambitious she was, echoing her brother's words, 'I have no ambition, or if I do have, it is so inbred in me, so closely bound up with my being that it is like the blood which flows in my veins or like the air I breathe.'

Caroline enjoyed the battle of will with her brother but the battle of will between herself and her husband she was already beginning to find exhausting as well as unnecessary; she was still young and arrogant enough to believe that her own methods were always better than his.

The goal she had fixed on was Murat's appointment to the immensely important post of Governor of Paris, but she was sure that if he took part in the delicate negotiations necessary to secure it he would ruin everything by his impulsiveness and gaucherie. Therefore she diplomatically suggested to him that he return to the department of the Lot to preside over the elections for the Legislative Assembly, a suggestion he welcomed for the opportunity of seeing again the family, and particularly the mother, to whom he was devoted. The little villages of La Bastide-Fortunière and Montgesty where his parents and brothers and sisters lived were charmed to find in the distinguished general the Joachim Murat they had known. He never assumed airs of consequence with his old friends, showed himself cordial and friendly, chucking the village beauties under the chin as he had done as a young trooper.

Caroline's diplomacy was shown to be excellent. When Murat returned to Paris with a large majority he found he had been appointed Governor of Paris and Commandant of the First Division of the army and of the National Guard, although it was a position in which he soon discovered that the difficulties outweighed the distinctions.

The First Consul was not securing his own position without running into opposition; the assassination attempt at the Rue St. Nicaise was followed by a royalist plot in whch General Moreau was implicated. Moreau's reputation as a soldier was too formidable to permit of more than a prison sentence being imposed on him while his fellow-conspirators were put to death but, after his release, when he went into exile, he remained a potential danger to the régime. Bonaparte reflected bitterly, for the memory still rankled with him in later years, that if only Moreau had married Caroline he would have been securely assimilated into the clan, but she had wilfully willed it otherwise: 'She does not appreciate my position.'

Bonaparte's bitterness was increased when Murat set himself up in opposition to the summary trial and condemnation of the Duc d'Enghien, the young Bourbon prince who had been kidnapped and brought to Paris under the pretext of complicity in the royalist plot.

The responsibility for the trial and its foregone conclusion rested on Murat as Commandant of the fortress of Vincennes where d'Enghien was imprisoned. Both he and Caroline realised that if he were implicated in the affair it might for ever damage his reputation. Murat, who in this instance showed more political acumen than the First Consul, did his best to reason with him, but was unable to withstand the threat to strip him of his honours and send him back to his mountains in the Quercy. His rage and illness availed him nothing. Faced with the prospect of losing all that he won for himself, Murat yielded to orders, bearing out Bonaparte's judgment of him that he was a lion when facing the enemy, a woman when not.

Once the order for the commission to be constituted to try

d'Enghien was given Murat's responsibility was at an end. It was Savary, the executor of many of Napoleon's unsavoury commands, who bade the adjutant give the actual order to fire when the farce of a trial was over, although Murat could not escape the moral responsibility.

On March 21st, 1804, Louis de Bourbon, Duc d'Enghien, faced a firing squad by the wavering light of a lantern. The platoon fired and, when he fell, his face was unrecognisable. Murat did not witness the execution but he knew how d'Enghien had been mutilated and he remembered.

The unveiling or engineering of plots made easier the slow transition towards monarchy, which had for so long been rumoured, and which the establishment of the consulate for life made inevitable. The climate thus created inexorably demanded that Bonaparte should assume some title and establish a new dynasty. Even the most ardent Revolutionaries were forced to recognise that without Bonaparte France had nothing; in spite of their repugnance to monarchical institutions, irresistibly the idea of an Empire appealed to their imaginations. Of one thing they were certain. If monarchy were an old story it would be newly clothed and shining with Bonaparte's achievements. On a lesser plane the re-creation of a Court with its magnificent apparatus of great officers of state and gorgeous ceremonies appealed to the French people, giving them back something which they had secretly regretted. For a long time the results justified their anticipation.

CHAPTER SEVEN

IMPERIAL HIGHNESSES

On Friday, May 18th, 1804, the Senate in a body, escorted by a regiment of cuirassiers, went to St. Cloud to proclaim Napoleon Bonaparte Emperor of the French. In reply to Cambacérès' long and solemn harangue he said firmly and with dignity,

'I accept the title which you believe contributes to the glory of the nation. *I hope that France will never repent of the honours with which she will clothe my family.* Whatever comes to pass, my spirit will no longer be with my posterity on the day when it ceases to merit the affection and confidence of the nation at large.'

The choice of words was significant. At this crucial moment in his career Napoleon might still have repudiated his family, electing to found his dynasty on merit alone. In spite of the resentment he felt towards some of its members and his impatience with others he could not do so. It was contrary not only to the hereditary principle he had adopted with all its inherent dangers, but also to his traditions, his beliefs and his own affections. Bound by his own deed Samson delivered himself tied hand and foot to the Philistines.

Napoleon's first act as Emperor drew the cords a little tighter. Joseph Bonaparte was nominated as Grand Elector and Louis Bonaparte as Constable of France. Both, with their wives, Julie and Hortense, were raised to the title of Prince and style of Imperial Highness. Lucien, the self-imposed exile, and Jerome, who had forfeited his brother's favour by an unauthorised marriage to a young American, Elizabeth Patterson, were ignored as were the Emperor's mother and sisters.

At the family dinner held to celebrate the creation of the Empire Napoleon maliciously took every opportunity of punctiliously addressing Julie and Hortense by their new titles, which served only to increase the anger of Elisa and Caroline, who were both affronted by their exclusion from the distribution of honours.

Caroline convulsively swallowed glass after glass of water as if at the same time to wash down her humiliation and wounded pride. What had her exertions served her to ingratiate herself with Josephine and Napoleon? If her relationship to him did not suffice to gain her the same distinctions as her brothers then Murat's services demanded them. More controlled, but equally angry, Elisa sat stiff and silent throughout the meal.

Pauline was not present at this painful dinner. The authentic princess, Princess Borghese, was in Rome, straining at the leash for permission to return to Paris. Nor did Napoleon's mother witness her son's apotheosis. At this glorious hour in his fortunes she elected to remain in Rome with the brother who had defied him.

The next day saw one of the old glories of France revived when eighteen of her most outstanding generals were created Marshals of France, including Joachim Murat although he was one of the youngest in seniority, but the honour conferred on her husband did not prevent Caroline, in company with Elisa, from waiting on their brother later in the day and enacting a scene reported to be worthy of the furies.

Napoleon was wont to remark amusedly that with Caroline he always had to fight a pitched battle but at this contest it was she who carried off the victory, which was officially gazetted in the *Moniteur*. The Emperor's sisters and their husbands were invested with the rank of Prince and Princess and the girls were given the style of Imperial Highness. His mother, significantly, was still passed over, remaining Madame Bonaparte, mother of the Emperor. Not till a year later was she given the title 'Madame Mère' and the style of Imperial Highness.

It is probable that Napoleon intended to confer Imperial status on his sisters but he could not resist the temptation of teasing them, nor of making them sit up and beg for it. It is equally likely that he wanted to teach them the subtle lesson that henceforward every honour, every distinction and every advantage lay solely in his gift.

On this occasion his calculations had once more gone amiss for to bestow freely is one thing, to appear to be forced into giving is another. Experience ought to have taught him that, where Caroline at least was concerned, he was a bad psychologist and that she had the habit of getting her own way. By establishing the precedent of yielding to his sister's importunities he made himself vulnerable in the future to conceding demands which, like those of the horse-leech's daughter, grew ever more pressing.

Once his sisters were temporarily appeased the new Emperor turned his mind to matters of greater moment. After fourteen months of uneasy peace war had again broken out with England. Since there was nowhere on European soil that the French and English could meet Bonaparte decided to take the war to England, and began to assemble a huge camp at Boulogne and a fleet of flat-bottomed boats for an invasion. Plainly he had forgotten his words of 1798, 'The real moment for preparing this invasion has passed, perhaps for ever.'

To Pauline wars and peace were alike of little moment except the war of pinpricks which she was now waging with Camillo. Her new honour of Imperial Highness affected her only as giving her an added barb to use against him and, as Borghese's inadequacy fretted her nerves more and more, so did the friction between them grow. Hemmed in by her mother, uncle and mother-in-law, Pauline could find no opportunity of seeking consolation elsewhere. An unsatisfactory and disagreeable husband, a boring society and a brother who unsympathetically continued to remind her that her place was with that husband, and that she would forfeit the Emperor's affection if she tried to return to France without Camillo, combined to make Pauline really ill, so that there were times when she wished she was still Madame Leclerc with a modest income rather than Her Imperial Highness, the Princess Borghese, with millions.

To regain her health was of cardinal importance and the first step was to leave the insupportable climate of Rome, so the Borgheses, in great state, travelled north to Tuscany, leaving Dermide at one of the Borghese villas at Frascati in the care of his nurse.

From Pisa, which she found pretty and pleasing and where she tried the waters, Pauline moved on to Florence where she posed for Canova for the now world-famous statue. If society was scandalised that the Emperor's sister sat for a sculptor, or one should say reclined, with the bare minimum of drapery, Pauline's own practical point of view was that she was as beautiful in form as in face, that the perfection of her body was as great a work of art as any to be found in a gallery, and how much more pleasure was to be had from looking at an animate than an inanimate form ! Beauty was a gift to be shared, not hoarded ; however prudent she sometimes was in her expenditure of money, she was always generous with her person.

This propensity to be careful with money was one Pauline shared with her mother. When Madame Letizia came to join her at Bagni di Lucca, which was the next spa which she visited, they both had great satisfaction in practising economy. Although their cheeseparing with the butcher, the baker and the candlestick-maker aroused a good deal of adverse local comment, neither of them cared, Madame Letizia because her conduct was always exemplary, Pauline because, apart from her brother's, her own opinion was the only one she valued. Whatever Elisa might protest, Pauline was unquestionably Madame Letizia's favourite daughter ; in her company she behaved irreproachably because she was most truly devoted to her mother.

The regularity of her life and the air and treatment of Bagni di Lucca, for which she formed a great affection, brought about a real improvement in Pauline's health and spirits so that she was even able to tolerate Camillo's presence and write kindly about him to Murat, when unexpected bad news darkened the sunnier scene.

Dermide, who had found it so difficult to draw his first breath in Italy, found it easy to draw his last. His illness was sudden, death following too quickly to allow Pauline to go to him. Both his illness and death were for a time concealed from her because she had had a relapse and her entourage feared the effect of the news on her.

Pauline cannot be reproached with neglecting her son for she had left him in good hands, but she did reproach herself; she had perhaps been a careless but never a bad mother. In an access of grief she made the same splendid if theatrical gesture she made for Leclerc and cut off her hair to be put in the child's coffin. Pauline was not unnatural and a letter she later wrote to Lucien is revealing. In it she said she loved his children as if they were her own and regretted that it did not seem likely that she would now have any herself.

There could be only one answer to Pauline's plea to be allowed to return to France to carry out the sacred duty of burying Dermide beside his father at Montgobert, although no doubt Napoleon was not for a moment deceived by her opportunism, but she had given evidence of better behaviour and earned herself some good marks by her recent decorum. So, in spite of the sadness of her errand, Pauline set out happily for Paris, a city in which the Bonaparte sisters spent actually only a few years of their lives, although it was always the place where they wished to be when they were elsewhere.

The only disagreeable factor to mar Pauline's pleasure in resuming her old habits was the presence of Camillo but she had now formed the easy habit of ignoring him and left him to wander about disconsolately by himself. Together in Paris once again Elisa, Pauline and Caroline gave themselves over to the excitement of the imminent Coronation, finding a pleasing occupation in setting up their households to accord with their new dignity. An almoner, two chaplains, a lady of honour, ladies-in-waiting, a chamberlain, equerries, an intendant, a private secretary, a doctor-in-ordinary, readers, all to the number of some twenty or thirty persons added to the consequence of the Emperor's sisters.

The great increase in their expenses was met by gifts from their brother, who in return required that they should keep great state and entertain lavishly, for France was to be paramount among the European nations, looked up to and envied not for her military glory alone but as the queen of luxury and gaiety.

The Bonapartes found it easy to submit to the Imperial wish because they had inherited from their father an inclination towards dress and outward show. Even their mother, in spite of her carefulness with money, had instilled in them the belief that one must always appear well-dressed and prosperous at the expense, if necessary, of economising at home.

The Coronation and its attendant festivities offered them a glorious opportunity for display since the costumes devised for the occasion by Isabey, the court painter, and executed by Leroy, were extremely gorgeous, a riot of Imperial purple velvet, brilliant white satin, and lavish gold embroidery with everywhere the emblem of the Empire, the golden bees which had superseded the Bourbon lilies. 'It is not,' remarked Philip Guedalla, 'until the bees are round the lilies that we get their true savour.'

Of all the Marshals of France it is probable that only Murat, with his passion for the flamboyant in dress, was quite happy with his mantle and coat of white velvet embroidered with golden bees and his lace cravat. Napoleon himself laughed at the purple velvet tunic that he wore for the procession, with a short cape *à l'espagnole* embroidered with the ubiquitous bees, and a toque of black velvet with eight rows of diamonds and three white plumes attached by a diamond knot, 'which hesitated in style between the Renaissance and the toreador'. At the ceremony itself his long white satin gown, lavishly embroidered with golden acanthus leaves and heavily fringed with gold, the buskins hidden under their weight of gold, looked more like an elaborate nightshirt than the dress of an Emperor.

The girls were more fortunate with their graceful dresses of white silk of French manufacture, their long sleeves embroidered in gold and the *chérusque*, the becoming Mary Stuart ruff of lace, and long court mantles.

The citizens of Paris sighed with pleasure at the treat in store for them. Never before had a sovereign of France been crowned in the city, nor a Pope come specially to crown him. Their pleasure was not shared by the Emperor's sisters. Elisa and Caroline, and to a lesser degree, Pauline, were dismayed when they found that they were to carry Josephine's train. It was unthinkable that they, Bonapartes born, should have to perform this menial service for a Beauharnais Empress. Once again they treated Napoleon to a display of temper more suitable to fishwives than to Imperial Highnesses, but their resistance showed only how little understanding they had of the nature of sovereignty, which inexorably sets the sovereign apart from even the nearest of his relatives.

A princess born to the purple never for a moment questions that she takes second place to the sovereign's consort. Her place in the hierarchy is known to her from birth and, whatever her private feelings may be, her public behaviour is always impeccable; where the consort leads she knows she must follow. But Elisa, Pauline and Caroline refused obstinately to recognise this immutable law, showing themselves to be the parvenus the world thought them.

Napoleon was justly impatient with his sisters' intransigence. He himself was well aware that, in assuming sovereignty, he accepted its traditional appanages. He did not ask his sisters to carry the train of Josephine de Beauharnais but the Imperial mantle, which was not a piece of velvet but a *mystique*, for from the tassels of that mantle hung their own fortunes, honours, even their very existence.

The Coronation brought out the very worst in the family. Joseph blustered a show of independence, narrowly avoiding a rupture with his younger brother, while Madame Letizia lingered in Rome with Lucien and on her journey home so that she arrived in Paris three weeks after the Coronation had taken place. The Emperor's brothers and sisters, and even his mother, grasped almost as their inherited right the privileges he granted them, but bitterly grudged submission to the responsibilities of rank.

It was, however, finally made clear to them that they either obeyed or they might take the same road as Lucien and Jerome, although it was not long before Jerome showed that he preferred the Imperial fleshpots to the domestic dish of herbs, divorced his American wife and married the princess of his brother's choice, Catherine of Württemberg.

In the end the sisters were forced to submit, having reached the compromise that they would ' hold up ' but not ' carry ' the Empress's train, but they took their revenge by performing their task as awkwardly as possible so that she was nearly dragged down by its weight, a symbolic gesture indicative of their unwavering determination to strip it entirely from her shoulders.

It was Murat who carried the Empress's crown in the procession and its winking gems fascinated him as they gleamed in the pale winter sunlight filtering through the great windows of Notre Dame. Eyeing her husband, Caroline may well have thought how much better that crown would look on her own head than on Josephine's.

She alone had a valid excuse for her ineptitude in carrying the train. She was again pregnant and said later that the weight of the mantle of purple velvet lined with ermine was intolerable, but anger was added to her malaise because she now knew that, whichever the sex of her child might be, it would stand no hope of succession to Imperial honours.

The question of the succession, which had been agitating the family since the institution of the Consulate for life, had, with the creation of the Empire, become pressing. Now definitely there would be no direct descendants, but the Emperor had no more desire than the First Consul to be succeeded by one of his brothers. His wish to adopt the child of Louis and Hortense met with unexpected resistance from Louis, who was morbidly sensitive about the rumours concerning Napoleon's relations with his step-daughter. Caroline was not entirely innocent of the whisper which reached him that their child might, in fact, be Napoleon's, although both knew that there were no valid grounds for the allegation. The idea of adoption was equally unwelcome to the rest of the family because, although little Napoleon-Louis was part Bonaparte, and they cared little whether he had been fathered by Louis or Napoleon, he was also part Beauharnais. The internal struggle in the family went on, provoking Napoleon to storm,

'I shall make a law which at least will make me the master of my own family.'

It was an illusion. Master of France he was, master of Europe he might become and narrowly miss becoming master of the world, but never master of his own family.

All uncertainty came to an end on the day before the Coronation, when it was announced that the Imperial dignity was to be hereditary in the legitimate descendants of Napoleon or, if he died without issue, of Joseph or of Louis. Lucien and Jerome and their issue were excluded and so were his sisters and their issue.

The exclusion of the Emperor's sisters was to be expected since the Salic law had always prevailed in France. Elisa at this time had no living children and probably cared more about rearing a child than that he should be named in the Imperial succession, while Pauline's son was dead and the possibility of her having any more children remote.

Caroline had two sons and a daughter and a fourth child was on its way, while Murat was one of the outstanding personalities of an Empire whose existence proved that talent and capacity might look to the highest honours. Achille was to his parents at least as endearing a child as Napoleon-Louis. Although the Emperor wilfully refused to show him the same preference Caroline rated his claims at least as high of those of Louis' sons.

Little though Napoleon cared for the idea of being succeeded by one of his brothers he was quite categorical that the French Empire was not to be the appanage of one of Murat's sons. Murat might be a hero, he might have distinguished service to his credit and a brilliant future before him, but he was a fool. There, for the moment, the matter rested, but not in Caroline's mind. As a passionate chess-player she was always thinking several moves ahead; she was convinced that the last move had not been made nor the last pawn played.

Private grievances were set aside as the sisters joined the rest of Parisian society in the splendid round of entertainments in honour of the Coronation at which, as wife of the Military Governor of Paris, Caroline was a prominent figure. Of her present position she had little cause to complain whatever her nagging irritation about the future. She was Her Imperial Highness the Princess Caroline Murat, young, beautiful, courted and with a keen appreciation of her own powers.

Aware for some time that Josephine's influence with her brother was waning, Caroline gradually transferred her attentions exclusively to him. She had a happy knack of knowing what pleased him, earning his approval by taking very seriously her new métier as princess, by devoting herself to mastering every detail of the strict etiquette laid down for the Imperial Court and by imposing a severe discipline on her household; there were also other ways in which she could earn her brother's admiration and gratitude.

After the birth of Caroline's fourth child, Louise, in March, 1805, the Murats moved into even greater state at the former Elysée-Bourbon, which gave Caroline an excellent opportunity of helping her brother. It was long since he had made any attempt to be faithful to Josephine, but his casual affairs were hampered by his own insistence that at least an outward decorum should be observed at his Court, which demanded the maximum discretion on his own part; he was still reluctant to bring his amourettes under the conjugal roof, even if that roof covered a palace.

This reluctance was seized upon by Caroline. One of her brother's fancies was for a beautiful lady-in-waiting of whom Caroline at once made much, indicating to the Emperor that he would find the Elysée a convenient *maison de rendezvous*, with the added security of Murat as a screen. She did not in the least mind that her husband should parade an apparent unfaithfulness since they both knew that they were performing a most useful service to the Emperor which would not go unrecognised, nor did it do so. Murat was appointed Grand Admiral, a horseman as a sailor being as absurd as a sailor on horseback, especially when he proceeded to take his wholly honorary duties seriously and attempted to meddle in maritime affairs, which attracted the customary reprimand.

More important than the previous affair was Caroline's throwing in Napoleon's way a young woman named Eléonore Denuelle, which was of vital importance in the history of the Empire. She bore the Emperor his first child and set in train a chain of events of great consequence. Had Caroline not introduced him to Eléonore he might never have known that it was not he who was sterile. He might never have divorced Josephine nor gone will o' the wisp hunting for a legitimate heir through the courts of Europe. He might have come home from the wars like Odysseus and with an ageing wife grown old with her. Caroline's eagerness to stand well with her brother may have altered the history of the world.

Napoleon's next move was as surprising as it was unexpected and one which Caroline had been unable to foresee.

In March, 1805, the Emperor was invited to assume the crown of Italy, an offer which he was graciously pleased to accept. The regions now to come under French rule were Lombardy, the Duchies of Modena and Parma and the former Papal Legations of Bologna and Ferrara. To administer these states in the name of France Eugène de Beauharnais was appointed Viceroy and when, on March 18th, the Emperor went in full state to announce to the Senate that he had accepted the crown of Italy, he announced at the same time that he had given the principality of Piombino to his sister, Elisa, to govern.

PART TWO

CHAPTER EIGHT

PRINCESS OF LUCCA

Surprise was general that Elisa should have been chosen to rule over even so small a state as Piombino, although its insignificance in territory and population belied the richness of its unexploited minerals and its strategic importance. Piombino commanded the narrow strait between Tuscany and Elba, from which British warships and Barbary pirates insolently menaced the Italian mainland, and to Piombino the Emperor promised that Lucca, of far greater area and value, would shortly be added; together these states formed a single defensive area against attack from the sea.

Caroline's chagrin was great because she could not perceive what either Elisa or Baciocchi had done to merit sovereignty. It seemed ridiculous to overlook Murat's real merit and as for herself, 'I am made of that self metal as my sister, And prize me at her worth.'

Elisa's services had not been quite so unimportant as Caroline thought. As a literary hostess she had won over to her brother's side many of the writers and intellectuals who were a potential source of disaffection. Her energy and organising ability had not gone unremarked. She had earned Napoleon's respect even if his personal feelings for her were no warmer.

Merely to be a Parisian hostess was, however, insufficient distinction for the Emperor's sister. Pauline's marriage had put her into the European princely hierarchy, while Caroline's destiny was linked with her husband's, who had every chance of increasing his stature on the battlefield, which Baciocchi was never likely to do. On the other hand he would always be available to perform those duties in a state which could only be carried out by a man while the actual government was entrusted to Elisa herself, although hedged about with French advisers.

Elisa was immensely gratified to have a sphere of activity worthy of the talents she believed herself to possess. She busied herself immediately with all the problems arising from her new status, learning about the political ramifications of Lucca and Piombino in the course of long discussions with their representatives and the French ministers responsible for Italian administration.

In spite of the glittering prospect before her Elisa delayed in leaving Paris, perhaps finally reluctant to leave the city where she had lived for the last six years, to exchange the known for the unknown, although she had no apprehension about her ability to govern her new states. Baciocchi preceded her to Italy but the couple arranged to meet at Milan and there attend Napoleon's coronation as King of Italy before themselves going on to Lucca to be crowned.

If the ceremony in Milan Cathedral was not as magnificent as in Notre Dame, Elisa's position was one of considerably greater importance. This time she was not required to hold up the Empress's train; she sat on a throne next to Josephine, who herself sat on Napoleon's right. Her Imperial Highness the Princess Elisa had repaired to the Cathedral immediately before the Empress, accompanied by her full suite of chamberlains, ladies-in-waiting and *dame d'honneur*. Even Baciocchi was distinguished on this occasion. He was allowed to carry the Hand of Justice.

On July 14th, 1805, Elisa and Felix Baciocchi, Prince and Princess of Lucca and Piombino, were themselves the chief personages of a state occasion. On that day they made their solemn entry into their city of Lucca in their state coach drawn by six bay horses, Felix in the ornate costume of a French prince and Elisa in a robe of white satin, heavily embroidered in gold, which did little, however, to conceal her bony décolletage.

The installation ceremony was very splendid although the choice of date was unfortunate. Only eighteen short years since the Bastille had fallen and new royalty in its panoply mocked its fall and the glorious Revolution!

While Elisa was revelling in her good fortune as she sped along the roads to Lucca her sisters in Paris were less happy. Caroline was ill, too ill even to attend the fête given at Neuilly to celebrate the coronation of the Emperor as King of Italy, while Pauline was suffering from what seems to have been some tubercular trouble in her chest.

Her feelings towards her husband, however, were at the moment kindlier, possibly because the Emperor had taken pity either on her or on him and summoned Camillo to Boulogne with the rank of major in the army. Pauline was so delighted to lose his company that she secured for him the title of a French Prince and the rank of Imperial Highness. It gave her great pleasure, she said, to hear that the Emperor was pleased with him because she had never doubted his aptitude—as a soldier.

Camillo, however, was now completely disillusioned about his marriage. From Boulogne he wrote bitterly to Angiolini, 'I shall no longer attempt the conquest of women except with money.'

In Lucca, her robes of state laid aside, Elisa was setting herself to the task of conquering her principality. First of all there was a strict definition of powers to be determined between herself and Felix who, however, had no illusions about his position. Not until clause VI of the decree establishing Elisa as Princess of Piombino and Lucca did his name appear and then only as the husband of the Princess Elisa who would take the style and title of Prince of Piombino. This clause appeared almost as an afterthought after those concerning the Princess's descendants, of whom he was nevertheless to be the father.

Felix was to command military manœuvres, organise parades, pass regiments under review and act as a rubber stamp for all that his wife decreed. Elisa, quite simply, undertook every other task of government. It says much for his humility or sweetness of temper that he dutifully accepted his subordination and displayed no desire to step outside the limits laid down for him by his wife.

Elisa was determined to show that she sprang from the same stock as her brother, that in her humbler sphere she was an equally capable administrator. Work, as she admitted, soon became her ruling passion. Much to her brother's irritation she imitated not only his industry, but copied his ways and speech, his curtness and his outbursts of anger. In spite of her formidable personality, natural or assumed, Elisa did also possess some of the family charm or she could not otherwise have made and kept so many friends.

From the moment she herself became a sovereign Elisa's attitude to her brother changed. She may have loved him no more than he loved her, but experience of government led her to a better understanding of his problems. She early decided to be a devoted subaltern, a decision easily seen from her letters, which form an amusing contrast to those written by her sisters. Pauline always wrote to Napoleon as a sister to a brother, Caroline as sovereign to sovereign, but Elisa as subject to suzerain.

She made it her guiding rule to refer and defer to his decisions, not because she considered herself incapable of making them, but because she perceived that the greatest safeguard for her sovereignty was docility. Graciously she condescended to concede that her brother did have qualities superior to those of the rest of the family, including her own. Assiduous cultivation of the Emperor and devotion to his interests was her watchword; she even intervened with Lucien to beg him to set aside his wife in order to reconcile himself with Napoleon, an act of officiousness which resulted in a break with this once dearly loved brother.

To her task of endowing her small States with the great régime of public order that her brother had instituted in France Elisa brought a personal energy remarkable in one whose health was always poor. She insisted on attending to every detail herself because, in her arrogant opinion, there was no one else in Lucca so well qualified. Even with the advantage of the order and method she had learnt at St. Cyr it is staggering the amount of administrative work, ceremonial duties, recreation and amusement Elisa was able to cram into twenty-four hours.

Administration and politics necessarily occupied a large part of her time but she also concerned herself with developing the industry and agriculture of her two States. Public works were undertaken on a large scale, the marshes in Piombino were drained, the port facilities improved and the fortifications strengthened, so that piracy was checked, although nothing could challenge British supremacy in the Mediterranean. Bridges and roads were built, timber felled and minerals mined, while she fostered the industries of Lucca, its tanneries, refineries, soap and silk factories which, during her reign, became exceedingly prosperous.

When she added the coveted territories of Massa and Carrara to her fief she at once set the marble quarries of Carrara in action again, providing much employment and more revenue. From the Academy of Sculpture she set up at Carrara marble statues were sent out all over Europe, the majority inevitably busts and statues of the Emperor. The marble miniatures of Canova's 'Venus Victrix', of which there is one in Pauline's old home in Paris, undoubtedly came from Carrara but they did not pose the same problem as the Director of the Academy encountered when executing a command for a statue of Caroline. The twelve busts of her which had been ordered presented no difficulty, but for a statue the only two female models they had at Carrara were of an amazon and of the Venus de Medici. The Director wrote apprehensively to Elisa, 'These two statues are naked and their pose cannot be that of a Grand Duchess.'

For Caroline was at last a sovereign.

From the time Elisa became Princess of Lucca Caroline was determined that she herself should have a similar honour and exerted herself to the utmost to push her claims with her brother. She and Murat followed him to the camp at Boulogne where their stay resulted in Joachim's being entrusted with a reconnaissance mission in Germany and thereafter with the command of Lieutenant of the Grande Armée at Strasbourg.

From Paris Caroline reported to her husband all that was happening in his absence, how the Emperor had suggested that, instead of remaining alone at Neuilly she should come to St. Cloud, share the apartments of Pauline, who was convalescing there, and dine with him every day. Josephine was markedly cool because she saw that Caroline was transferring her attentions to her brother, which was the more bitter because she had lavished genuine affection on her. But what really infuriated the Empress was that the Murats had been successful in securing Joachim's appointment to command the cavalry in the imminent war in place of her son-in-law, Louis.

Her angry words were retailed to Caroline by Pauline, always happy to report anything that showed Josephine up in a bad light and who, in anger, never had the slightest discretion.

'I am not surprised that the Murats were so eager to go to Boulogne to cozen the Emperor and that by cajoling him they got what they wanted. Murat and Madame Murat are certainly very attached to him but they are both very designing, and Murat wheedles everything he wants out of the Emperor.'

> You see, [Caroline wrote to her husband] that they are jealous of what the Emperor intends to do for us, so be very careful, because the Empress, Louis and all her family will never forgive you for having got the finest command there is.
>
> When I left her last night I said, 'Will you permit me to come and dine with you tomorrow?' and she answered with a mocking smile, 'But aren't you able to do everything you want?'
>
> You know that the Emperor advised me to be on good terms with her so I show her the greatest deference, and do everything I can to keep her happy, but without taking her into my confidence. This makes her most angry because she sees it is impossible to carry back to the Emperor about me anything which would distress him.

This revealing letter ended with a word of caution.

> I will let you know what happens, but only when I can send a letter by one of your aides-de-camp, because I don't

want to entrust it to a courier. The Empress tries to find out what our intentions are, and if she got hold of our letters she would show them to the Emperor and do us more harm, so in all your conversations with him pretend that you know nothing.

The resumption of general war in 1805 meant that Paris was cleared of its men as if by magic, an occurrence which repeated itself throughout the Napoleonic era, the knowledge that they were here today and gone perhaps for ever tomorrow lending a heightened tension to all the gaiety. When they returned briefly to the capital to recuperate from their wounds, or to carry out some duty, this gay and gilded troop was made doubly welcome by the women intolerably deprived of masculine society. For a few months they danced, gossiped, laughed and made love before disappearing again to exchange beds of down for the hard ground of a bivouac, the charms of silken dalliance for the rigours of the camp.

The Austrian campaign this time was short and sharp. In its battles Murat showed great courage and brilliance, which gratified Caroline for once content to enjoy the simple pleasures of Neuilly with her children. But she was delighted when the Emperor invited her to represent the family at the wedding of Eugène de Beauharnais and Princess Augusta of Bavaria at Munich in January, 1806. The distinction flattered Caroline until she found that the rigorous etiquette of the Bavarian Court gave her a lowly place in precedence but neither tantrums nor screams nor feigned illness prevailed with her brother; she was obliged to take her place, whatever it might be.

The Murats had, in fact, lost some ground lately. Murat had been called to account for making an armistice without orders, causing the Emperor to lose the fruits of a campaign, and he had been unwise enough to express himself too bluntly about Eugène's marriage. Boldly he told Napoleon:

'When France raised you to the throne it was because she thought to find in you a chief of the people, a plebeian chief, endowed with a title which raised you above all the sovereigns of Europe, but it was not her intention to recreate the monarchy of Louis XIV with all its abuses and all the pretensions of the old courts. Yet you surround yourself with the old nobility, you fill the salons of the Tuileries with them, they believe themselves restored to all their rights; they consider themselves more at home than they think you are. The old nobility regards all your comrades in arms, and perhaps even you yourself, as parvenus, intruders and usurpers.

Today you intend by the marriage of Eugène to ally yourself to the Royal House of Bavaria, and all that you are doing is to demonstrate to Europe how much value you put on that in which we are all lacking: the glory of birth.

You pay homage to all these titles of power which are not your own, which are in opposition to ours, you make clear to France and to these sovereigns that you want to be the continuation of an old dynasty and yet, if you are reigning, it is because France does not want an old dynasty and, believe me, your dynasty will always appear new to the other monarchs.'

This piece of very just observation earned Murat the haughty reply,

'Monsieur le Prince Murat, I know how devoted you are to me and I render full justice to your quality. I am always pleased to see you at the head of my cavalry but this is not a question of a military operation. It is a political operation and I have given it due thought. This marriage displeases you? Well, it pleases me and I regard it as a great success, as great a success as the victory of Austerlitz.'

In spite of his animadversions against parvenu kings Murat was very happy to be invested only a few months later with the title of Grand Duke of Cleves and Berg, a territory carved out of the Rhineland, while at the same time Joseph was created King of the Two Sicilies, Pauline Duchess of Guastalla and shortly afterwards Louis King of Holland.

While her brothers and sisters were being initiated into the arts of government Elisa, a year in advance of them, was serenely carrying out her duties, one of them a tour of inspection of Elba, which she thought had a very pleasing countryside. Her report on her visit has a wry significance.

> The Elbans are in general agreement that the greatest good fortune which could come to their country would be to be united under one master and to live under the paternal laws of Your Majesty.

Any ordinary woman would have been crushed under the weight of work Elisa assumed but her energies were boundless. In addition to her public duties she spent much time, and more money, in the furnishing of her many palaces, at Piombino, Lucca, Massa, Viareggio on the coast, and Bagni di Lucca, which she visited frequently for the waters, but the pearl of them all was Marlia, her country home outside Lucca, which had the most exquisite gardens, including an English garden, and an *al fresco* theatre.

Elisa had neither lost her interest in amateur theatricals nor thought it incompatible with her sovereign dignity to take part in them herself; Phèdre was the rôle in which she thought she excelled. If anyone showed signs of criticising her she could retort that the dissemination of French culture to the Italians was part of her task. She was a most ruthless patroness of the arts; no cultural activity escaped her vigilance. She founded literary and musical prizes, presided over séances of learned societies and educational establishments and even kindly allowed Felix to organise an Académie Napoléon on the model of the Académie Française. The number of her cultural foundations was prodigious—two large libraries, a medical college, chairs at the University in French law and history, communal schools for boys and girls as well as the Institut Elisa for the education of girls of good family, a project very near her heart.

It was little wonder that her court at Lucca soon became famous for its erudition and refinement as well as being one where the strictest etiquette was maintained, for the Bonaparte sisters piqued themselves on being more Imperial than the Empress. Felix was always resplendent in a white uniform or in the blue and gold of a French general, with diamonds in his epaulettes and the collar of the Golden Fleece and plaque of a Grand Eagle of the Legion of Honour. While he paraded the salons like an affable shopwalker Elisa sat on her throne, smothered in cameos and diamonds, and wearing the latest creations from Leroy; yet all this magnificence did not hide the awkwardness of her movements, in such contrast to Pauline's grace. In private she relaxed her stiffness while Felix who, in public, behaved with proper deference to his wife, treated her in the family circle as if she were an ordinary human being.

In Lucca it may have been his influence, exerted in this alone, which made music a dominant part of Court entertainments and ceremonies. Either his passion for the violin, or the predilection Elisa shared with her family for the company of musicians, made Lucca an outstanding musical centre. Her *maestro di cappella* was named Puccini, a name made world-famous by his grandson, Giacomo. Spontini dedicated his opera, *La Vestale*, to her and Paisiello a cantata and an opera, *Proserpina*, for which he was rewarded with a gold medal. Paganini was the most important member of her musical entourage; he became her *virtuoso di corte* although his other less public duties were possibly even more appreciated.

During his many years at Lucca Paganini was prolific in composition, composing at least one sonata for solo violin in honour of his patroness, and a sonata for violin and orchestra, known as 'the Napoleon', in honour of her brother. To his music Elisa listened, as once she had listened to Chateaubriand reading *Atala*, lying on a couch, but how much more romantic was the atmosphere, under the starry Italian night sky, on the terrace of her villa at Marlia or in her palace at Massa looking out to sea. Now she was not obliged to fan herself; the office was performed for her by her ladies and attendant pages.

Paganini was accorded the extremely odd distinction of being made Captain of the Royal Bodyguard, although perhaps less odd when one considers the most important of his functions; and he gave Baciocchi violin lessons, which may have compensated Felix for the occasional loss of her intimate society.

Elisa's satisfaction with herself reached its summit when she at last gave birth to a child who survived the dangerous months of infancy, a daughter, Napoleone. Shortly after the child's birth Angiolini visited Bagni di Lucca and wrote his impressions to Borghese.

Remarking that Princess Elisa was the member of the Imperial family whom he knew least, he said he was charmed to find that she had more wit and erudition than he had expected:

> Her manner, and her way of doing things, are those of the Emperor, and I should be very surprised if her character was not similar to his. Since her confinement she has put on weight. Her complexion is excellent, in a word she has become pretty.

Angiolini was a courtier because no one else has ever so described Elisa, although no one went so far as to anticipate the nineteenth-century Member of Parliament, who stated categorically that all strong-minded women are ugly!

It was Elisa's inclination as well as her duty to foster French commerce by parading French fashions, but she had to rely on others to do her shopping for her in Paris, a commission generally undertaken by her *dame d'honneur*, Madame de Laplace, whose husband, the eminent astronomer and mathematician, was also President of the Senate so that her own duties obliged her to be in Paris for half the year. Here she was a useful link between Elisa and the capital and a faithful reporter of the Imperial family's doings and the latest modes.

Most important was to gloat over the remarks made by the Emperor. The sycophancy of Madame de Laplace's letters is exaggerated to the point of high comedy, were it not that the adulation showered on all three of the sisters induced them to believe in their own legend. Invariably she laid at Elisa's feet the homage of devotion, respect and submission!

> My only consolation, Madame, at being so far away from you is to hear your praises constantly sung by distinguished men who regard you as a model. One of his ministers told me the other day that the Emperor had said that the best of his ministers was the Princess of Lucca.

Another sweet crumb was gathered up from Caroline, who told Madame de Laplace how the Emperor had praised Elisa for the wisdom she showed in government, while Caroline added a message of her own to say how happy these words had made her. Certainly this does not bespeak envy and the interest she took in all Elisa's concerns sounds genuine. She was also particularly helpful with suggestions about the staffing of the Institut Elisa.

Madame de Laplace frequently met the Imperial family socially or else she paid them visits in order to give news of Elisa or to collect messages to send to her. Caroline had had her portrait painted by Gérard to send to her sister; the Court was moving from St. Cloud to Fontainebleau; Jerome, now King of Westphalia, was very well and sent tender messages to his dear sister; his new wife, Princess Catherine, was most anxious to meet her sister-in-law, for Elisa was too busy to go to Paris for the wedding; Madame Letizia had been unwell but was better and had charged Madame de Laplace with kind messages for her daughter; Pauline, of course, had also been ill but was now somewhat better; at a dinner followed by a concert at the Tuileries Caroline looked brilliantly beautiful in rose-coloured silk embroidered with silver and a bandeau of turquoises.

Always Madame de Laplace made careful notes about Caroline's toilettes, her hair styles and her entertainments, sending back faithful reports to Elisa. The rose-coloured dresses Caroline affected became her blonde beauty, but Madame de Laplace tactfully chose white for Elisa which suited her swarthy complexion better. Anxiously she warned her mistress that garlands were now worn to one side of the head not to hide the tiara and, when the Court went into mourning for the Empress of Austria, she took it upon herself to order mourning for Elisa, hastening to tell her that a wreath of black flowers might be worn during the period of deep mourning but not for half-mourning.

In one month alone Madame de Laplace sent to Lucca two ball dresses, a redingote, one full dress and four other dresses and another consignment included sixteen pairs of white satin sandals and eight dozen pairs of gloves. No wonder she complained that everything was fearfully expensive, especially since Elisa bought at Leroy's, disdaining Pauline's economies.

Finding money for her wardrobe, for furnishing her palaces, for maintaining the dignity of her Court, and above all for paying her tribute to the French treasury, constituted one of Elisa's greatest problems. The Emperor's praise was gratifying but she was not so pleased with his constant demands for money.

With due submission but also with great firmness she pleaded for a reduction in the amounts levied on Lucca. Of course if he insisted she would do her utmost to get the money for him, but where was it to come from? There was an answer. The monasteries and nunneries were extremely rich, owning a disproportionate amount of the wealth of the community, a source which so far had not been tapped. Elisa had no scruples about dissolving the religious communities, having long since left behind her the piety of St. Cyr, but there were difficulties to be overcome, the Pope's antagonism and the attachment of the Luccans to their monks and nuns. Consequently Elisa hesitated until she received the categorical order, 'This must come to an end once and for all. I desire that the religious orders should be suppressed.'

The Emperor's command was naturally carried out but it was much resented by the people of Lucca and engendered some political unrest. To conciliate a minority of the population, Elisa extended to the Jews of her States the full civil rights they now enjoyed in France.

To make up the deficits in her personal expenditure Elisa

asked her brother to buy back from her the Hôtel Maurepas in Paris; she felt that, in future, the city would see little of her and she no longer needed to maintain a home there. She also asked him to pay back on Pauline's behalf money she had borrowed from her; it was a habit of Pauline's to borrow money from her sisters, although she always ultimately paid it back.

Elisa plumed herself on her punctuality in congratulating the Emperor on his victories and in arranging for Te Deums to be sung on every possible occasion; these ceremonies consumed a great deal of time during her years at Lucca. In 1805 there were the victories of Ulm and Austerlitz over the Austrians to be commemorated, although there was no Te Deum for Trafalgar. In the following year came the Peace of Pressburg with Austria and the defeat of Prussia at Jena. Russia was crushed at Eylau and Friedland in 1807 and there was the Treaty of Tilsit between Napoleon and the Czar Alexander I to be celebrated.

The Emperor became extremely weary of receiving the special emissaries sent to his headquarters by the Princess of Lucca. He disliked the way she fawned on him, yet he could not resist her slavish request that she might henceforward be known as Elisa-Napoleon, an outrageous piece of sycophancy which was copied by Murat and Jerome.

Elisa was satisfied that she had made Lucca a model state. True, there were always difficulties about payments to France, taxes and customs duties, but in every other respect she had shown marked efficiency. She thought it time to extend her sphere of influence for which an opportunity presented itself when Napoleon visited Venice and he allowed her to meet him there.

This was an apotheosis for which Elisa had longed, to appear in public at the Emperor's side, share in his triumphs and in all the great ceremonies of welcome. With unctuous compliments she thanked him for all the benefits bestowed on her and, in the course of conferences with him, learned of an opportunity for gratifying her ambition to rule over a larger territory;

Tuscany was shortly to be incorporated in France but its sovereignty was going begging.

Elisa pleaded eloquently that her devotion to her brother and French interests had earned her the right to increase her consequence. For three years she had acted at Lucca strictly in accordance with their needs while Baciocchi had faithfully reviewed every tiny Luccan regiment. In putting forward her claims Elisa did not, unlike Caroline, have to exonerate her husband from some stupid act or ineptitude, and was secure in the knowledge that there was little anger or irritation on her brother's part to counter.

While she thought she had convinced Napoleon of the justice of her claims, to make assurance double sure she wrote, on her way home from Venice, to the French Minister of the Interior, so that there should be no doubts as to where she stood.

> I am very anxious to have an extension of territory. Since I cannot live near His Majesty in Paris I wish to have a State which would not be unworthy of belonging to me. I have very little ambition but, since I am the Emperor's sister, I ought to want and have a right to more than the 150,000 inhabitants who make up the Principality of Lucca. . . .

Right? Elisa was falling back into the error of believing that the Emperor's family had rights not privileges, an error which Lucien echoed when, on his way home, Napoleon had a definitive interview with him, the first time the brothers had met since Lucien's disgrace. On this occasion the Emperor offered Lucien any European throne he would like if only he would renounce his wife.

Lucien was older now and wiser but even more attached to Alexandrine than heretofore, and he had been looking at the Empire objectively from the outside. His words expressed what the other members of the family felt but did not dare to say.

'I do not want to be your prefect—if you give me a kingdom I want to rule it in accordance with my own ideas, above all according to its own needs. . . . I do not want the people whose ruler I would be to curse my name. I would want them to be happy and not slaves as they are in Tuscany or the rest of Italy.'

It was Tuscany that Napoleon wanted to give Lucien but not to rule according to his expressed ideas. Tuscany was too large and too rich to be allowed independence or to be the appanage of a prince of the family. As a feoffee of France the new sovereign would be a Governor-General just as Eugène was merely Viceroy of Italy. Whoever held Tuscany would reign but not rule. As Lucien rejected it it must go to Elisa since no other member of the family was available or competent to take it.

Even with these disadvantages Elisa still coveted Tuscany but, in spite of her intrigues, slavering and even rages, Napoleon delayed in handing it over to her. It was not until March, 1809, after a year's impatient waiting, that Elisa was at last created Grand Duchess of Tuscany, a territory which, at her insistence, included Elba.

CHAPTER NINE

GRAND DUCHESS OF CLEVES AND BERG

Caroline's satisfaction at finding herself at last a reigning Princess was marred by the fact that her State was only a Grand Duchy. Although Grand Duchies did not yet have their frivolous association with musical comedy a Grand Duchess was in no way comparable with a Queen.

While Murat went off to Germany to claim his new honours Caroline remained in Paris, for she did not intend to copy Elisa; Cleves and Berg provided her with a title and revenues, but she saw no reason for exiling herself. However disappointed she was with her new status, she still took her position very seriously. Laure d'Abrantès observed that she now talked a great deal about herself and her person with much consideration and a slight sneer for others, and developed a schoolgirl snigger which was most displeasing. Even discounting the Duchesse's malice, there is no doubt that Caroline was feeling the same intoxication with her elevation as Charles James Fox observed in her brother.

Vigée Le Brun recalled with no pleasure her assignment to paint Caroline's portrait, which she undertook for 1,800 francs, half her normal fee, including, for the sake of her composition, little Letizia Murat in the same painting for the same price... 'It would be impossible for me,' she wrote in her Memoirs, 'to describe all the torments and annoyances with which I had to put up while I was painting this portrait.'

For the first sitting Caroline arrived with two maids to do her hair but, as throughout the sitting she constantly changed her hair style, her headdress and her dresses it was obvious that she had not the smallest idea of sitting for a portrait. All these changes obliged the poor painter constantly to paint out and to repaint, but even more irritating was Caroline's failure to keep her appointments, which made Vigée Le Brun hang about Paris throughout the summer. Finally she became so exasperated that she remarked to a visitor in her studio, loud enough for Caroline to hear, 'I have painted real princesses who never caused me so much trouble nor ever kept me waiting.' And her final devastating comment was, 'The truth of the matter is that Madame Murat was completely ignorant of the fact that punctuality is the politeness of kings as Louis XIV so truly said, and he indeed was no parvenu!'

Vigée Le Brun had her revenge because her portrait of Caroline is the least flattering ever painted of her. She appears awkward, stout and badly dressed with the vapid expression of an amiable cow.

Murat was called away from the congenial occupation of squeezing as much as he could out of Cleves and Berg to take part in the next campaign, in which he again brilliantly distinguished himself at Jena in October, 1806. His conduct earned him not only compliments from Napoleon but naturally a letter of congratulation from Elisa, whose couriers were kept busy posting about Europe with her eulogies.

From Jena the Army moved on to Berlin where Napoleon issued his decrees instituting his Continental System, the blockade of English goods and bottoms to the Continent. This policy greatly annoyed his sisters who were not prepared to renounce their India muslins and cashmere shawls for which they were now, with Leroy's connivance, obliged to pay the inflated price of all smuggled goods.

By November Murat reached Warsaw where he was so flattered by his reception that the idea of becoming King of Poland now entered his head, for which he was rebuked; 'Do not let them think I am seeking a throne for my family. I am not short of thrones for them.'

The winter was very gay in Warsaw. Murat enjoyed himself greatly, one of his pleasurable activities being to lay siege to the charming and witty Countess Potocka. But siege warfare was not his forte and he found himself outgunned by his own aide-de-camp, Charles de Flahaut, the son of Talleyrand and the Comtesse de Flahaut.

Murat would have been considerably deflated had he known the Countess's assessment of him :

> Prince Murat was supposed to be handsome, but his countenance was lacking in nobility and entirely devoid of expression. He had the majestic air of an actor playing at being a king, and it was easy to see that his manners were assumed and not natural. He did not talk badly because he was very careful in what he said, but his Gascon accent and some expressions that smacked of the camp rather gave the lie to ' the Prince '. He did not converse, he talked, flattering himself that he was listened to, if not with pleasure, then at least with respectful deference.

Borghese was also in Warsaw with the army but was regarded as an absolute cipher as well as a subject for mirth.

> I shall never forget, [wrote the Countess] how, when the conversation took a slightly serious turn for a very few brief moments, he went off to look for chairs, arranged them two by two right in the middle of the drawing-room, and amused himself by humming a tune and dancing with these dumb partners.

In Paris the winter of 1806–7 was equally brilliant in spite of the absence of so many young men scattered all over Europe ; Caroline was now the leading figure in society for Josephine had given up dancing and Pauline went out only when the whim took her. To Hortense in Holland Caroline wrote, describing how she spent her days,

> I dance all night, sleep part of the day, and the rest of my time I spend attending to my letters, receiving visits and waiting for the couriers. Why are you not here, my dear

Hortense? You would enjoy our balls so much. I think the movement of the legs calms the head !

But Caroline did not tell Hortense all that was in her mind. She shared with Elisa supreme self-confidence in her own capacity. It was her judgment which had singled out Murat as a husband, acknowledged the most brilliant cavalry commander in Europe, and who was rapidly fulfilling all her hopes of him. Her marriage was happy even though she now appreciated the weaknesses in Murat's character but she was fully confident that her influence and guidance would direct him aright.

Caroline was not sufficiently introvert to see that so much success and adulation were leading her to megalomania nor that she had come to love power, not as her brother did, as a musician loves his instrument for the chords and harmonies he draws from it, but for itself, a love that grew until it developed into a passion as compulsive as that of a gambler chasing elusive gains until the pursuit destroys him.

Caroline was obsessed by the question of the succession to her brother, ignoring the fact that it was now regulated by decree. She no longer wanted the divorce since, if Napoleon re-married, he would probably have a child which would rule out her new idea, that Murat was far and away the logical choice to succeed to the throne. To those who doubted his capacity she would have pointed to her own.

Supplanting her brother was impossible but even a commanding general is subject to the hazards of war. So far, in spite of slight wounds at Toulon and Marengo, Napoleon had escaped a fatality, but if he should be killed or incapacitated ? Prudence and patriotism alike demanded that France and its Empire should devolve upon capable hands, her own and Murat's rather than those of Joseph or Louis.

How long this idea had been evolving in Caroline's brain is difficult to assess, perhaps from the time Achille was born and unsuccessfully dedicated to be the Emperor's favourite nephew, but it was not longer a question of Achille first. This new plan, however, was something to be kept from her brother since she was scheming for an eventuality when he would have disappeared from the scene.

Caroline was convinced that this was a favourable moment to move her next piece on the board. Both Napoleon and Murat were far away in Warsaw, so that one should not get wind of her plans nor the other interfere with them. The man who held the key to the situation should the Emperor be killed was Junot, who had succeeded Murat as Governor of Paris and Commander of the First Military Division. His would be the duty of maintaining order in the capital in the event of Napoleon's death and his was the vital position should a new *coup d'état* be necessary. Junot's devotion to Napoleon, to whom he had been attached since the early Toulon days, ruled out the possibility even of sounding him about a hypothetical future, but he was a man of Murat's stamp, coarse, vulgar, swaggering and a tremendous lady-killer. He could be wooed by other means.

Coldly and deliberately Caroline set out to seduce Junot, riding roughshod over the friendship which had linked the Murats and the Junots in the early days of their marriages. Fate must be seized by the throat, no matter who got strangled.

It is difficult for a man to resist when a young, charming and pretty woman, who in addition wears the aureole of being sister to a man one adores, sets out to enslave him. Junot found the gradation from falling in love with one Bonaparte sister to another easy, although he made the mistake of falling genuinely and sincerely in love with Caroline.

Part of her plan was to parade her affair with Junot. Soon everyone in Paris knew that the Governor of Paris opened the ball with the Grand Duchess of Berg, that he rode beside the Grand Duchess of Berg, that he danced attendance on the Grand Duchess of Berg, that the Grand Duchess of Berg sat in his box at the opera, and that his livery was seen at all hours in the courtyard of the Elysée.

Even Pauline, paying a morning call on Laure Junot, adopted an unusually serious tone to say,

'If Junot is out so early he's probably gone to the Elysée. He is the chief director of everything that happens there. You really ought not to put up with it.'

'There is nothing I can do,' Laure answered sadly, with no pretence that she did not know what Pauline was talking about.

Laure herself was in no doubt that Caroline's pursuit of Junot was with the object of attaching him to Murat's party. No one talked about it, she said, but once the comic side of Murat taking Napoleon's place vanished, and the idea became familiar, then the moment would inevitably follow when one would become impatient that the enemy's bullets were taking so long to reach him. 'And from this germ the idea of anticipating the enemy's bullet inexorably follows'.

This may have been going too far, but Caroline was going far enough in the insolent way in which she flaunted her conquest. The climax came with the amateur theatricals performed at Malmaison for Josephine's saint's day. Neither Pauline nor even Caroline now cared a pin for her, but it gave them one of their cherished occasions for displaying themselves on the stage, and for Caroline endless opportunities for rehearsals with Junot, who played opposite her lead.

Neither sister shone as an actress but the play went off as plays go. Afterwards, for some unexplained reason, Caroline chose to return to Paris in the company of Junot—and Laure. When they reached the Elysée Junot handed Caroline out of her carriage and followed her into the palace. Laure waited—an hour, two hours, then ordered the coachman to whip up his horses and take her home. The vulgarity of Caroline's behaviour on this occasion was unpardonable and unpardoned by Laure; it is always dangerous to antagonise people who may write their memoirs because writers, like artists, have the last word.

Although Caroline thought her brother would not get wind of her exploits he was informed by his efficient police but, when he returned to Paris in July, 1807, after an absence of ten months, it was Junot who was reprimanded for having compromised his sister and sent into gilded disgrace at Lisbon. Thereafter Laure nursed a bitter hatred against Caroline, convinced that by this unhappy affair she set in train the chain of events which led to Junot's madness and suicide.

Caroline did not escape scatheless, but her brother credulously believed that Caesar's sisters were above suspicion, guilty of nothing more serious than flirtatious and frivolous conduct. Her punishment was that Junot disappeared from his position as Governor of Paris and all her intrigues went for nothing, but the idea continued to obsess her. She found new allies where they were least expected. Neither Talleyrand nor Fouché, the diabolical duumvirate of the Empire, could be classed as dreamers; their previous enmity made their present alliance more formidable. They both shared Caroline's anxiety about the succession, with graver doubts as to the future of France should Napoleon be killed since Joseph and Louis were generally held to be of a ' revolting incapacity '. As a popular soldier Murat, allied to the Emperor by marriage and with sons to secure his dynasty, was a more acceptable successor to the kingmakers because his weaknesses would ensure that he might reign but they would rule. Napoleon, however, obstinately refused to be killed and, when this scheme also came to nothing, Caroline was obliged to seek a new outlet for her activities.

When Hortense's son, Napoleon-Louis, died, Caroline showed real affection by going to Holland and bringing her back to Paris to distract her mind from her grief, which was intensified by the unhappiness of her marriage. This kindliness was obliterated by Caroline's passing affair with Charles de Flahaut, with whom Hortense was deeply in love, while Flahaut was in love with Countess Potocka.

It would take a mathematician to work out all the permutations and combinations of the lover-mistress-husband-wife relationships of Imperial society, because often the scarcity of men in Paris led to an obliging stallion like Flahaut being the lover of at least four women at the same time, with all the consequent intrigues, counter-intrigues, jealousies and complications.

Caroline was said to choose her lovers strictly for political motives. If this was not true of Flahaut it may have been partially true of the next object on whom she practised the arts of higher prostitution, although Count Metternich, the Austrian Ambassador, was also a very attractive man. He, as well as Caroline, realised the advantages of finding his extra-marital adventures in a milieu which would serve his interests. If Caroline sought to use Metternich she found herself used as a listening-post, but her association with him did bring her to appreciate the great importance of Austria in European affairs. It was only rough justice when Laure Junot took Metternich away from her.

Murat did not compete in this amatory gymkhana, partly because he spent little time in Paris, and partly because he preferred to take his pleasures in a lower order of society. His prolonged absences were responsible for the weakening of the important physical influence he had over Caroline and friction between the couple grew as Murat made more mistakes off the battlefield. Caroline felt herself to be increasingly his superior in political manœuvre, while he grew more irritated by her authoritarianism which made him feel insufficient. Concord between them was not helped by the kind of rebuke Murat was earning himself.

> Your rank in my palace is fixed by the rank you have in my family, and your rank in my family is fixed by the rank of my sister. Her elders must pass before her. I cannot accord to you in my Court the rank of a foreign Prince. You are the most fortunate man on earth from every point of view, but you are spoiling your own happiness. You do not appreciate that to earn consideration in matters of rank you must not ask for more than your due.

It is wounding to a man's self-esteem to be constantly reminded that he owes a great part of his advancement to his wife, particularly when he feels that he has earned it by his own deeds.

It is not therefore surprising that, when he was taken to task for mismanagement in his Grand Duchy, Murat exclaimed, 'The Emperor wants me to be a sovereign in order to obey and receive orders ; it is impossible. There is a strange contradiction here. Why didn't he leave me as a colonel or general of brigade? I should not have degraded myself by obeying orders.'

No doubt it came as a relief both to Caroline and Murat when, in April, 1808, he was appointed as the Emperor's Lieutenant in Spain, which had become a French satellite. Here Caroline could not outshine him and she was more confident that, in a military command, he would show his real capacity.

In his own estimation he fulfilled his mission with distinction and, since it was clear that the Spanish Bourbons were to be ousted and the throne of Spain was going to fall within the gift of Napoleon, Murat once again began to dream of a crown. But, although his brother considered him to be the worst Head of State imaginable, the crown of Spain was awarded to Joseph. Murat was so violently disappointed that he developed a severe attack of jaundice and a nervous breakdown, which led him to leave the army to nurse his chagrin and his illness.

The year 1808 was the predatory year of the Empire in which the Bonapartes growled round their brother's cave, seeking ever larger bones from his kill. In Lucca Elisa was clamouring for Tuscany; in Paris Caroline shared Murat's disappointment that Spain had fallen to the civilian Joseph's share, rather than to Joachim's, who had played so large a part in the Spanish business.

At last a letter from Napoleon invited the Murats to meet him at Bayonne where he offered them the crown of the Two Sicilies which Joseph had doffed. It was a small crown when compared with that of Spain or Poland but for Murat it was at last a kingdom.

'If they put a crown on that head,' someone remarked sapiently, 'both will fall.'

He spoke with more justice than he knew.

Alone of the sisters Pauline was not interested in ruling over anything other than Parisian society or the hearts of her admirers, but nevertheless her pleasure at finding herself a reigning Duchess turned to dismay when she learnt that Guastalla was a mere village. She willingly traded in the sovereignty for hard cash, while keeping the title of Duchess of Guastalla. If Elisa was a reigning Princess and Caroline a Grand Duchess then she could not remain simply Princess Borghese! But the title in which she gloried most was Queen of Hearts.

Pauline Borghese's reputation as a *grande amoureuse* was such that it was enough to be seen in her company to be branded as one of her lovers. It is unfortunate that the word 'lover' in English is used to translate both the French *amoureux* and *amant*, the distinction being between one who sighs in vain and one who sighs with fulfilment. Pauline certainly had innumerable *amoureux* but not perhaps quite as many *amants* as she is credited with.

To enter into details of both categories would require volumes, but on analysis they fell into two classes of society. One would have expected her to take her pick of the gay, handsome and gallant young officers of her brother's armies, so paying him a subtle compliment. It was one, however, that he did not appreciate and brother and sister waged a private guerrilla war about these young men. Napoleon believed that Pauline as well as Caroline was no more than a giddy flirt, but he did demand that she should behave with circumspection so, as soon as a dashing hussar or grenadier showed too great an interest in the lovely Princess Borghese, he was whisked away on a tour of duty. Not the least fascinating part of the game to Pauline was outwitting her brother.

There was less hazard in the irresistible attraction that men of the theatre and the world of music had for her. The Bonapartes were full of unexpressed artistic temperament, and they were all attracted in others by the creative talent they lacked. Elisa, married to a musician, if Baciocchi's scraping on the violin entitled him to be called such, found great satisfaction in the company of artists, musicians and writers. Napoleon's amatory excursions in the theatre were many, and Pauline had chosen Lafon, an actor, while later there was Talma, the greatest actor of the age, and later still the composers, Blangini and Pacini.

During the years since her marriage to Borghese Pauline had been leading a life of great prudence, with no serious attachment, which she found extremely irksome because her heart was functioning in a vacuum. Her health during this period had been worse than usual although she could on occasion rouse herself when there was pleasure in prospect. This capacity for shaking off her illness when amusement offered has been seen as a sign of hypochondria which is in part correct. There was probably a psychosomatic element in her recurrent illness but also, like all chronic conditions, it was subject to fluctuation and, in her better moments, she found the energy necessary to take part in the brilliant entertainments which kept Paris so continuously gay.

Borghese's return to Paris from the army coincided with an urgent desire on her part to go and take the waters, and it may have been by design that at Plombières she met the Comte de Forbin, whose acquaintance she had probably made in Rome.

Forbin, handsome, aristocratic, extremely charming, was neither soldier nor actor but an artist. Whether they met in Rome while he was studying painting there or not is immaterial, for at Plombières Pauline fell madly in love with him. Her love affair with him was intense, passionate and almost fatal because her obsession with him was so great that she declined visibly, although nothing would persuade her to detach herself from him; no doubt in temperament Forbin had much in common with Murat.

To ensure his perpetual presence Pauline named Forbin as her chamberlain, but there were too many of her attendants to inform her mother and her uncle, Fesch, of the alarming state of her health. At their instigation a famous gynaecologist, Dr. Hallé, was called into consultation with her own doctor, Peyre, who had been her personal physician since San Domingo.

Hallé informed Peyre of his conclusions in a famous letter.

Her habitual and constant state is one of uterine excitement and if this state is continued and prolonged it can become alarming. The spasms I saw in her arms were hysteric and so were the headaches. Her general condition is one of exhaustion. I talked to her in general terms about everything which contributed to the uterine irritation and I thought she listened to me but I'm afraid not sufficiently. One cannot always make douches responsible and one must suppose that in a young, pretty, sensitive and solitary woman, who is visibly fading away, there is a constant cause for this decline. Whatever this cause is it is time and more than time to eliminate it.

Neither Hallé nor Peyre had any doubt that the cause was named Forbin but Pauline had no intention of giving him up, although she did not want to precipitate a full-dress quarrel with her mother, who would undoubtedly inform the Emperor; if he commanded her to dismiss Forbin, she would have no alternative but to obey.

To checkmate her family and her doctors Pauline sent most of her entourage home, except the very few whom she could trust not to tell tales, and moved ever southwards until she ended up at a small spa, Gréoulx, where she could be safe from outside interference. Here Forbin rejoined her. They passed an idyllic few months, but the fire had been too fierce and in the end it burnt itself out. Either Forbin solicited an appointment in the army or perhaps Napoleon, who had inevitably discovered who Pauline's latest preoccupation was, politely invited him to take a commission.

So the lovers parted but it is noteworthy that Pauline rarely quarrelled with any of the men to whom she was attached, with the exception of Borghese, and they always kept a kindness for each other.

After Forbin's departure Pauline remained in the south of France, drifting from one place to another in her chair or litter carried by porters, when she found the movement of a carriage too painful, until she finally came to rest at Nice where she spent the winter of 1807–8.

Her most urgent problem was to find a successor to Forbin so she called from Paris her *maître de chapelle*, Felix Blangini. Like all her lovers Blangini was young and handsome but he was not an aristocrat nor as cultured as Forbin. On the other hand, on account of his humble position, he was much more biddable but also much more overwhelmed by his sudden rise to the honour of being the *amant en titre* of the Princess Borghese; nor was it a situation without its dangers. Timorous by nature, Blangini went in some terror when she insisted on parading him in public: 'I was not in the least anxious to run the risk of being offered a lieutenant's commission to go and sing my nocturnes in Spain to the accompaniment of whistling balls and bullets.'

The harum-scarum household at Nice was very musical—even the cook played the guitar all day long. Pauline's new idyll was one of harmonies and romances, composed by Blangini, and duets which they sang together, she always slightly off-key.

For Pauline this interlude was one of pure distraction, a mere indulgence of the senses; Blangini did not touch her heart as Forbin had done but for him 'if my slavery was sweet, it was none the less slavery.' He may have been relieved, although Pauline was extremely annoyed, when her stay in Nice was cut short by the arrival of Borghese, who had been appointed Governor-General of the Italian departments north of the Alps. Flanked on one side by Eugène de Beauharnais and the other by Elisa he could not really do much harm in this position, certainly less than in Portugal. Although it is scarcely credible Napoleon had toyed with the idea of making Pauline Queen of Portugal.

Pauline was sufficiently put out that she would have to assume the fatigues and obligations of the wife of a Governor-General, especially as she must now keep house again with Camillo. Their journey from Nice to Turin was one of high comedy, since

Pauline alternated between venting her ill-humour on him and quarrelling about who was to receive the honours on the various stages of their journey. Although she had not the faintest desire to listen to or answer speeches, Camillo had to understand that *she* was the Emperor's sister and it was through her that he had reached his eminent position. Her lady-in-waiting's feelings can only be imagined as she listened to the bickering—particularly as Pauline was using her as a foot-warmer.

Blangini was not included in her new household but Pauline insisted on his accompanying them. He, however, had had more than enough of his position and was even more apprehensive in Camillo's presence of the signal favour shown him. Why did Pauline always insist on receiving him when she was in her bath? A little intrigue and Blangini was offered the position of music master to Jerome in Westphalia. Much to his relief Pauline nobly said that she would not stand in the way of his advancement and the affair was settled to their mutual satisfaction.

Pauline's new office brought her the usual stream of exhortations from Napoleon; she was to make herself loved, to be affable to all, to be good-tempered and to make the Prince happy. She was naturally inclined to heed the first three pieces of advice, although she differed from her brother as to the degree to which she was to make herself loved, but she was annoyed by the admonition to make the Prince happy. Since, in spite of his fortune and his Roman nobility, he owed everything to his marriage to her, the onus was on him to make *her* happy.

His efforts to do so made Pauline ill again. Camillo was evidently trying to put into effect the advice urged on him again by Angiolini: 'If Pauline has a son everything will go well for you and for her. To have a son is of first importance to her, and also to you, and for all those who love you and wish you well.'

A resumption of married life with Camillo found Pauline as bored with it as before, nor did she like Turin and the duties her new status required her to fulfil. It was so dull to hold court in imitation of the Tuileries, while naturally the climate of Turin did not agree with her! To entertain the Murat children on their way south to Naples was only a brief distraction as their visit was short.

As often as she could Pauline escaped from Turin to a little hunting lodge at Stupigini, but when Joseph visited her there on his way from Naples to Madrid he was alarmed by her health and counselled her to leave at once for a spa without waiting for Napoleon's permission to absent herself from her post.

Pauline needed no urging and, by the time the Emperor's order came that she was to go to a spa within her husband's government, she was already at Aix-en-Savoie.

From Aix she wrote to Napoleon:

> I feel it is quite impossible to return to Piedmont as the climate is very bad for me since in six weeks I have lost the benefits of a year of treatment and a strict régime. I can now only hope to improve by means of continual denial which will take time.

Pauline complained that she was suffering from fits of vomiting and that more than ever before she must be allowed to return to Paris: 'It is impossible for me any longer to endure an existence so wretched and painful.'

Whether Napoleon took her seriously or not we do not know but he allowed her to return to Paris and chided her no more. On the contrary he was very kind to her, gave her the property at Neuilly which had been the Murats' and lavish gifts of money. In all probability he was glad to have her back in Paris because, although he sent his family far and wide, he seems never to have been so happy as when they were all around him.

CHAPTER TEN

QUEEN OF NAPLES

When, in September, 1808, Caroline Murat made her state entry into her Kingdom of the Two Sicilies she should have been a very happy woman. The crown she had so long coveted was at last hers, but the satisfaction she thought to find in wearing it eluded her.

First of all the Murats' kingdom was only titularly that of the Two Sicilies; in Sicily itself the Bourbons, supported by the British fleet, remained entrenched and a constant menace to the security of the mainland. This truncation of their territory robbed the Murats of consequence and revenue, the more exasperating because Joseph had left the public finances of Naples in a deplorable state, having, in addition, virtually sacked the royal palaces so that they took possession of bare rooms and little else. They could not furnish their new homes from their properties in France because they had had to cede them to the Emperor with all their furnishings, valued at four million francs, against an annual compensation of 500,000 francs which, in fact, was never paid.

To the disappointment which still rankled about Spain Caroline added other sources of unhappiness. She faced an indefinite absence from Paris—after all Elisa had not been back even once since she went to Lucca in 1805—and from her family. She did not feel well and complained of the climate, although she admitted that the country was beautiful and the palaces superb, Caserta being in her estimation much superior to Versailles; but to reach her apartments in Naples she had to climb nearly three hundred stairs, while the noise of the arsenal below prevented her sleeping. Greater than these inconveniences was her fear lest in Naples she lose her influence with Napoleon, ever more important to maintain as Murat's behaviour was already giving her cause for anxiety.

His military reputation, his swagger and panache delighted the Neapolitan populace, but the nobility were more reserved. Certainly Murat pleased them more than Caroline, whose hauteur was sharply criticised. The general consensus of opinion was that he played his part of king extremely well, talked and received people with ease and dignity, with nothing in speech or manner to betray his origins, a verdict that the Countess Potocka would have found surprising. It was conceded that Caroline bore herself like a queen; even Vigée Le Brun would have been perfectly satisfied with her behaviour because she had learned much—even punctuality.

At Court the Neapolitans still regarded the French as intruders and usurpers, while the small French colony was a minority always on the defensive. There were very few French in Naples and Caroline felt lonely, so lonely that she invited Madame de Cavaignac, wife of the general who had once been Murat's colonel, to visit her often and without wearing a train, a remarkable concession from one to whom a rigid etiquette was essential.

The etiquette she instituted was, like Elisa's, even stricter than at the Tuileries. To maintain her royal dignity Caroline required a Grand Marshal of the Palace, a Master of Ceremonies, a Grand Huntsman, innumerable chamberlains, equerries, ladies-in-waiting and pages, all obliged to wear full dress from their first appearance of the day. Although dazzled by the colour and flamboyance of the uniforms even little Louise Murat found it all very absurd, particularly the costumes of the *dames d'annonce* stationed at every door of Caroline's apartments. They wore dresses of canary-yellow satin, the sleeves and hem slashed with white satin, and on their heads toques of white satin and tulle with the inevitable white plumes.

Etiquette weighed heavily on the children as well as the shadow of the Emperor who influenced their studies and their amusements. Because Tasso was one of his favourite poets they had to learn his stanzas by heart; because he might one day ask Letizia to play chess with him she had to learn the moves. Only their father threw the exaggerated manifestations of royalty to the winds where they were concerned. He adored them all, but Letizia was his idol. Always he carried with him the charming moustache comb of gold, the handle inlaid with turquoises, which Letizia and Louise had given him.

The children returned his adoration, going so far as to address him by the familiar 'thou', but only when Caroline was not present because she would not have tolerated this liberty.

Of Caroline they went in some awe; they loved her but they were afraid of her. Her affection was not demonstrative. Days went by without her seeing the children, which she excused by saying that she kept them at a distance because she was afraid of spoiling them as Murat did, but it is notable that her daughter, Louise, writes of her with some reserve.

Even during a bitter war with England, Napoleon's sister, the Queen of Naples, thought it indispensable for her children to have English governesses. Mrs. Pulsford and Miss Davies were probably among the earliest of the host of English nannies and governesses who left their indelible stamp on generations of foreign families. Caroline, also, seems to have come under their influence because it must have been from them that she learned to love tea in real English style, with toast, muffins and crumpets, a taste no doubt largely responsible for her increasing plumpness.

Miss Davies has left an artless memoir about her eleven years' residence with the Murat family; she tells how Caroline furnished her palaces, more like fairy palaces to Miss Davies than anything she had seen in England or France.

> The Queen, who was a person of great taste, made many improvements in and about the palaces at Naples, which had been till then in a very neglected state, having little of the appearance of a royal residence: but the alterations she made were very magnificent and suitable to the rank she held.

But there was a reverse to the medal, which shows that being a member of Caroline's household was no sinecure.

> Everything in her palaces was conducted in an admirable manner and with perfect regularity. Moments passed without employment were irksome to her; nor did she allow others to spend time unoccupied.

Caroline's deepest concern, however, was neither with her Court nor her household, but with her husband. In a few months a matter of common gossip was the open discord between them, founded on Caroline's determination to rule as well as reign, a determination fiercely resisted by Murat.

Nagging at Caroline's consciousness was that clause in the Treaty of Bayonne which ensured to her, should she survive Joachim, the crown in her own right, she alone to have the title and powers of monarchy to exercise fully and independently. This was a notable advance on the letters patent creating Murat Grand Duke of Cleves and Berg, in which she did not figure, although he himself had wished to insert a clause that she should be regent in the event of his death.

The Treaty of Bayonne marked the change which had taken place in the Emperor's estimate of his sister and of his brother-in-law. 'This unique exception to a fundamental law', ran the clause, 'is inspired by the fact that this cession of the Kingdom which places her family on the throne has been made primarily in her favour.'

This clause was title enough to Caroline's intention to have an equal share in the government of Naples and to show her brother and the world that she had at least as much capacity as her sister, Elisa.

Madame de Cavaignac remarked that Elisa's example had turned Caroline's head; she had never, during a four years' association at Naples, seen in her any qualities which justified her claim to govern. She thought that Caroline's ambition came from being born a Bonaparte, and that her vanity had taken the wrong turning; the rôle of pretty and charming woman was the one for which nature had fitted her, had she not been obsessed by the desire to ape Napoleon—and Elisa.

But Madame de Cavaignac had once seen that pretty and charming face distorted into one of hardness, evil and hate, a memory that remained with her, so that always she saw the other face as if behind a mask.

Elisa, however, had had the foresight to provide herself with a husband who was content to be her first lackey, who arrogated to himself no rights other than those of conjugality, and even these he amiably ceded when Elisa's fancy temporarily fell elsewhere. In Tuscany nothing changed for him except that Elisa now encroached on his province and was at his side on horseback in a magnificent hussar uniform when he reviewed the troops.

Immediately Elisa received notice that she was at last to be Grand Duchess of Tuscany she and Felix scrambled into the Palazzo Pitti in Florence, determined at all costs to stay there. It was immaterial to her that her brother made it quite clear that her position was not to be the same as at Lucca. There she might be as independent as he allowed any of his satellites to be, but at Florence she was his lieutenant and nothing more.

Nothing daunted Elisa was convinced that she would soon show how well she performed her duties in the larger sphere now hers and she began at once to inaugurate activities similar to those which she had pursued at Lucca.

Her first task was to show herself to her new subjects. By her ceaseless round of visits throughout the province she bent herself to achieving popularity but, in spite of all her efforts, the Tuscan nobility remained cold. Elisa both earned her brother's disapproval for being too precipitate in what she did and found that her larger responsibilities were not bringing her the satisfaction for which she had hoped.

Tuscany, moreover, was not as calm as Lucca and there were disturbances when the Pope passed through the State on his way to France. Elisa was now too fearful of displeasing her brother to go and meet the Pontiff, which might have prejudiced the extremely delicate political manœuvre of taking him prisoner.

Elisa, anxious about the British squadron operating in the Mediterranean, was glad to have Murat's reassurance that they were not making for Tuscany. Moreover, if she was frightened of their appearance on her coasts, 'I shall not forget that in Naples I have the Achilles of France and I should be perfectly reassured that his heart and his strong right arm are with me.' The Prince had just come back from Leghorn and sent tender messages to Murat, messages which he received with some contempt for he shared Napoleon's opinions: 'Baciocchi has done nothing, he is incapable of governing, but Murat has earned his crown.'

Nevertheless, Murat was haunted by Baciocchi. He feared that, if Caroline was allowed to gain too much ascendancy over him, he would soon be reduced to the same position and would be merely husband of the Queen, so that he took umbrage at the slightest encroachment on his powers.

This jealousy and suspicion made normal relations between husband and wife extremely difficult and Murat's feelings towards Caroline reached a psychopathic point of violence. His daughter, Louise, thought that he was wrong to fear that he might ever dwindle into a Baciocchi as his own personal qualities were too great and Caroline's sense of her own dignity too strong for her to try to impose so ridiculous a rôle on her husband.

It is probable that Murat had by no means recovered from his nervous breakdown in Spain. His temper, always violent, was more uncertain than normally, and he was exacerbated by Caroline's attempts to be admitted to the Council of State and to take an active part in government. He was the more susceptible because, behind Caroline, he saw the brother who continued to hold him on a tight rein.

Murat's great defect in character was that he had no self-knowledge. He was irresolute except on the battlefield and thought he could extricate himself from any difficulty by a gasconade. Although he boasted that 'The Emperor thinks I will yield, but I am like iron, and I shall show him so,' he was in fact flabby in willpower and unable to impose himself either on Napoleon or on Caroline.

During their years at Naples the Murats went through recurrent periods of crisis, fighting a battle of wills as to which should dominate the other. When Caroline could make no progress against her husband's obstinacy she resorted to intrigue and subterranean efforts to undermine his obduracy.

News inevitably reached Paris of the disharmony between the couple, provoking a letter to Murat from his mother-in-law, written in the Italian she reserved for her most intimate communications, in which she warned him of the consequences of this news reaching the Emperor's ears. She sounded the tocsin: 'The well-being of the family depends on its unity.'

A further warning from Paris came from Agar, Comte de Mosbourg, Murat's man of affairs, who told him plainly that his quarrel with Caroline provided useful ammunition to the members of the Imperial family who were his only real enemies; the brothers-in-law had not wanted the crown of Naples to go out of the direct line and Josephine, once too friendly to him, had become inimical because she knew Murat had expressed himself openly in favour of a divorce.

In addition to their personal rivalry there was an irreconcilable divergence of view between the Murats which persisted throughout their reign in Naples. Caroline believed in submission to the Emperor's wishes, and subordination of Neapolitan interests to French, while Murat constantly and conscientiously tried to promote the welfare of his subjects, an aim incompatible with the increasing demands made on Naples in finance, commercial preference and manpower.

'When I mounted the throne of Naples I swore to make my peoples happy, and I shall keep my oath. I shall overcome all the obstacles, combat all the bad faith and strike at those who would like to prevent my doing good, wherever I find them, whatever the rank or the place they occupy.'

It was an admirable concept. Unfortunately it ran directly counter to Napoleon's.

'If I put a king of my family at Naples it was not in order that my trade should be worse treated than when I had an enemy on the throne. I want above everything that which is suitable for France. If I have conquered kingdoms it was in order that France should get advantages from them and, if I do not get my wish, then I shall be obliged to incorporate these kingdoms within France. That is what I shall do in Spain, and the other States, if they do not want to enter into my system.'

Here was the fundamental cause of the duel of reproach, reproof, recrimination and extenuation fought for years not only between Murat and Napoleon but between the Emperor and his brothers, although he had made his standpoint crystal clear. They had all been placed on their thrones as being more likely than anyone else to carry out his policy; if they did not wish to do so they need be under no illusions as to their fate. Either they would be removed or forced to abdicate. Napoleon was not going to tolerate requests as unbelievable and peremptory as Joseph's to be left in peace to carry out his duties as king.

Part of Murat's resentment against Caroline was just this, that he had been put in an impossible position; it was her ambition rather than his which had made him mount the throne of Naples, yet he felt that 'no other throne offers such opportunities of doing good to a nation which has so many claims to happiness' and finally, in spite of his feelings, he must stay where he was because 'there is no promotion for kings'.

Yet at times Murat could not forgive Caroline for having taken him away from the life for which he was most fitted, the life of the camp. His real throne was the saddle, his real sceptre the sword, his most eloquent speech the one made on 18 Brumaire,

'Drums, sound the charge! Grenadiers, forward!'

Murat's nervous depression and his bad temper were redoubled when he was not called to take part in the new Austrian campaign; Caroline had to suffer for the fact that the victory of Wagram in 1809 was won without his aid. He made a bogy of her and her ambitions, perhaps with the subconscious thought that she would find her position so intolerable that she would ask her brother to release them from the burden of a crown.

It was small consolation to him, resentful of having been robbed of fresh laurels, for which the grinding day-to-day problems of administration, of revenue, of imports and exports offered no substitute, that Napoleon said,

'If I had had Murat at the head of my cavalry at Wagram not a single Austrian would have escaped.'

Caroline watched Murat's discontent with alarm, anxious that his show of independence and threats to step down from the throne should not exasperate her brother, but he rebutted all her efforts to counsel him, since he held her responsible for his present discomforts. If only she could be in Paris and talk to the Emperor himself, were it but for an hour!

She made Hortense her chief confidante, the coolness between them because of Flahaut forgotten. To her she wrote that she was so sad, so cross and so low-spirited that she found no pleasure in life.

> I am sure that you think there isn't a pleasanter Court than mine, but things have changed. Since the day I left Paris I have renounced all pleasures and even happiness.

She had some small satisfaction in the archaeological excavations at Pompeii in which she was greatly interested and in the school she founded at Naples, modelled on Elisa's Institut Elisa at Lucca, but the vicissitudes of her married life marred it all. Her only respite came from Murat's absences in pursuit of the brigands and the English who infested Calabria.

Release for the Murats came at last in a message from Napoleon, telling them that they were free to come to Paris as soon as they liked and the situation permitted their so doing. Even more welcome to Murat was the autograph postscript to this letter. 'If you come you will find me the same for the King of Naples as for General Murat.'

It was not in Murat's nature to suspect the Emperor of irony.

The winter of 1809 was a glorious one in the annals of the Empire for almost everywhere in Europe French arms were victorious, and the Emperor had dictated peace to Austria from Schönbrunn itself. For the Bonapartes the year was marked by an event more glorious still. On December 14th, 1809, the whole of the Bonaparte family, with the exception of Lucien and Elisa, who was in the early stages of pregnancy and feeling unable to undertake the journey to Paris, assembled in the Grand Cabinet of the Tuileries. They were there to hear the divorce by mutual consent pronounced between Napoleon Bonaparte and Josephine de Beauharnais.

It had taken the Bonapartes thirteen years of effort and intrigue to get rid of her and their long struggle was at last rewarded. They saw her go without pity, but their joy was not shared by the people of France, who cared more for Josephine's real kindness of heart and graciousness than they did for the dynastic principle. Never, in spite of the gaiety the Emperor commanded at Court—as though gaiety could be produced to order—had Paris been sadder in the midst of its most splendid entertainments. A gloom hung over everything and the Court itself, missing its central point of reunion, was disunited.

Caroline could not take Josephine's place because her arrogance and inflated idea of her own importance made her disliked at her brother's Court and people did not enjoy themselves at her balls. The only source of pleasure she gave was when she sang duets with the Grand Duke of Würzburg because they both had the most shocking voices, although princes always sing in tune!

Tired and unwell as she was Caroline, unlike Pauline, was never too tired to carry out the Emperor's wishes. Deep as ever in her passion for chess—her gift to the Emperor was a set of chessmen made from the lava of Vesuvius and the coral of Naples—she decided to make the quadrille she was asked to produce a living chess game.

The Kings and Queens glittered with rubies and sapphires,

and the red and blue pawns were dressed in Egyptian style, their headdress copied from the Sphinx, but the quadrille itself was not so successful since only one dancer could move at a time, but Caroline was pleased with her complicated conceit. As she modestly assigned herself the rôle of a blue pawn, blue won the game.

Although the prettiest women of the Court were chosen for this quadrille, including Laure d'Abrantès, who could not refuse the honour of dancing for the Queen of Naples, Pauline did not take part; she had other and more important duties to perform for her brother.

At Schönbrunn the Emperor had had as companion Marie Walewska, perhaps the only woman, apart from his mother, whom he ever really respected, but now he was at a loose end emotionally until his new marriage was arranged. During this interregnum between the divorce and his re-marriage it was remarked that he saw a great deal of Princess Borghese. At St. Cloud, in Paris, or at Fontainebleau they were always together and the rumours long current about an incestuous relationship revived.

> 'Never', said Fouché, 'did she show so much love and adoration for her brother. I heard her say (for she knew *I* knew everything that went on),
>
> "Why should we not reign together in Egypt? We would do as the Ptolemies did. I would divorce my husband and marry my brother."
>
> I knew she was too ignorant to have used such an analogy herself, and I recognised her brother's voice.'

Fouché heard that voice next day raised in great anger; there was a tremendous scene between him and the Emperor about which he says nothing in his memoirs, but one may guess that Napoleon had heard of Fouché's allegation and taken him to task for it.

Fouché was wrong. The object of the Emperor's assiduity was not his sister but one of her Italian ladies-in-waiting, the blonde and charming Christine de Mathis, who seemed not to appreciate that *immediate* submission to the Emperor's desires was necessary. This liaison was, of course, known in Court circles, but was disregarded by those who preferred to believe in the slander of incest. It was not until the discovery in 1939 of letters written by Napoleon to Pauline at this time, which were published by M. Fleuriot de Langle, that the lie has been definitively nailed.

Perhaps it was not very creditable that Pauline should adopt Caroline's rôle of *entremetteuse*, but neither of them saw anything wrong in pleasing their brother and sovereign; Pauline, in particular, could render him no other service. The truth, however unpalatable, was that their co-operation resulted in solid financial gains for themselves as well as Napoleon's gratitude less materially expressed.

Fouché preferred to see Madame de Mathis as a cloak for Pauline's design to subjugate Napoleon to herself, professing a Tartuffian horror at the licentious scenes witnessed by the walls of her voluptuous château at Neuilly and her magnificent hôtel in the Rue du Faubourg St. Honoré. His version is that the affair between her and her brother lasted a year, but there was no passion in it, for Napoleon was completely dominated by his lust for power and conquest. Fouché does not attempt to explain what, if there was no passion, there was in this unnatural relationship.

Josephine's evidence was called on as corroboration of these lies. It is possible that, in her jealousy and despair, she had made statements as wild as they were unguarded and that she did not stop to think that in traducing her sister-in-law she was also blackening her husband. But Josephine had at last disappeared from the scene and everyone's attention was fixed on the Emperor's second marriage.

To Caroline the marriage brought new honours and fresh responsibilities because she was chosen by the Emperor to collect the new Empress's fabulous trousseau and charged with the duty of escorting her to France from the Austrian frontier, but

Caroline's mind was full of other things, and strangely enough most of all of her husband. Nothing could console her, not even the Emperor's company and kindness, for Murat's absence when, after the divorce, he returned to Naples.

Their reconciliation had been startling and complete and the writers who say that it was purely for the sake of their political interests have ignored one significant detail of their ménage at Naples. The king's apartments were separated from the queen's by a very long terrace, the only interior access from one to the other being by a long and complicated system of corridors, so that everything connived to keep them physically apart. In Paris they were housed together in the same apartments at the Tuileries and it seems plain that they recaptured the attraction they always had for each other.

> Each time they saw each other after several months of absence, each time Murat executed some equestrian movement at the head of his cavalry, which recalled the old paladins, all their old resentments disappeared, and they were more closely attached than ever.

Louise Murat was an old woman when she wrote those words, realising perhaps the implications of these reunions which, as a child at Naples, she would not have understood. Hortense, too paid tribute to Caroline's attraction, saying that she had all the Asiatic softness and seduction of an odalisque; it is clear that after Murat's adventures *de bas étage*—for there was no Pompadour at Naples—he found his wife again most desirable. As for Caroline, letter after letter followed Joachim to Naples to tell him how much she missed him and how great was her affection for him.

These are letters of a lovesick young girl who wrote that, although she was petted and spoiled in Paris more than in Naples, perhaps in future Murat would spoil her so much that she would never want to leave him again! Yet the woman who had been married for nine years could not avoid warning her husband to refrain from opposing the Emperor's marriage in much the same terms that he had used about Eugène's marriage to Princess Augusta; Napoleon had firmly decided that the *autre ventre* he was marrying, as he brutally put it, was to be Austrian.

> It is in your interest and in that of our children that you do not alienate the Emperor's affections . . . do as he says. If you don't come to the wedding your enemies might suspect that you are acting only in your own interest and insinuate it to the Emperor.

We have no replies to these letters because Caroline had the habit, so tiresome to posterity, of burning all those she received. Very few Murat wrote to her escaped her anxiety not to preserve any evidence which might be incriminating.

Her new honours kept Caroline busy from morning until night; she confessed herself as terrified that the Emperor might appoint her as Mistress of the Empress's Household, an appointment which would have given her precedence over the Queens of Spain and Holland, but would have meant an absence of two years from Naples. This, in her present mood, she could not contemplate. In spite of the high favour in which she now stood with the Emperor she longed only to be back with Murat and her children but, before she could obtain her release, she had to earn it.

Caroline's outward journey to Braunau on the Austro-Bavarian frontier was pleasant, but the return was a nightmare. Some one hundred persons in nineteen carriages set off in three convoys with one hundred and twenty-two horses and four travellers to each berline. The Empress's own cortège consisted of six carriages, each drawn by six horses, her own carriage, in which she was alone with Caroline, drawn by eight white horses.

The journey was in every sense an uneasy one.

'It's like being on a forced march,' Caroline complained, because the Emperor was so impatient to meet his bride that the journey was done in record time, never mind to what inconvenience. For sixteen hours Caroline had to sit in the carriage, surrounded by escort and equerries, not permitted by the

Emperor's orders to leave it even when the horses were changed at lightning speed.

'It is all right for the Empress,' Caroline wailed to her husband, 'for she is young and it doesn't worry her, but for me who has had children it is very tiresome and painful.'

It was almost as enervating to travel shut up alone in the company of a young woman, brought up to fear and despise one's family, with the mission of putting her into a frame of mind where an Ogre was transformed into an ardent and eager lover. The fact that Marie Louise's disposition towards the Emperor grew more kindly as the journey progressed must, in some part, be attributed to Caroline's efforts, although to Caroline herself she took a great dislike.

The noise and hubbub of the journey were insupportable. All day long the sound of *vive l'Impératrice* beat in Caroline's ears. On one of their brief night stops, after her obligatory letter to the Emperor, she wrote to Murat,

> All night long I hear the words in my ears and I wake up, shouting *vive l'Impératrice* ! Please tell Paulette and the rest of the family that, when they see me, the first thing I shall say to them will be *vive l'Impératrice* as I can no longer say anything else !

But at the end of the journey Murat was waiting at Compiègne and, as soon as she had handed over her charge, Caroline was thankful to fall into his arms.

The marriage on April 2nd of the Emperor of the French and the Austrian heifer, the Archduchess Marie Louise, was yet another glistening Imperial ceremony of white satin, gold embroidery and diamonds, but on this occasion the parvenu princesses made no demur about carrying the Imperial mantle. They had either learnt their lesson or they still felt the need metaphorically to touch their forelock to a member of one of the most ancient ruling houses of Europe.

In view of the services she rendered by escorting the Empress to France Caroline was excused from carrying the train but

Elisa, in spite of her pregnancy, could not beg off. She had felt reasonably safe in handing over the sceptre to Felix while she journeyed with all precautions to Paris for the wedding. Camillo Borghese, very gay and very mad, had come from Turin and once again nearly all the family was assembled in Paris.

Murat's reception by the Emperor, however, was less cordial than both he and Caroline expected. For fourteen days he cooled his heels waiting for a personal interview. When he was at last received, it was only to meet an urgent demand for money; vast expenses had been incurred for the marriage and the French treasury was once again empty.

Murat, too, needed money for he had set his heart on mounting an expedition to Sicily to make his kingdom *de facto* the Kingdom of the Two Sicilies, but in face of Napoleon's inflexibility Murat showed himself to be made not of iron but butter.

For once even Napoleon's dissatisfaction did not weigh with Caroline, enjoying a second honeymoon with Murat. When he again returned to Naples, leaving her in Paris, he was followed by letters more tender and loving than before.

She loved him and their children tenderly; he must know how dear he was to her, and how impossible it was that she should for a moment dream of separating herself from the father of her children; she was anxious about the Sicilian expedition but she reassured Murat that the Emperor seemed very well disposed towards him. She had been dreadfully distressed to see him leave; above all she was touched by his kindness to her,

> You have never been like that before and I admit that it filled me with tenderness and has given me the courage to ask you for what I want, without being afraid that you will get angry as you always do, which made me unwilling to ask anything of you or owe anything to you.

Constantly Caroline reverts to Murat's tenderness to her which made her long to return to Naples, to her children, but above all to him.

> You were so good, so perfect to me in the last minutes of your stay that I was touched to tears, and am still full of tenderness. I must admit that, when you render justice to my feelings for you, I am the happiest of women. Believe me when I say that all the happiness of my life consists in the happiness of the father of my children, of him whom I consider my best friend.

The proof of Murat's tenderness was apparent when Caroline began to write of her hopes, an even clearer indication that there had been a long physical separation between them because it was five years since their last child, Louise, was born.

CHAPTER ELEVEN

1810

After the Imperial wedding the three sisters remained in Paris to await the return of the Emperor and Empress from their honeymoon journey to Holland and Belgium. They had not been together for a period of five years, a time during which they had all developed very differently. Elisa was an efficient, if subordinate; sovereign, Caroline a Queen Consort, who longed for some of Elisa's freedom from marital interference, and Pauline a brilliant and successful Queen of Hearts.

Countess Potocka, who had come to Paris from Warsaw to see the Imperial wedding, was very interested to meet the sisters, and particularly Caroline, after Murat's pursuit of her in Warsaw. She thought Caroline's face most expressive, her complexion still dazzling and, in spite of her smallness of stature, her bearing most truly royal. Pauline was the epitome of classic beauty, although she repaired the ravages of time by a little art; to her perfect face was added a figure which was admirable and too often admired. In Elisa the Countess recognised her brother's features, although of a much harder cast but, in spite of her reputation for wit and character, she did not find her an attractive personality nor had she ever heard of anything outstanding that Elisa had said or done.

Caroline and Pauline saw a great deal of each other but rather less of Elisa, who was feeling her pregnancy very much and was unable to go out in the evening. To Murat Elisa wrote that she hoped to visit Naples soon and was delighted at the prospect of bringing her little daughter to meet his charming family. She had had a cold and some fever which had lasted three weeks but she was feeling better. Since she was unable to go out in the evening she had a little music at home. 'We much regret, my dear brother, the absence of a King so handsome and so amiable. Caroline has just left me. She is keeping well and is pregnant.'

The two sisters who were pregnant were keeping an eager eye on their new sister-in-law but Caroline had to report that she as yet showed no signs of an heir, perhaps a little pessimistic since Marie Louise had only been married for a month. Of more real interest to Caroline was to revisit the places where she and Murat had been together. At Neuilly, now belonging to Pauline, she thought only with nostalgia of their happy days there together; at Mortefontaine she recalled that it was here that she had first begun to have for Murat those feelings which she had still, but to which were now added esteem, habit and a deep friendship. She loved him, she was grateful to him; it was very sweet to her to owe to the one she loved so tenderly all the pleasures and happiness of her life.

Caroline's biographers believe that she was constantly actuated only by the desire to gain as much power for herself as possible at her husband's expense, but no one reading the series of letters written by her during this long stay in Paris could possibly regard them as false and calculating. She wrote at all times of the day or night, when she was feeling tired or ill and, if she was dissembling, then she was indeed the Machiavelli she was called rather than a woman clearly drowned in love. It is obvious that to find Murat again after the rift with him was a source of real happiness to Caroline, for it is more than possible that the lovers she took for political motives were not his equal as a man prodigious in love. The reconciliation opened out to her prospects of happiness for the future of greater importance to Caroline as a woman than playing a man's part in her kingdom, and she ventured a prophecy.

> You will see that one day we shall be the happiest creatures in the world, and we shall owe it to our children. They will give us back all the love we have lavished on them, and our old age will be glorified by their virtues. See how far I can look into the future!

Caroline's crystal ball was clouded; a serene old age was not written in the Murats' destiny.

When at last the Emperor returned to Paris Caroline said that she would ask him if she might leave in a week; she could not stay in Paris any longer for she was bored and anxious and existing like that wasn't living.

> I am afraid for you of the fatigues, the heat, failure, your little worries, and all the dangers to which you are exposed. It's no use my telling myself I am wrong. My imagination is stronger than my sense and I am angry with myself without, however, being able to do anything about it, for being such a child.

But Napoleon would not let Caroline go, nor Elisa. He wanted his sisters to remain in Paris to take part in all the post-wedding festivities and to become attached to their new sister-in-law; there was to be no repetition of their enmity to Josephine.

Pauline was the first to fête the newly-weds. With infinite pains she organized the most splendid entertainment at Neuilly in their honour, recreating in her grounds with exquisite tact the façade of Schönbrunn, its huge courtyard and porticoes alive with people, carriages, strollers, dairymaids in their traditional golden bonnets, valets running about in the Imperial Austrian livery and groups of Tyroleans dancing the national waltz.

To this charming fantasy the Empress remained as phlegmatic as ever but Napoleon appreciated Pauline's gracious intention, thanking her repeatedly and warmly for the efforts she had made and the expense she had not spared.

Both Caroline and Elisa felt the festivities an increasing burden as their pregnancies advanced, but there could be no question of staying away. The Emperor immediately became angry when they talked of going home while Pauline soon lost the credit she had gained by her fête by asking leave, which was refused, to go and take the waters.

Against Caroline's desire to go home was her feeling that it would be politic to remain in close proximity to the Emperor in case direct approaches had to be made to him since, although her tenderness for Murat suffered no diminution, he was now writing letters to the Emperor which alarmed her. Murat was afraid he had lost the Emperor's confidence, and he was at a loss to understand why.

> Have I not heard you say, 'Murat is the only one of my family who has never given me cause to complain of him?' Love me as you did in Prussia, as you did in Poland, and I shall still be in love with life.
>
> Did I not write to you in Vienna that, if you wish to incorporate the kingdom of Naples in France, I would see that it was your desire, and I would work with that idea in mind? And why not incorporate Naples today? Recall me to your side. You spoke to me at Compiègne of a dignity of Cavalry General of the Empire. Create it for me! Sire, at the first battle, under your own eyes, I will justify so much kindness.

Alas, for Caroline! Murat's love had to be a thing apart in his life and he was still beset by the same problems of conscience and even expediency. Once again he made a wrong move.

Lucien had resisted every plea from his sisters and his mother to become reconciled with the Emperor. He had ignored Madame Letizia's plaint that his obstinacy in refusal was shortening her life and her appeal to Alexandrine to sacrifice herself for the good of her children. It seemed better to leave the orbit of the family and make a new life for himself in America. He asked Murat to lend him some money, pending the disposal of his Italian property, and to get him a passage on an American ship. Murat, always kindly when the family was concerned, did as he was asked, thereby incurring Napoleon's displeasure.

He had been too hasty, Caroline told him, although she admired his inability to see his brother-in-law unhappy, and confessed that she would probably have acted in the same way but, she reminded him, it might have been Napoleon's plan to force Lucien's hand by making him apply to him for money. In the event Napoleon was proven right because Lucien and his family were captured by one of the British ships in the Mediterranean and were taken to England where they spent nearly five years in Herefordshire as prisoners of war.

Caroline herself did not incur the Emperor's anger; she continued to spend every day with him and he was exceedingly kind to her. He did not appear to take Murat as seriously as he seemed to do in his letters and rather regarded him, when he was in a good temper, as a comic figure, laughing at his rages. 'Oh, he's angry with me, what an odd creature! He gets angry about everything,' and he teased Caroline frequently about her 'king of the lazzaroni'.

The birth of a son to Elisa in July caused little stir in France because the Empress was now pregnant and the country was anxiously waiting for the months to pass, but naturally in Tuscany the news that there was an heir to the Grand Duchy was rapturously received. No sooner had Elisa recovered from his birth than she was once again back at work, eager to show the Emperor on the spot how devoted she was to her charge. Nevertheless he was angry with her when she insisted on returning home in September.

Elisa was not sorry to leave Paris behind to return to Tuscany where she was first in importance. She had enjoyed seeing her brothers and sisters again, particularly Jerome, whose gaiety and charm made him a great favourite with his sisters and who had taken Lucien's place in her affections, but she felt increasingly that her future lay in Italy. She did not foresee that this was her last visit to Paris.

During her stay she had seen far less of the Emperor than Caroline; it is obvious that she had preserved her unhappy knack of irritating him. To Savary, who had succeeded Fouché as Minister of Police, he wrote with annoyance:

The Tuscan papers give detailed accounts of what the Grand Duchess is doing and too often the Paris papers copy

> them. You must instruct the Director of Police to stop this nonsense being printed. The less the Grand Duchess is talked about the better—get someone in Paris to drop her a hint that she is making herself ridiculous. Europe doesn't care a snap of the fingers about what the Grand Duchess is doing . . . it is a matter of great interest what sovereigns are doing, but as to what Grand Duchesses do, who cares?

The snub was severe, but not so wounding as the Emperor's sudden decision to take Carrara away from Tuscany, which meant a loss not only of territory but of revenue. Elisa, like Murat, was feeling the squeeze Napoleon was putting on his satellites. She was provoked into writing to him, pointing out that the birth of a son now made his benefactions more, not less, necessary. 'I fear, moreover, that this reduction in territory is a reduction in tenderness for Your Majesty's sister, and that is the main cause of my grief.'

Nevertheless Elisa's grandiose ideas and the magnificence of her Court at Florence continued to irritate her brother who, this time, sent his warning through Pauline that she was putting herself forward too much. To which Elisa, who kept up a rather cool correspondence with Pauline—she had been heard to say that she did not believe in Pauline's illnesses—hastily answered: 'My dear sister, be kind enough to tell the Emperor that I have always done what he wanted me to do, and that I should never do anything with the intention of displeasing him.'

To cling to Tuscany, to her position as Grand Duchess, her work, her patronage of the arts, her way of life, were all-important to Elisa and to maintain them she was prepared to grovel as much as was necessary.

Caroline found the same difficulty as Elisa in being allowed to leave Paris. Although she was delighted with her release, at the final moment of departure she did regret leaving the Emperor after so long and so close an association yet, in spite of his gaiety, charming and perfect behaviour to her, it was with

Murat she wanted to be. ' When we are together again we shall be perfectly happy.'

When Caroline at last, after a gruelling journey in the heat, reached her capital of Naples Murat was not there to meet her. He was still in the royal camp at Piale, still hoping to launch his expedition against Sicily.

> Don't let yourself be overcome by the difficulties and the discouragement of the people around you, advised Caroline. If you find that the expedition is impossible come back to me. Don't distress yourself so, look about you and see what you should do for our benefit and the benefit of the Kingdom, and rest assured that the world will approve your decision.

It may be that at this moment all Caroline did sincerely long for was domestic happiness. She was pregnant, ill and tired and the life of a private person may have beckoned with great charms; she insists continually that their supreme felicity was in their family and she may well have contrasted her life with the emptiness of Pauline's. Perhaps the Murats were never so much at one as at this moment, but with a husband as mercurial as Murat the unexpected was the expected and clearly Caroline gave a great deal of thought to her final letter to him before he returned from Piale to Naples.

She begged him to heed what she had to say and concern himself with the present rather than torment himself about the future. She had reassured the Emperor about their personal relationship, had told him that she was happy and content, that Murat was very good to her and the trivial disagreements between them did not merit his attention. Her brother had insisted that the Murats' relationship to each other touched him more than she realised and much of Murat's own reputation depended on the way in which Joachim treated his wife. She allowed the Emperor to speak for himself:

' I am fond of the King, and I am very pleased with the attachment you have proved to me during these seven months, and I am not looking for means of hurting you. Nevertheless, I want you to speak frankly to the King and tell him what my intentions are. This is what I want from him—that he favours French commerce and it should not be as it was during the time of the Bourbons. I also wish that the King should treat you well.'

Caroline reminded Murat that, if their situation was bad, that of the others was worse. All Europe was crushed under the yoke of France. Joseph could not hold out much longer in Spain, Louis had abdicated from the throne of Holland and Jerome in Westphalia could not carry on for more than six months:

> So you can see that you are still the one who is least badly treated, and I advise you therefore to reconcile yourself to the situation in which you find yourself, to endure it and to give no cause for any complaint. Overlook the little things so that later on you can obtain the bigger ones and keep us friendly with the Emperor.

It was vital, Caroline insisted, to obey the Emperor.

> What is your aim? It is to keep us where we are and to preserve the Kingdom. Therefore we must do as he wishes and not anger him when he asks for something, for he is stronger than you are, and you can do nothing against him. Perhaps one day he will become calmer and then you can get everything which is due to you. You will obtain more by making sacrifices than by irritating him. By doing what the Emperor demands it is possible that you will impoverish yourself, but at least you will preserve the Kingdom and if, nevertheless, you are reduced to leaving it, you will have no reproaches to make to yourself with regard to your children.

Caroline now had doubts about the success of the Sicilian expedition, advising Murat to defer it rather than expose himself and the army to defeat. If he was courageous enough to give up the plan and return to her, she would try and console him for the troubles he had undergone—the perpetual illusion of a woman in love that she can compensate a man for the loss of a cherished ambition.

She would do everything she could to please him, go to no fêtes nor see the police reports nor anything which had been suggested to her. She had refused everything.

> My intention is not to concern myself with anything but what will be pleasing to you, and I do not wish to give rise to rumours that I have come here to govern during your absence, and in order to concern myself with administrative matters. I want to prove to you that I have come back to show you how attached to you I am. I hope that there will be no more people who try to distress you by making you believe that I concern myself with intrigues, that I am making a party of my own, and that I am trying to get into the Council of State. Those who say so have their own reasons for so doing.

Here, if one ignores her previous letters, there is a faint indication of a guilty conscience, but also a firm determination to shut the book of the past if Murat will only be sensible enough to play the part written for him by Napoleon. If he will do so then Caroline is ready to abandon her personal ambitions.

> We can be happy, but for that we must be content with what we have. You must cool your head a little, which gets inflamed so easily, and you must wait, with rather more patience than you have hitherto shown, for the time when we shall be more peaceful and independent. The happiness of our family life will compensate us for many of our difficulties, and you will find with me, with our children, and with all those whom we truly love, sources of joy which are worth more than all the others put together.
>
> Everything I am saying to you is dictated by the desire I have that you should be happy and you know that my happiness depends on yours.

It seemed for a moment that Murat was in a frame of mind to recognise the justice of all that Caroline said and we are fortunate that this is one of the rare letters to her which have been preserved.

> I am going to try, my kind Caroline, to reply to your letter of August 3rd. You are absolutely correct in all that you say and I can assure you that your thoughts echo those with which I have been seriously occupied. My system of conduct as well as my feelings have always proved that I think in the same way as you do. . . .
>
> The Emperor is now imposing on me most difficult conditions, he has made me sign an unjust treaty and accept a debt which is still more inequitable. He diminishes our revenues, crushes my trade, paralyses our factories, orders me to undertake a ruinous expedition, demands me to maintain a fleet, forbids my exports, in a word he puts me in the impossible position of supporting this enormous burden with which he has saddled me. And when his policy or caprice make him decide to push me off the throne it will be the same with me as with Louis.
>
> It is my belief that the Emperor must be the master of wishing us to follow his system, and that we should consult him about measures of policy or important decisions that we have to make, but he must be our mentor and not our master. One is not a King merely to obey. Then how can he tell the peoples whom he has entrusted to the princes of his family that the interests of the French come before their own?
>
> My dear Caroline, there is no end to the wrongs I could list, but that would serve no useful purpose. Let us act in such a way that there is no basis for any accusation, and await with resignation what it pleases Providence to decide about our destiny.
>
> I have made up my mind to do all the Emperor desires or will desire; when I can no longer carry the burden I shall ask him to take it off my shoulders.

Had Murat only been capable of following the line of conduct he had laid down for himself his future might have been very different, but all too often his susceptibility to imagined insult overruled his judgment. He allowed himself to accept as facts suspicions which in his rational moods he well knew to be groundless. Twenty years of war, of fighting, of intrigue, of womanizing and of constant nervous tension had, however, left their mark on him. His nervous breakdown in Spain should have been a warning; from the time he became King of Naples it is probable that Murat was suffering from a mild form of schizophrenia.

He was well aware that his terms of reference were to act merely as Napoleon's viceroy, that, galling though it was to his self-esteem, he *had* been made king in order to obey. In vain did Marshal Berthier, the Emperor's confidant and Chief of Staff, urge him most kindly, 'Be an entirely French king!'

He could not. And when, after so many hesitations, the Sicilian expedition was at last abandoned and his cherished hope of re-uniting Sicily with the mainland lost, his temper and disappointment gained the upper hand. Everyone else was to blame.

Caroline suffered a grievous disappointment when, on his return, instead of meeting the kindness and love she expected, she found that the weathercock had changed direction again. After a difficult and trying year in which she had poured out all the love and tenderness of which she was capable, after all the fatigues and illness she had endured, the final deception was too great. She had a most serious miscarriage and her reconciliation with her husband and her child were alike stillborn.

Caroline was blamed by Murat for much for which she was clearly not responsible, but to a mind whose values were distorted by jealousy it was she who appeared to be the source of every difficulty and disappointment. When the old, bitter mood revived Murat once again cut Caroline off from all connections with the world and made her virtually a prisoner in her own palaces.

News of Murat's behaviour did not fail to reach the Emperor who exclaimed furiously;

'He is king only because of her, of my sister.'

That he owed his crown to his wife and not entirely to his own merits was something Murat was never willing to admit. He was constantly at war with himself—one part of him, the best, longed only for a simple family life, the other, inflated by his success on the battlefield, led him into the folly of believing that he had more capacity as a king than he, in fact, possessed.

Murat's lack of self-control was at this moment such that scenes between the couple were held practically in public and it was seriously thought that he was losing his reason. It is true that most of the time he was in a high fever, appearing to have little control over his actions.

His intransigence made Caroline furious in her turn, her revulsion less because of the political issues involved than because, as a woman, she had been rejected. If he did not want what she offered him and what, in Paris, he had been so happy to take then she, too, would turn her back on the past. As Napoleon had made it clear that she and Murat were where they were because of her then she would be queen in actual fact.

In her frustration at being deprived of a secure and happy married life she sought compensation in the exercise of power, or at least in seeking to exercise it, and she again looked elsewhere for physical gratification. The lovers she had taken in Naples had always been those who would be useful to her, La Vauguyon, one of Joachim's aides-de-camp, Daure, the Minister of War, and others. It seemed that this infidelity was something that Murat could forgive, perhaps because he knew well the weakness of the flesh.

When one of her love affairs was disclosed to him and Caroline wept and blamed her enemies, Murat said heavily, 'She is there and I am here and we will not speak of it again.'

Nor did he.

But he continued to exaggerate the rôle Caroline wanted to play, his judgment now too clouded to realise that his constant opposition made her more obstinately determined to take an even larger part in government that she had intended. Murat, with the parvenu's acute jealousy of his own position, continued to be haunted by the thought that, if he allowed Caroline too much leeway, he would indeed become ' the very humble husband ' of the Queen of Naples.

No doubt it was the soundness of her advice and her interpretation of the Emperor's wishes which irritated him most; he longed to be free while she constantly reminded him of his chains. Of the two parties into which the Court was divided Caroline supported the French party, Murat the Italian, which showed signs of preferring even the oppressed independence they had enjoyed under the Bourbons to subservience to a foreign power.

At this juncture in their fortunes the Murats received news of the birth of a son to the Emperor on March 20th, 1811. More than ever it seemed vital to Caroline to hold on to what they had, since now the prospect of succeeding Napoleon had faded for ever.

She was much gratified to be invited to be godmother but weighed carefully the question as to whether she should go to Paris for the christening; finally she decided not to go. Nor was Elisa present. While all France was rejoicing at the birth of an heir to the throne she once again had the bitterness of losing her son, and was too ill with grief and shock even to join in the celebrations at Florence in honour of the baby King of Rome.

Murat, who had not been invited, went to Paris in his wife's stead, but his visit was ill-timed. In spite of his personal happiness at the birth of his first legitimate son the Emperor was so angry with Joachim for his treatment of Caroline that he cut short his stay and returned to Naples, once again to vent his ill-temper on her, a manifestation to which she was now accustomed but not reconciled.

Then Murat made a very bad mistake indeed. Pursuing his policy of Italianising his kingdom, he decreed that all the French in his service should be naturalised Italian. Even his daughter, Louise, admits that his decisions were not always prudent and here he had made a bad miscalculation for Napoleon immediately and furiously annulled the decree.

Caroline was now seriously alarmed at the consequences of Murat's lack of political intelligence and decided that it would be in their best interests if she once again went to Paris; whatever their personal disagreements, the interests of the ménage were paramount in her eyes. Hortense summed up her attitude neatly when she said,

'The Queen of Naples could always defend her husband's interests to the Emperor, but when she was alone with him an equal desire to govern created a cloud between them.'

This cloud was considerably bigger than a man's hand, too large to be hidden from the family. The Emperor was, perhaps, more than usually glad to see her, therefore, and installed her in the Pavillon de Flore at the Tuileries. Her presence was of great use to him because the winter of 1811 was from all points of view a bad one. To distract the attention of the public from the stalemate in Spain against the English and his preparations for another war in Eastern Europe he determined that the music should be louder and the gaiety, to order, more intense. Caroline could, in this, help him more than Pauline.

Pauline again was somewhat in disgrace for she preferred to be at Neuilly when the Emperor wanted her at St. Cloud. Now that Borghese had again returned to Turin after the wedding she was free to do as she liked, this time to parade her handsome and charming hussar, Jules de Canouville, who held first place in her affections and ranks with Forbin as one of the great loves of her life, but her lack of discretion attracted her brother's notice. Canouville found himself entrusted with despatches for Marshal Masséna in Spain, and a private message that the Marshal should keep Monsieur de Canouville with him until further notice.

The ardent and impetuous Canouville did not wait for the Marshal to open his despatches before he remounted his horse and rode like a whirlwind to Paris and his mistress, having accomplished the journey to Spain and back within a week. His haste served him nothing for the Emperor promptly sent him back to Spain with definite orders to remain with the army.

It was clear to Pauline that her brother was winning this round on points so she prudently removed herself to take the waters at Aix-la-Chapelle. Her mother's presence there made it difficult, although not of course impossible, to pursue her normal avocations, so she decided to make the short journey to Spa in Belgium. Under the lime-scented avenues of the Parc des Sept Heures beneath the aromatic and bosky Montagne Annette et Lubin, she lived a month's brief idyll with a famous figure in Parisian society, *le beau Montrond.* But he was too old and too much of a roué even for Pauline and the affair had no sequel except for Montrond, who found himself exiled to Antwerp for too much assiduity in attendance on the Emperor's sister.

Back to Paris went Pauline, rejoicing sincerely in the birth of her nephew, and ready to fall in with the Emperor's wishes to make this season the most brilliant in Paris for years, in spite of the shortage of money.

But the Emperor this year was difficult to please. When Caroline and Pauline together staged an elaborate allegory, representing the union of France and Italy, they earned only a reprimand for giving a political bias to their quadrille. Hortense was much more successful with her politically impeccable ballet of the Incas.

The toll of this unremitting round was heavy for Caroline. Ceaseless journeyings across Europe, mental strain, the necessity of being always on the alert with the Emperor, the constant friction with Murat and her bad miscarriage all combined to bring on a serious illness with recurrent sickness and headaches, symptoms which were not new. Very often she returned to her apartments after some official ceremony and there collapsed with fits of vomiting, a condition which required absolute rest, so that she had to adopt Pauline's habit of lying on the day-bed which was always prepared for her. No one, apparently connected these symptoms with her father's illness; even had they done so medicine had no solution to offer.

It was with some relief that Caroline, after another nine months' absence from Naples, once more took the road southwards for she was now sincerely attached to her kingdom, her early disappointment long since forgotten.

'It is only at Naples that one reigns well,' she told Marie Louise proudly.

Now at last she had the opportunity of ruling as well as reigning. In April, 1812, to his great joy, Murat received an invitation to join the Grande Armée massing in Eastern Europe. On his way to the east, Murat met Caroline in Paris and there entrusted her with the regency of Naples during his absence.

CHAPTER TWELVE

TRAGEDY OF ERRORS

To everyone's surprise but her own Caroline carried out her duties as Queen Regent extremely well; in her years of apprenticeship she had learned a great deal about government and handled her ministers with tact and good sense. She had neither time nor desire for amatory adventures thus showing that had Murat only had more of the compliance shown by Baciocchi and Borghese he would have been a happier man.

Borghese, having long since given up the attempt to alter a Bonaparte temperament, had taken into his household a distant cousin, a widow, the Duchessa Lante delle Rovere, who was far from being a decayed gentlewoman. She was extremely beautiful, in a more opulent style than Pauline, and for the first time in his life Borghese was enjoying real connubial bliss, which was just as well for the year 1812 marked the apotheosis of his wife's career as Queen of Hearts.

When Napoleon set off in May, 1812, to come to final terms with Alexander I of Russia, Pauline set out on yet another of her arduous campaigns, her chosen terrain being Aix-en-Savoie, on the Lac du Bourget, whose beauties are familiar to every French child who dutifully recites Lamartine's *Le Lac*. It was particularly suitable that her companion here was the great actor, Talma, who fitted admirably into the romantic décor.

Many of Pauline's friends, among them Laure d'Abrantès and Désirée Bernadotte, now Princess Royal of Sweden, and Madame Letizia, gathered at Aix this summer, as Paris was once again emptied of its men who were riding or marching to their assembly points in the east, Murat among them. At Danzig he met the Emperor, who enacted a scene worthy of Talma. First of all he greeted Murat sternly and with biting language, then suddenly changed his tone to that of a friend who had been sadly misunderstood and appealed to Murat's affection and their association in the past, *commediante*, *tragediante* of Alfred de Vigny's phrase. With his emotional nature Murat was unable to resist the appeal ; there was a grand reconciliation with Joachim near to tears.

Pauline was more fortunate than her friends in having a man to herself as men were so scarce that they had to be shared, a state of affairs to which long experience had made them more than equal. At Aix Maurice de Balincourt, with his wasp waist in his befrogged hussar uniform, his titillating whiskers and windswept hair, was fought over by Laure d'Abrantès and Désirée Bernadotte's lady-in-waiting. More than Forbin, who also was at Aix, now dancing attendance on Laure, more even than Flahaut, Balincourt was the pride of the herd but, surprisingly, he was not one of Pauline's lovers.

When Talma left Aix to fulfil engagements in Switzerland, putting an end to the romantic boat trips on the lake when he declaimed Racine and Corneille into those ears which were the only blemish on Pauline's perfect beauty, she fell into the arms of another hussar, the handsome and wholly admirable Colonel Duchand, who remained in favour for a comparatively long time.

Talma had made the foolish mistake of falling deeply in love with Pauline, an eagle in love with a butterfly. His ardent letters followed her for many months, until he became bitterly resigned to the fact that he was forgotten. In spite of his inevitable use of the language of the theatre Talma was patently sincere.

> Ah, tell me, do you not recall those moments of passion and delirium in which you plunged me before my last journey to Grenoble ? Alas, if I must one day renounce possessing you, if my destiny demands that I should never again find you as you were for me, then let Providence allow me to die ! Seven months without seeing you—dear one, never, never in this world has anyone loved or will love you more than I !

Pauline, now enjoying moments of passion and delirium in the arms of Duchand, remained as indifferent to yesterday's lover as to yesterday's hat.

> Is not my love for you a constant pain? But my own happiness means nothing—I see only you and I bear with constancy the torments which make for your own tranquillity. . . . Do not tire of being loved by me and, if you promised me the happiness I see fading in front of my eyes almost before I have enjoyed it, be indulgent to my sufferings and let me seek some consolation from the kindness of your heart. . . . Even the past is like a dream for me and my heart can foresee no future.

Talma's prescience was right; a lover at Aix was worth two in Paris. Although neither of them had any idea of it, Pauline never returned to Paris again. As the early autumn leaves drifted on to the lake and the ladies drew their cashmere shawls more closely round them a chill descended on Pauline's heart—Canouville had been killed at Borodino.

'It is dangerous to love princesses,' said Laure d'Abrantès with bitterness. It leads to disgrace as in the case of Junot or a premature death like Canouville's.

Pauline was not given to looking backwards but she was much affected by Canouville's death and, as autumn closed in, she left Aix and moved southward, naturally not so distressed that she went without Duchand. When he was obliged to leave her sadness settled on Pauline. She was depressed by the bad news coming from Russia which reached her although her entourage did their best to withhold it. She was now thirty-two and had reached the moment of truth in the life of a woman when she realises that she has only a few more years at her prime. Perhaps she recalled Napoleon's words:

> Tell her that she is no longer as pretty as she was and that, in a few years' time she will be less so, but all her life long she should be good and held in esteem.

She talked of going back to Paris but could not make the effort yet, with some animal sense of impending danger, began to reduce her household and order retrenchments in her expenditure.

If Pauline was depressed that winter by a sense of coming disaster Caroline for the first time for many months was completely happy, in spite of Murat's efforts to exercise a jealous remote control over her acts of government. Wherever there was fighting in Russia there he distinguished himself, but his temperament could not reconcile itself to the long marches, to the winter climate after the sun of Naples, nor to the slow erosion of the army on the long retreat from Moscow.

After the final débâcle of the Beresina and Napoleon's sudden departure for Paris, the command of what remained of the Grande Armée was entrusted to Murat, an error of judgment which could only have been dictated by the Emperor's haste to be gone.

Five vital weeks elapsed between Napoleon's departure and Murat's abandonment of the command to Eugène de Beauharnais, time to inform Caroline of his intention and to receive her anguished reply that he should reconsider it. What led Murat, a Marshal of France, a soldier who longed only for battle, the clatter of accoutrements, the thin calls of bugles and the thudding of horses' hooves in a cavalry charge, to disobey orders, to relinquish the command of the greatest army the world had ever seen, even if it was an army in full retreat? The reasons he gave, the state of his health and of his kingdom, were neither of them adequate. The answer had been given by Napoleon himself after Austerlitz.

'To command is to wear out!'

When Murat tried to re-group the army he found that the majority of its leaders were themselves exhausted and disheartened. Already many of them were anxious only about maintaining their rank, their place in society and the lands in the conquered territories which were their endowments.

Murat could no more cope with this partially disaffected

band than he could cope with the Emperor himself. The Comte de Ségur remarked that, though as a king Murat had not feared to die like a soldier in the front line, he could not bear the thought of living without a crown, and the Russian defeat was heavy with menace for the future. It was not *aux champs* but *sauve qui peut* which now rang in Murat's ears as once *vive l'Impératrice* had rung in Caroline's.

The King of Naples assembled the General Staff and addressed them.

'It is no longer possible to serve a madman; there is no hope of success in his cause—no prince in Europe now believes in his words or in his treaties', and more in the same vein until he was interrupted by Marshal Davout, who scorched him with reproaches,

'You are only a king by the grace of Napoleon and of your French blood. You can only stay a king through Napoleon and remaining united with France. You are blinded by black ingratitude.'

Although this taunt from a fellow-Marshal may have shamed Murat a little he was already beyond the range of reason. The final decisive occasion which led him to abandon his command was the receipt of a letter from Naples, which upset all his better intentions. Spectators observed that, as he read it, the bile mingled so quickly with his blood that, in a few moments, he became yellow with jaundice.

The news contained in the letter was that Caroline had carried out some act of government which ran counter to his wishes. At this moment in his career his jealousy of his own authority won a shameful victory over his honour, his duty and his love of glory. Within a few days he had left the army and his command and was on his way back to Naples.

'Murat is either a traitor or a madman, he deserves to be shot or sent to Charenton, one or the other,' exclaimed Napoleon in fury when he heard of his defection.

Caroline found it difficult to apprehend her brother's defeat in Russia but still harder to understand why her husband should have abandoned his command and, of all people, to a Beauharnais. She remembered, if he had forgotten, that Napoleon had said,

'I have always considered and I still consider Murat as a general in my army.'

Generals did not arbitrarily relinquish their commands because they felt their wives were not properly carrying out their duties.

Husband and wife were again drawn together by mutual resentment when the Emperor inserted a notice in the *Moniteur*, severely censuring Murat's defection, and by the letter he wrote to Caroline, castigating Joachim as a defaulter, an ungrateful traitor, incapable of sound policy, unworthy of his relationship and deserving of public and severe chastisement.

Insult and counter-insult were hurled from Paris to Naples, but the unforgivable retort came from Murat. Doubts have been cast on the authenticity of this letter but Joachim was goaded to the point where it is very likely that he did, in fact, write it.

> You have insulted and calumniated an old companion in arms, faithful to you in your dangers, not a small part of your victories, the support of your greatness, and *the re-animator of your lost courage on the 18 Brumaire.*

The final taunt was the more unpardonable because of its truth; it was with justice that Murat, harking back to Brumaire, had exclaimed to Bourrienne,

'He says that he made us kings! But did we not make him an Emperor?'

The news of French defeats in Russia came as an even greater shock in Florence than in Naples. Elisa had dutifully sent her comic opera regiments to Russia and, even though few of her soldiers returned, she failed for some time to appreciate the realities of the situation. Her correspondence with Pauline, now at Hyères, showed no signs of undue anxiety; she mentioned complacently and only in passing that she was aiding the Emperor to remount his army, with a troop of cavalry numbering three hundred men. Her earnest reassurance that she had made arrangements to get news of the latest hair styles from Paris seemed of greater urgency.

In spite of the deep malaise settling over Europe there was no apparent alteration in the way of life in the Bonaparte states of Tuscany or Naples and, as the Emperor demanded more and more gaiety in Paris to cover up his fevered preparations in raising new armies, Elisa saw no reason to abandon her normal course of keeping up a shuttle service between her palaces at Bagni di Lucca, Leghorn, Marlia and Florence.

But from Dresden Napoleon ordered Borghese in Turin and Elisa in Florence to be prepared for attack, showing particular concern about the provisioning of Elba against a possible British onslaught from the sea. More strangely still he summoned Murat to take part in the new battles to be fought and equally strangely Murat went; but he stayed only to take part in the battle of Leipzig and, after the defeat of the French armies there, sped back to Naples.

Just one year had elapsed from the French army's entry into the burning city of Moscow and the defeat at Leipzig and the alarm which had been rumbling grew into a roar—was it possible that Napoleon was not, in fact, invincible? When Wellington and the British army crossed the Pyrenees and Napoleon began to fight a rearguard action the possibility became an awful certainty.

Pauline was the first of the sisters to be really roused because it was the safety of her beloved brother which was in question. She alone had entire faith that he would overcome all obstacles but at the same time felt he might need the kind of help she could give him, so, after Leipzig, she had sent him a diamond necklace, a practical proof of affection which touched the Emperor greatly, although he sweetly told her that he had as yet no need of it.

Elisa's alarm was all for herself; she was now told to prepare for a full-scale invasion of Italy, most inopportunely since she was again recovering from a severe illness. Her own forces were quite inadequate for the defence of Tuscany; it was on

Eugène, the Viceroy, she depended, but he was fighting in the north and evasive about his plans, so Elisa wrote to the Emperor himself, in terms how different from heretofore.

> Things in Italy are going badly. There have been some insurrectional movements and brigands have appeared in the north. I shall leave the Grand Duchy only if the enemy should occupy Florence, and then I would withdraw via Piombino to the island of Elba, and wait there until matters improved.

She was still confident that matters could improve.

On his way through Florence Murat had promised that he would come to Elisa's aid if required but he had gone on to Naples and no word had come from him. What was she to do? Was she to believe in his promises of help in the event of an attack? The situation was now becoming alarming. The Austrians had already cut her direct communications with Paris and were threatening Bologna. At this juncture she received orders from her brother:

> Even if the enemy arrives on the Mincio you must not leave Tuscany so long as he is held by the Viceroy and so long as the enemy has not won a big battle. You will always have your retreat assured on Naples.

But would she? Strange things were happening at Naples.

When Murat returned to Naples from Russia condemnation of his action was general, but after Leipzig he was met by the profound silence which greets an overwhelming defeat. Although he was not too confused in mind to see very clearly that Napoleon had everything to lose, and nothing to gain by continuing to fight, he still lacked sufficient foresight to perceive that the shocks in France must have volcanic repercussions in Naples. The question which agitated Caroline and Murat was what, if anything, they themselves would lose. In December, 1813, Murat appealed passionately to the Emperor to make peace.

> In the name of all that you hold dearest in the world, in the name of your glory, do not persist any longer. Make peace, make it at any price. Gain time and you will have gained all. Your genius and time will do the rest. If you refuse the wishes of those who are your friends, of your subjects, you will be lost and you will have caused us all to be lost.

And he added that while Italy was still faithful because, in remaining attached to the French Empire, she perceived a better future for herself, she would not long remain so if her hopes were dashed.

Italy's problem was the Murats' own problem, either to remain faithful to the Emperor and, if he could not be influenced to make peace, perish with him, or to save their people and their crown by attaching themselves to the Allies. A waiting game was the only line of conduct not open to them.

Louise Murat herself admits that the first course was the only one for her father to take, or at least the most heroic, had he been in a position to act only as a private individual and according to the dictates of his heart, but he was a king . 'On his decision depended the fate of the people over whom he had been called to reign, with whom he and his family had completely identified themselves, and to whom honour and duty demanded that he should devote himself.'

If Murat abandoned Naples to the Austrians and the English he knew they would at once restore the Bourbon dynasty; the Neapolitans would have been betrayed without profit to France or the Emperor. If he entered into an arrangement with the Allies, and incidentally ensured his personal position, he could still expect to gain real advantages for Italy. His daughter stresses that it was rather in the interests of Italy he acted than in his own, but she does not conceal that he was dreaming of a united Italy, in whose rule he himself would naturally play a major part.

While Murat and Caroline were searching for a way out of the impasse in which they found themselves the English landed a small force at Viareggio and, encountering little opposition, marched on to Lucca which capitulated. The foray was merely a warning for they re-embarked and withdrew.

It was to Pauline, still at Hyères, that Elisa wrote now of her serious apprehensions and, as a precautionary measure, began to send her valuables out of Florence.

Whatever her public face, Elisa's decision to start unloading at Florence was an indication of her personal anxiety, intensified by the fact that she could get no clear ruling from anyone as to the course she was to take. Once again she enquired of Murat what help he could give her, to which his reply was that if Tuscany were attacked he would come to its defence, but in that case he must be given supreme command in Italy. This, in effect, meant eliminating Eugène, which troubled Elisa not a jot since he was a Beauharnais, but it did instil in her mind some doubts as to the part Murat was proposing to play, for she was not unaware of his ambitions to rally the whole of Italy. If he succeeded in this dream then perhaps her future lay with him rather than with her brother.

She sought advice now from the Emperor who told her,

> If it should happen that the King (of Naples) declares war on us, France is not dead yet, and so infamous a treachery, if it could exist, would redound only on its author. Let the King imprison or kill you, but do not permit of any failure of duty to the nation.

Napoleon knew that the Austrians were making advances to Naples and that the black-avised Count Neipperg, a name destined to become even more hateful to him, had arrived in Naples with offers of an alliance with Austria. While he found it difficult to believe that Murat and Caroline could contemplate allying themselves with his enemies his experience of Murat's changeability inspired him with no confidence as to Neipperg's reception.

Murat's struggle between two rights was a cruel one. He

knew that the Neapolitans, who disliked leaving their sunlit home to fight all over Europe, were in favour of peace nor could he ignore the weight of public opinion. Caroline's dilemma was even greater. She could not forget that it was because of her, as Napoleon had so often reiterated, that Murat was King of Naples and that, had he remained simply a Marshal of France, his duty would have been obvious.

Throughout the year 1813 Caroline had been torn by doubts. It was clear to her that Napoleon's power was on the wane, but it is probable that all she foresaw was a restriction of his dominion, not a complete collapse; it seemed inconceivable that his father-in-law, the Emperor of Austria, should turn irrevocably against his son-in-law or destroy his daughter's position as Empress of the French. If Caroline and Murat made an alliance with Austria they would consolidate their position and, without fundamentally harming Napoleon's future, achieve that independence of which they had so long dreamt. That Napoleon did not share their view is shown by his letter to Elisa.

While Murat was hesitating, and seeking some sign from Napoleon before taking the final step, Caroline made up her mind. They must choose the Allies. Her decision was no doubt influenced by her new lover, Mier, the Austrian Ambassador, and by the fact that her old lover, Metternich, was the most powerful man in Austria. In her turn she was able to influence Murat by impressing on him that, should it suit him, Napoleon would not hesitate to sacrifice them to the Allies.

For Murat this was a situation which could not be met with a gasconade. Intrigue had played its part; phrases must now give way to action. Murat wrote to the Emperor, reproaching him with giving him insufficient resources to resist the forces lined up against Naples. Austria was pouring troops into Italy and on his seaboard the English were poised for the kill. 'What can I do, menaced thus on all sides and unable to count on any aid? If I commanded a French army, I would dare all . . .'

Murat had few illusions about the fighting quality of his Neapolitan troops. He knew he could not lead them now beyond the Alps, even if he could lead them as far. Whatever their devotion to him personally might be would they not abandon a sovereign who was abandoning the interests of their country?

Napoleon thought otherwise. If Murat joined the Franco-Italian army commanded by Eugène together they would force the Austrian army on to the defensive in northern Italy which, with a large body of troops thus pinned down, would delay an offensive until the spring, giving him time to recruit and re-group his forces.

As the Allies crossed the French frontier in January, 1814, Napoleon wrote caustically to Murat,

> The title of King has turned your head; if you want to keep it, behave yourself and be careful what you say. I don't imagine you are one of those who think the lion is dead. If you did, you would be badly out in your reckoning.

But the lion, if not dead, was dying. Once again Murat recalled that, even before Dresden, he had been entreating the Emperor to make peace and once again he implored him to do so.

> Sire, if bitter necessity leads me, as I believe it must, into a course apparently contrary to your interest, but which perhaps all the same may be useful to Your Majesty and to France by giving me some influence in the peace negotiations, I hope that you will judge me with calm and impartiality.

Now came what Murat himself called the unhappiest day of his life, the day when he must make his final choice. On one side he saw the inevitable loss of his kingdom while on the other were his commitments to his subjects and his family, yet over all were his eternal devotion to Napoleon and his unalterable attachment to France.

Two days later he wrote the fateful words, 'I have just concluded a treaty with Austria', but he repeated vehemently that he would fight neither against France nor the Emperor. Napoleon might castigate him as 'the Bernadotte of the South' but he would never, like his quondam friend and fellow-Marshal, now Prince Royal of Sweden, take up arms against the country of his birth.

'The Marshal of France who, on his own admission, owed his sword, his blood and his life was wrong,' said Bourrienne. 'The King of Naples was right.'

But Joachim Murat, Marshal of France, and King Joachim of Naples were one and the same man.

Murat still sincerely nourished the hope that the course of action he had chosen, or which had been forced upon him not by his own actions but by the Emperor's, might still be of some benefit to France.

> In the midst of the pretensions and the prejudices of all the old reigning dynasties I have dealt with them as equals. I have been able to take and hold my rank among all the débris that covers Europe. Your pupil, your brother-in-law, has kept the crown you gave him and, after this short storm which separates us, you will find again the man who is eternally devoted to you.

It was not so much against Murat, furious with him though he was, as against Caroline that Napoleon exploded; he believed rightly that she was the decisive influence in Joachim's volte-face. If it was true, as de Ségur said of him, that Murat could not now, after being six years a king, envisage life without a crown, the corrosive acid of power for itself had not eaten as deeply into him as into her.

Caroline evidently thought it politic at least to appear distressed by the Emperor's anger. Her mother wrote uneasily to Elisa:

> I have had letters from Caroline in which she writes to me of how unhappy she is at the Emperor's displeasure on this head. I hope it will end all right.

But, in fact, Caroline was serenely confident that their action had been the right one.

They say that the Emperor is furious with me, she wrote to Joachim. You know my attachment to him, and his anger certainly distresses me, but I am sure that on reflection he will feel that I have only done my duty and that I could not have acted in any other way. A woman who had done otherwise would not have merited his esteem. My conscience is clear, and I have nothing with which to reproach myself so, even when you see in the newspapers disagreeable things printed about me, do not worry nor think that is what has made me ill.

When one does one's duty one may wait with calm for the end of the storm and hope still to have fine weather.

The storm still seemed to the Murats to be almost one in a teacup. Together with Elisa they thought that independent action on their part would have no decisive effect so far as the Emperor was concerned. They believed that they would preserve their sovereignty and that, henceforward, with Napoleon still Emperor, even if with a curtailed Empire, they would be able to govern as they wanted without excess interference. This may have been miscalculation and faulty reasoning, but it was not in their minds treachery.

Elisa was now leaning heavily on Murat as crisis showed up her weaknesses. A good administrator she undoubtedly was but nothing of a statesman and she stood in urgent need of an adviser. To Pauline she wrote of the cruel position in which she was placed, in which she could see no favourable outcome for herself. Acting on the advice of Fouché, she withdrew to Lucca, a tactical error because the Florentines thought she was abandoning them and her departure was attended by hostile demonstrations.

Murat, at the behest of his new allies, marched north to Bologna, if need be to fight against Eugène, but this he could not bring himself to do, temporising until warned that his vacillation might cost him his throne. His new partnership showed no signs of being easier than the old but there could now be no looking back for the Murats. The decision they had made must be abided by.

Murat's aid to Elisa had not worked out as she had imagined. The Neapolitans occupied Florence, and Lucca was at Murat's mercy, but she was determined to make a strenuous defence of Elba. Nevertheless, when all the fortified places in Tuscany had been handed over to the King of Naples, and peace negotiations with the Allies were opened at Châtillon, Elisa had already reconciled herself to the loss of Tuscany. She pleaded with Caulaincourt, the French delegate, at least to be allowed to retain Lucca, a plea certainly doomed to disappointment even had Lord William Bentinck, the British Minister to Sicily, not taken the law into his own hands and, acting without authority, precipitated events in Italy.

Landing at Leghorn, he issued a proclamation calling on all Italians to rise in defence of their liberties, at the same time asserting that Great Britain would maintain the rights of the Sicilian Bourbons, an arbitrary action which roused Murat immediately to resume negotiations with Eugène.

Lord William, virtually master of the Tuscan coast, imperiously demanded that Elisa withdraw from her States, overriding the clause in the Peace of Pressburg which guaranteed to her, as their legal sovereign, the States of Piombino and Lucca. Elisa had no alternative in face of superior odds but to go entreating, even as the waggons were loaded with her goods and chattels, that at least the institutions she had created for the good of her peoples should be preserved. With a last look at their city of Lucca the Baciocchis took the road to Genoa and exile.

To Italy in turmoil came the news that, on April 6th, 1814, the Emperor had signed an act of abdication, renouncing for himself and his heirs the crowns of France and Italy. On the 20th he said farewell to the Guard in the courtyard at Fontainebleau then, with an Austrian escort, he left for the south.

It was the Marshals who betrayed him in the end. They had lived too hard and lately too soft. Many of them, like

Murat, were exhausted and their minds confused. No longer were they the gay and brilliant young men of Mombello, and it was Marmont who led the rout, Marmont whom Napoleon had wanted to marry to his sister Pauline, and who showed his feet of clay as he took the road from Fontainebleau to treat with the Allies, Marmont who remarked composedly,

'Today it is probable that as a result (of refusing to marry Pauline), I have more to congratulate myself on than to regret.'

Since, alone of the family, Pauline still believed in her brother's future, it had been particularly distressing to her to receive a letter from Murat, of whom she had always been fond, in which he attempted to explain to her, and perhaps also to himself, his attitude of mind. It was hard for her to entertain divided loyalties but she tried to understand.

> The Emperor is at grips with the Allies, France is unhappy, and yet everything requires me not to go and die to defend them. Everything attaches me to my new fatherland—the destiny of my children and that of my subjects has prevailed with me. I have taken up arms for them and apparently against the man whom I revere, and whom I love still more. However, I am not yet an enemy, and I hope that peace will come before the King of Naples must decide to act.
>
> Pity me, my sister, you love me and know how much I love the Emperor. . . . Remember that you have and will have in me always a friend in every difficulty who will love you all his life.

Did Pauline understand? Gay, brittle Pauline who had played so completely passive a part in the Imperial destinies now seemed to be the one person to whom all the Bonapartes turned, if not for help, at least for comfort.

There was one who needed her most. Pauline stayed where she was at the little town of Luc to await the Emperor's arrival, hoping that he would allow her to accompany him to exile, never to leave him again. If he did not want her she would go to Naples but when the Baciocchis, who had arrived at Marseilles, invited her to go with them to Rome she would not go. She must wait for the Emperor.

The Baciocchis had been on the road for a long time. Their first intention was to go to Paris but, when they found the Austrians barring their way, they changed direction and went on to Montpellier, where Carlo Bonaparte had died. Here Elisa met her Uncle Fesch in flight from his see at Lyons, but it was a mistake to have chosen the south-west which was in a state of royalist effervescence. They found it wise to move on to Marseilles, a painful experience for Elisa who had lost her first child here.

Their indecision was that of all exiles; they hoped to go to Naples, perhaps to Rome. Elisa refused to abandon the hope that their final destination might still be Lucca, as always over-estimating her own importance. She had none of the value in the Allies' eyes that Murat had and they treated her as being of the same political nullity as Pauline.

Napoleon's abdication made her hope vain and, cruellest of all, her former subjects did not want her return. No sooner had the Baciocchis left Florence than the vultures gathered round their régime, pecking it to pieces. The good she had done was forgotten, only the extravagance of the Court and her pursuit of Church property remembered.* They had yet to find that with Elisa's energy and creative ability went their prosperity but they learnt that they had made a change for the worse. The Tuscans missed the gaiety and colour of Elisa's Court and their new taskmasters, the Austrians, offered them no mortar for their bricks.

It was unfortunate for Elisa that her qualities did not measure up to her estimation of them and that she lacked essential powers of acumen and statesmanship. When her testing time came she was caught between the stronger will of Caroline and Murat and stigmatised for betraying her brother when, in reality, she was embroiled in events that she had no capacity for influencing.

* To this day she is known in her former Grand Duchy as *la Baciocca*—a play on the word which means a woman of easy virtue.

At least she was fortunate in being allowed to return to Italy, if not to Tuscany. The Baciocchis at last found a home in Bologna where Felix, in an unfortunate access of independence, issued a declaration of adhesion to Louis XVIII, now sitting on the throne of France at the Tuileries where fleurs-de-lys had hastily been sewn over the Imperial bees.

Elisa settled down with her accustomed obstinacy to the task of winning the Allies' approval of her living if not ruling in Tuscany, which she must have known to be an impossible request but, nevertheless, she sat all day writing, writing, writing until disillusion and discouragement affected her health and spirits.

Even more important than finding a permanent place of residence was to assure herself of her fortune. She asked for a passport to Vienna to plead her own cause with Metternich, a move which aroused Pauline's extreme indignation. She wrote to her mother,

> I am distressed to hear that Elisa has been to Vienna. She wrote to Queen Caroline that from there she would like to go and settle in Paris. I should never have thought her capable of such conduct, yet she wrote to the Emperor that she would like to go to the island of Elba. I am sure that her determination will grieve the Emperor very much, for he did not conceal from me that it would be unpardonable treachery for any member of our family to establish himself in France. . . . It is now when he is unhappy that we must show him our devotion—at least that is the way I see it.

And that is the way Pauline went on seeing it. When the Emperor of the French who had crumbled into the King of Elba stopped at Luc to say farewell to his sister they spent four hours alone together. No one knows what they said to each other! Then he went on his way to that island which now had its wish to live under his paternal laws. In those brief hours the Queen of Folly died and the real Pauline, for so long unknown except to those who truly loved her, came to life.

Henceforward she determined to dedicate herself to the man who had loaded her with kindness and with love.

'I never loved him as my sovereign,' she said simply. 'I loved him as a brother, and I shall remain faithful to him until death.'

It was a promise she kept.

She had said she would join him at Elba but for a few weeks she lingered with Duchand. It seemed that he represented to her all that had been gay and happy in her past life and she could not bear to leave him; but she was Bonaparte's sister, and once again she showed the same courage that she had manifested at San Domingo.

In spite of her fear of the sea she embarked for Elba, arriving at Porto Ferraio on June 1st, 1814, in the frigate *Letizia*, sent to her by Murat. Napoleon went on board to greet her and she spent the night on the island. Next day she re-embarked on the *Letizia* and sailed for Naples.

CHAPTER THIRTEEN

'THE BURNT-OUT HOUR'

> It was through the intervention of some members of the Bonaparte family that the desired rapprochement took place between the two brothers-in-law, and Princess Pauline Borghese was the principal negotiator. Her frivolity and flighty reputation inspired no misgivings and it was, therefore, easy for her to come from Porto Ferraio to Naples to carry out her mission of peace, without arousing any suspicion as to the important messages with which she was entrusted.

This information must have come to Louise Murat from her mother and gives the lie to those who assert that Pauline played no part in the changed climate between Napoleon and the Murats. In fact, the rupture between them was of short duration.

Pauline settled down at the Villa La Favorita at Portici, one of the favourite country homes of the Neapolitan royal family, where she remained for five months, in spite of her expressed wish to join her brother at Elba. There must, therefore, have been some reason for her delay more important than her reluctance to put to sea again.

She spent her time drawing up more budgets and entered into negotiations for the sale of the Hôtel Borghese in Paris, a clear indication that she was resolved never to return to France so long as Napoleon remained in exile. This move on her part was wise because in December, 1814, in contravention of the Treaty of Fontainebleau, signed by Napoleon, and which assured their rights to the Bonapartes, they were deprived by decree of all their property in France. Pauline thus lost her homes at Neuilly and Montgobert which she had been unable to sell in time.

Pauline was happy to be with Murat and Caroline for whom, according to her daughter, she had a tender affection, of which until her death she continued to show the most touching proofs. Of little Louise herself Pauline was particularly fond, although one might have thought she would prefer Letizia, who was outstandingly pretty. She was always delighted to see the Murat children but their governesses did not allow them to visit her very often because of the frivolity of her conversation.

From Naples Pauline wrote to Lucien who, with the peace, had been released and returned to Italy from England, that the king and queen were charming to her, but she regretted being so far from her dear mother. Although the others might talk of going, Madame Letizia was the only one of the family who actually went to Elba.

In her letter to Lucien Pauline added, 'Tell me about Prince Borghese. I have had no sign of life from him but I should nevertheless like to be on good terms with him if he wants to do the same.'

When the Emperor abdicated Borghese was deprived of his Governor-Generalship in Turin but, as an Italian, the collapse of the Empire meant very little to him. He had palaces in plenty in Italy and he simply moved his household goods and chattels and the Duchessa Lante delle Rovere from Turin to Florence.

The world, however, heaved a great sigh of relief that peace had come at last and the powers settled down at Vienna to their Congress whose aim was to ensure that 'Europe's wormy dynasties rerobe themselves in their old gilt, to dazzle anew the globe!'

Of the new dynasties only Bernadotte in Sweden and Murat in Naples remained, which justified Caroline and Murat in the step they had taken. By entering into secret relations with Napoleon they had insured their position so that, whatever happened, they should still be on the right side. Superficially their situation was fortunate although they were now isolated in a largely hostile Europe. Since all their French friends had left the Court they personally were both glad to have Pauline with them as well as to welcome the many foreign visitors who flocked to Naples.

The English in particular, in their eternal quest of the sun, came in large numbers. They were graciously received at Court by the Murats who were especially happy to show them the excavations at Pompeii which aroused their great interest.

They were all very gay. Miss Davies, the English governess, repeats an anecdote about the king, 'who dearly loved a joke', which shows that Murat was not wholly given over to care.

One morning at breakfast in the pavilion he surprised and amused his guests, among whom were some of the English nobility, by having a pair of dwarfs served up as the middle dish at the dessert.

> They came through the aperture in the table, resting quietly in their china car; and when safely landed, they rose up, and lightly tripping along the table, presented an offering of flowers to the royal pair.
>
> Their unexpected and ludicrous appearance drew peals of laughter from the light-hearted guests.

A greater but less avowable subject of amusement was provided by Caroline of Brunswick, Princess of Wales, whose visit to Naples of four months might better be described as a visitation, although her presence greatly gratified the little English governess.

The Princess developed a violent passion for Murat, whose extravagance in dress and person no doubt touched a sympathetic chord; she even affected an enormous blonde wig with long curls floating on her shoulders which, she happily thought, gave her a resemblance to him.

To return the hospitality she had enjoyed the Princess of Wales gave a ball at carnival time in 1815 in honour of her host. When Murat arrived he was led to a dais by a group of pretty English girls, dressed as goddesses from Olympus. Then the Princess of Wales, who represented Glory, took a feather from the wing of the girl representing Fame, and wrote in great golden letters on a tablet she was holding the names of Murat's battle honours.

Scarcely able to restrain their laughter, the guests applauded loudly, but Murat was annoyed while the parvenu Queen Caroline shrugged her shoulders at the eccentric and un-royal antics of the authentic Princess Caroline.

Murat forgave the Princess of Wales sufficiently to present her with an equipage in which, to the delight of Europe, she rode about, preceded by her favourite, Bergami, dressed exactly like Joachim, whom he did his best to resemble in manner and gesture. The little phaeton was shaped like a shell, gilded in mother-of-pearl and upholstered in blue velvet; it was drawn by two little piebald horses, led by a child dressed like a cherub. The whole entourage looked like the advance party of a circus. Murat, who did not like being the subject of ridicule, was not amused.

Pauline was not in Naples to take part in all the gaiety. Her mission there apparently accomplished, she left Naples in October, 1814, for Elba to fulfil her promise on the inappropriately named *L'Inconstant*. With her beauty, grace and gaiety she did her best to distract a man overwhelmed with memories and heavy with plans for the future, playing the same part she had played in San Domingo. What the Emperor missed, and what his mother was unable to give him, was the atmosphere of elegance, of fashion and sophistication, to which he was accustomed, which was equally beyond the power of Elban society to provide.

To the little island and the miniature Court Pauline brought a whiff of Paris, organising daily receptions and parties in her own apartments, dining with the Emperor and allowing him to criticise her dress or anything which occurred to him, so long as it gave him pleasure. In all things she was sweet, affectionate, kind and above all gay, although it grieved her greatly to see her brother, once master of Europe, attempting to confine his genius within the boundaries of his petty kingdom.

She gathered round her the prettiest women on the island, willing to act as she had done in the case of Christine de Mathis, but once again it was her own presence at Elba on which the pamphleteers seized as an opportunity of discrediting the fallen meteor with their squalid stories of incest. To them Pauline could have no other reason for going to Elba than to resume hcr guilty relationship with her brother. Family feeling, sisterly devotion? These reasons could only be creditable to the Bonapartes whom now, more than ever, it was essential to discredit.

First the 'Revolutionary Plutarch', then Fouché, then the Englishman, Lewis Goldsmith, who had served, then fallen out with, Napoleon, established the line of libel, the last-named in an edifying work, entitled *The Secret History of the Cabinet of Bonaparte*, published in 1810. He wrote:

> Napoleon has much immoral intercourse with women, but he has shewn himself addicted to that vice with which Socrates is accused, perhaps falsely, with respect to Alcibiades. I should not wonder if he should, like his prototype, Nero, marry a boy . . . he has been guilty of the most nefarious transgressions of decency; he lived in a state of undisguised concubinage with two of his sisters, Mesdames Murat and Borghese; the former made a public boast of it.

From here it was easy to go on that Pauline, even under her mother's eye at Elba, was once again part of the dark picture, although no one has been graceless enough to suggest that Madame Letizia connived at incest between her son and daughter.

The 'evidence' rests on two letters, allegedly written by Pauline to two of her lovers, although these letters have never formed part of any archive, nor have they actually been seen by any human eye. One letter was reputedly addressed to Colonel Duchand, a man of great personal integrity who would have been revolted by the terms of the letter. The other addressee is not even known, nor are the dates of the letters, but their authenticity was accepted without question.

The substance of one of the letters was Pauline's complaint that her only lover in Elba was 'this rotten old man'—'*ce vieux pourri*'—identified unhesitatingly as Napoleon, although Pauline never referred to her brother either in speech or letter in any but the most respectful terms. Apparently he was too jealous to allow her to summon the gentleman to whom this complaint was addressed but, by the time the second letter was written, he had evidently relaxed his vigilance, because this correspondent is invited to come to Elba and bring with him, or send in advance, a remedy, known as '*Rob l'affecteur*', for the 'inadmissible illness'.

Had Pauline really stood in need of such a remedy she could have obtained it through the normal correspondents in Paris who supplied her wants, and why the gratuitous information that she was suffering from a malady rarely alluded to should have been considered as an inducement to her lover to join her can be explained only by its inventors.

The truth of the matter is different. It was now a matter of national policy to give free rein to a campaign of vilification, to cast the man who had been the national hero down from his metaphorical pedestal as his effigy had been toppled from his column in the Place Vendôme. Fears of a Bonapartist revival dictated what had been the prerogative of spite.

There were other reasons as well. Marie Louise's father, the Emperor of Austria, was at great pains to prevent her going to Elba to join her husband with her little son, the King of Rome. The main deterrent in the Austrian armoury was the one-eyed charmer, Count Neipperg, who had been their emissary to Naples to win Murat over to the Austrian alliance. If he failed in his task of seducing Marie Louise calumny was their reserve weapon, and what could render a husband more repugnant to his wife than to learn that he was enjoying an incestuous relationship with his sister, while at the same time assuring his wife of his whole-hearted devotion and eagerness to be re-united with her. To share him with Pauline?

The confidence the Austrians put in Neipperg was not misplaced; the letters also served their turn in blackening the Emperor's character. These stories are now known to be fabrications, based on the mischievous gossip of royalist police spies. All correspondence from Elba was read by the police on the Italian mainland and forwarded to Talleyrand at Vienna. Little skill or ingenuity was needed to infiltrate these forgeries into a bundle of intercepted letters. They had other uses also. Louis XVIII delighted to roll salacious morsels about the Bonapartes under his impotent tongue and the time-servers and vicars of Bray who, in Frédéric Masson's phrase, served under every régime with the same infidelity, learned early that an important element in gaining the favour of the new monarch was vilification of the Bonapartes.

Napoleon had far more serious preoccupations at Elba. On February 17th, 1815, he addressed a letter to 'his brother and very dear brother-in-law', Murat, which was taken to him by the Chevalier Colonna, his mother's chamberlain, with urgent and important messages.

> The Chevalier is authorised to sign any convention that Your Majesty may desire with regard to our affairs. Your Majesty should in particular regard with all confidence what he will tell you about my attachment and deep consideration . . .

It is plain that the reconciliation Pauline had been instrumental in effecting between her brother and her brother-in-law was now complete.

She was not informed of her brother's plans to leave the island, although this was obviously what the Chevalier Colonna had to tell Murat, but she guessed what was afoot. Once again she gave Napoleon her diamonds although she now could not really afford to part with them.

On the point of departure on February 26th, 1815, Napoleon took Pauline into the garden of the Palazzo Mulini and there said his farewell, leaving her sad and overwhelmed by the premonition that she would never see him again. All that she could say, between sobs, to his entourage as they made their cautious way to the harbour to embark on *L'Inconstant*, was,

'Farewell, my friends. All my thoughts and prayers go with you. Love my brother always and protect him.'

> If, wrote Pons de l'Hérault, an Elban memorialist, all the princes and princesses of Napoleon's family had the same disinterested devotion as Princess Pauline, Napoleon would perhaps still be on the throne. . . .

Elisa, certainly, had no time for devotion except to her own interests, but some excuse may be made for her as she was most inopportunely pregnant and as time passed she became increasingly apprehensive as to where her child would be born.

The peace she had hoped to find at Bologna proved only temporary, The Austrians made her stay uncomfortable so she drifted first to Graz to be near her brother, Jerome, then to Trieste, and there were times when she thought her child would be born in a common inn. In fact, her son, Jerome-Frédéric, was born in August, 1814, at the villa at Passeriano where Napoleon had stayed to negotiate the Treaty of Campo Formio in 1797, in the long dead days when she was a young and happy bride.

At last she was allowed to rejoin Felix at the Villa Caprara at Bologna, where he had settled down to the life of a country gentleman. The new Grand Duke of Tuscany visited her on his way to Florence, moved either by pity or curiosity or because the Allies were anxious to know her state of mind. It gratified Elisa to receive a reigning prince again and gave her a little spurious hope for the future.

Wearing now the incognito of Comtesse de Compignano, one of her pretty Tuscan estates, Elisa began the slow apprenticeship from royalty to private life until Napoleon escaped from Elba and her peace was at an end. Four days after the Emperor made his entry into the Tuileries Elisa and the little Napoleone were seized by the Austrians and carried off to the fortress of Brünn. The world's contempt of Baciocchi was shown by his being left in Bologna with the baby, Frédéric.

In Naples during 1814 the appearance of stability and peace had been resting on foundations far from solid. The Bourbons were in no wise reconciled to the retention of an upstart king on a throne which had belonged to a branch of their family, even if the Emperor of Austria would rather have a Murat as King of Naples than a revival of Bourbon hegemony in Europe. Unfortunately for Murat it was Metternich, not the Emperor Francis, who dictated policy. Legitimacy was now the catchword, while Metternich also feared Murat's devotion to Italian nationalism. If Murat were successful in promoting the unity of Italy, it would mean the loss of her Italian provinces to Austria.

In January, 1815, a secret treaty was drawn up by Talleyrand, acting for Louis XVIII, Metternich for Francis of Austria, and Castlereagh for the Prince Regent, enacting the agreement of the Three Powers that Murat should be expelled from Naples and the Bourbons restored.

This treaty Napoleon found lying on a desk when he returned to Paris with the violets, as he had promised, in March, 1815, and it is certain that he communicated its contents to Murat. The Murats may already have been aware of the Treaty because in those moments when Caroline invited Mier, the Austrian Ambassador, to view the Bay of Naples from the windows of her private apartments, she gleaned from him much of importance.

For Napoleon it was now vital, since Murat was his only ally in Europe, to have his flank protected by a Neapolitan army. One of the first letters he wrote from Paris was to the King of Naples.

> It is my sincere desire, as you can realise, to keep the peace, especially as Your Majesty's future depends on it, but if we are forced to take up arms again, I should reckon myself perfectly ready from that moment to face whatever may happen. . . . My confidence is increased by Your Majesty's support. If your attachment to me has not changed, it will be a pleasure to me to give you fresh proofs that you can always count on my friendship.

Murat was happy to be back within the fold. He had not really understood that his action the previous year had been regarded as treachery until a word of Madame Récamier's, who was visiting Naples, brought it home to him in all its horror.

Now Austria had turned its back on him and his future again lay with the Emperor, with the added prospect of himself as the author of a *risorgimento* which beckoned like a *fata morgana*; it was not he but Pauline's godson, Camillo Cavour, who made that dream a reality many years later.

While Madame Letizia made her way to Naples after Napoleon's departure from Elba, thus realising Caroline's cherished wish of receiving members of her family in her kingdom, Pauline had precipitately taken to flight. She was so alarmed by the threats of Colonel Campbell, the English commissioner whose short absence from Elba had made Napoleon's escape possible, that she decided to leave the island without further delay, embarking on an Italian vessel which landed her next day at Viareggio from where she went to Elisa's villa at Compignano.

The new Austrian governor of Lucca, Wercklein, was so seriously alarmed at the close proximity of this redoubtable Bonaparte that he at once sent a squadron of cavalry to surround the villa. Murat and Caroline were most indignant that two inoffensive women, Elisa and Pauline, had been made prisoners of the Austrians. Pauline's own distress was due to the fact that Napoleon had given her instructions to go to Rome, which she had failed to do because of Colonel Campbell's intimidation, and 'I am the more upset about this because it is the very first time in my life that I have disobeyed the Emperor.'

Her brother ordered a frigate to be sent to rescue Pauline but the order was not carried out nor was Murat in a position to use his influence with the Emperor of Austria to obtain her release. He had received a letter from Joseph Bonaparte telling him how enthusiastically Napoleon had been welcomed back to France. Joseph continued,

> You can associate yourself with the actions of the great nation which you have helped to glorify. You can do it effectively both by negotiation and by force of arms. This is the moment of decision . . . your throne will be consolidated by your alliance with France and with Austria. I

> hope that the Prince of Sweden (Bernadotte) will support this movement against the Bourbons of France and Italy. Let Austria send the Emperor back his wife and his son. Speak, let your heart dictate your actions, march to the Alps but not beyond. I guarantee that you will be happy because your policy will be in accord with your duty as a Frenchman, as a good relation, as a man of the Revolution, who owes everything to the people and nothing to divine right nor to the ideas of the eighth century. No more Bourbons! Honour to the men of the great Revolution!

It was a long time since anyone had appealed to Murat as a man of the Revolution, an appeal which he could not resist. He did not perceive that the part it was hoped he would play would be that of an intermediary with Austria or, at the very least, to keep the Austrians guessing about his intentions. Murat did, in fact, write to the Emperor Francis, what was an apologia for his conduct in 1814:

> As your Majesty, as well as I, is united by family ties to the Emperor Napoleon, I knew that in making war on him at the head of the Coalition, you never intended to dethrone him but only to induce him to accept moderate terms of peace. Knowing, too, that the Bourbons have an implacable hatred for the House of Austria, I believed that the Emperor's return to France would satisfy both Your policy and Your personal affections.

Murat went on to express his surprise that the Emperor Francis not only intended war but that he should have seconded his Allies in branding Napoleon, his son-in-law, as an outlaw. He then realised that the complete ruin of the Imperial House of France had been determined and 'that my own ruin went with it'. He ended by imploring Francis to think again, but it was too late for second thoughts.

Joachim had no real faith that he could influence the Emperor of Austria but Caroline was loath to face reality. She believed that her influence with Metternich could sway the issue, that his former tenderness for her would prevail over political expediency, that old and common error into which women fall.

Heedless of Caroline, and basing himself only on Joseph's inspiring instruction, which he believed erroneously came directly from Napoleon, Murat precipitately left Naples at the head of his army to march north to the Alps. It was his last mistake. Joseph did not have Napoleon's authority and the Emperor's tactics demanded that Murat remain in Naples for, once he moved, Austria would move too.

Pauline did not see Murat on his march through Italy. With the aid of a battery of doctors she had succeeded in getting leave from the suspicious Wercklein to go to Bagni di Lucca to take the waters. Less pleasantly Murat was followed by the adoring Caroline of Brunswick who, although a very zealous Bonapartist, feared that Napoleon's actions might compromise the king—a title she reserved exclusively for Murat, which would have enraged her poor, demented father-in-law, George III, had he known of it.

But it was Murat who compromised the Emperor. On May 3rd at Tolentino he met the Austrians and the hero of a dozen battles was defeated in this, his last.

> While the broken line enlarging,
> Fell or fled along the plain,
> There be sure was MURAT charging,
> There he ne'er shall charge again!

The battle was decisive. Shorn of all the panache in which he gloried, harassed and exhausted, Murat returned to Naples to take farewell of Caroline, the man in all his nakedness at last.

'Madame,' he murmured, 'I have not been able to find death.'

Miss Davies, who was much affected by his departure, wrote: 'He left her almost immediately, and entered a vessel which conveyed him to Ischia; and on this side of eternity they met no more.'

In spite of her predilection for chess Caroline had guessed her opponent's moves wrong. Now she could only watch helplessly while he swept the board of kings and queens, castles and knights—nothing left but humble pawns.

In Naples she was left to rule over confusion and disorder. Murat was absent from her counsel and her influence nor did she even know where he was. He was in fact in France, near Toulon, hoping to be summoned by the Emperor to take part in the imminent campaign against the Allies. From the bay of Cannes he wrote to Napoleon on May 25th,

> If you are forced to make war, I offer you my services to do as you please with. If you hope to preserve peace and my presence in the Empire is a hindrance to Your negotiations I beg Your Majesty to give refuge to my wife and children and I throw myself at Your feet to disown me. I have lost none of my courage and I feel myself capable of enduring anything while the hope of being useful to You through a new misfortune would lift my heart even above its grief. At this moment consider only the interests of Your subjects which is what I did a year ago in the hope of being able to serve You better one day.

And then, pathetically, for he now, too late, saw the consequences of his impetuosity, he added:

> It is most unfortunate that Prince Joseph wrote to me when he did. I could have been much more useful to You today, and I should not have made so many people unhappy.

Napoleon found himself unable to forgive Murat's failure at Tolentino. His offers of service were rejected; he was forbidden to go to Paris, but what wounded him, he who had once been the pride of the French army, was the Emperor's allegation that they would not tolerate his presence among them. The army marched to the Belgian frontier without the King of Naples.

In the stormy sunset of her glory Caroline showed that she had learned her métier as queen. Although she was forced on May 20th, 1815, to sign the Convention of Casalanza, which ceded her dominions to the Austrians, she insisted that a clause be inserted whereby an amnesty was assured to all those who had been attached to her government. Still she remained in Naples with the object of calming the populace but she took the precaution of sending her children to the fortress of Gaeta where they would, she thought, be safer than in the city.

Madame Letizia and Cardinal Fesch, who had succeeded in reaching Naples, accompanied the children and would willingly have taken them to France but Caroline refused to be parted from them. All the family who were able to do so were rallying in Paris. Jerome managed to escape Austrian vigilance in Trieste and make his way to join his brother while Lucien, the outcast, the rebel, left Italy to see if he could again play the part in his brother's fortunes that he had played on 18 Brumaire. Only Pauline chafed at Bagni di Lucca, borne up, however, by the good news which reached her from France. She was convinced that it would not be long before she, too, was able to join Napoleon in Paris.

Although Caroline was clinging tenaciously to the last shred of her dignities and power, banking perhaps on Metternich's kindness for her, she was in the end forced to submit; the forces piled up against her were too strong. She had finally to face the ruin of all her hopes, her efforts, her intrigues and her loves.

'One only reigns well at Naples!'

The reign was over.

The Neapolitans did not let her go quietly. A conspiracy was formed by galley slaves to murder her and she was obliged to seek the protection of Captain Campbell of the English man-of-war, *Tremendous*, 74 guns. Caroline Murat, Queen Regent of Naples, sister of the Emperor Napoleon, spent her last days in her palace of Naples under the protection of British marines.

She was still a queen. From her own purse she gave money for the soldiers' pay and, before she embarked on the English vessel to take her to France to join her husband, of whose whereabouts she was still ignorant, she made one royal gesture to inspire confidence in the people and to ensure order and tranquillity.

Dressed in a blue habit and mounting her charger for the last time, she went to the Royal gardens to thank the volunteers for their kindness and for the protection they had afforded her. She tried to smile but her tears could not be restrained. Bowing her head, she patted with her diminutive hand the neck of her horse, seeming to bid a long farewell to all that belonged to her former greatness; nor could the most indifferent person have felt uninterested in her, so lovely did she at the moment appear.

As by the private staircase Caroline left her palace for the last time the Archduke Leopold, with his Austrian troops, entered by the Grand Entrance.

From Naples Caroline took only what was her personal and private property, disdaining to strip the royal palaces as she had found them stripped seven years before. With her went a favourite cow with one horn, named Caroline after herself, to give milk to the children on the ship, and an entourage of seventy-three persons, among them the Murats' faithful adviser, Agar, Comte de Mosbourg, and General Macdonald, the Minister of War. Caroline's feelings as she boarded a British ship and turned for a long, last look at her royal palace can only be imagined. At once she was made aware of bad faith. Although it was agreed that she should be taken to France, Captain Campbell, by the direct order of the Admiral, refused to take her there; she might go anywhere, except to France. Believing that from the Emperor of Austria she would get the consideration denied her by the British, Caroline decided to make for Trieste.

During the eleven days of her voyage Caroline spent most of her time on the bridge, calm and serious, talking to her attendants while following the children's games with an indulgent eye. Perhaps she remembered what she had written to Murat:

> You will see that one day we shall be the happiest creatures in the world, and we shall owe it to our children. They will give us back all the love we have lavished on them, and our old age will be glorified by their virtues.

There might still be some happiness in store for her. Her brother was once again Emperor and might he not maintain himself on the throne of France? As so often in the past, she would be able to win his forgiveness for Murat and perhaps one day she and Joachim and their children might see Naples again—an exile's dreams.

Caroline was brought up sharply against the realities of her situation. When those of her entourage who wished to leave her at Trieste addressed a memorandum to her as 'ex-Queen of Naples' she drank the first drop from a cup of bitterness which already seemed full but which would overflow. At one moment people were subservient courtiers, at the next . . .

Tragedy often turns to banality. Of all the people in Caroline's suite no one could speak English properly and Captain Campbell was most irritated at not being able to make his orders understood. The children, however, thanks to Miss Davies and Mrs. Pulsford, spoke excellent English. As they acted as interpreters all went smoothly henceforward, but there were some distresses he could not avoid.

Tremendous passed the ship which was bringing Ferdinand of Naples to resume the throne so lately occupied by Joachim, and Captain Campbell was obliged to fire a salute of 21 guns. He apologised to Caroline for the noise they would occasion but she proudly replied that, as the sister of Bonaparte and the wife of Murat, the noise of guns occasioned her no concern.

Caroline's anxieties were many. Little Louise remembered hearing during the night some big packages drop into the sea. They were cases of papers, but what they contained the child did not know, nor did she ever discover what was in one case of papers which her mother kept always with her.

Before she disembarked from *Tremendous* Caroline royally distributed gifts to the crew, a hundred pounds to the sailors, diamond rings, pins, brooches and gold seals to the officers. Captain Campbell, who insisted on accompanying the royal party ashore, was so overcome with emotion that he flung himself back into his launch, unable to utter a word. It is less pleasing that, for his kindness and sympathy to Caroline, he was severely reprimanded and fell into disgrace.

When on June 6th, 1815, Caroline landed at Trieste she stepped ashore between an Austrian guard of honour of twelve men and one officer. This time the salvos rang out for her; Napoleon was still Emperor of the French even if she was no longer Queen of Naples. She was still treated with deference, and was still the Emperor of Austria's dear sister as of Her Majesty he was the good brother. Nevertheless, Baron Spiegelfeld, the Austrian governor of Trieste, kept a close watch on her movements.

Metternich wrote to her that anywhere she might choose to settle in Austria would be agreeable to the Emperor Francis, to which Caroline replied firmly that she intended to go to France and was, therefore, unable to adopt his suggestion that she go to Graz. She would leave Trieste at her own convenience.

At Cannes Murat was in a state of ferment about his family, writing in agony to the Emperor.

> My position is no longer tenable. It is appalling. The Queen, I learned, has left Naples but has not arrived here nor at Toulon. I fear that the English have not lived up to the Convention whereby she was to be brought to France with my family. She must, therefore, be either in Germany where the Austrians would like to hold us prisoner, or in England. . . . In coming to France I hoped to find asylum for my family. I must await knowing the Queen's fate before I can take a decision myself.

However much the Austrians might have disclaimed at the term, Murat's fears were justified; Caroline was in effect their prisoner. Baron Spiegelfeld continued to keep her under surveillance, not even allowing her to receive the French newspapers. His vigilance was intensified when, on June 12th, 1815, Napoleon left Paris to join his army, and once again there was war.

In Trieste Caroline was fighting a battle of her own, a brave battle but a losing one. She was anxious about Achille who was ill; she was anxious about Murat, from whom she had had no word. Her time was taken up with letters and consultations and she had the added worry of finding a name for herself. Call herself ex-Queen she could not, nor would she again wear the name of Madame Murat. She thought of calling herself the Comtesse de Bari, but it was pointed out to her that this sounded too much like the Comtesse du Barry, an unfortunate association. Finally she chose to call herself the Comtesse de Lipona, an anagram of the beloved name of Napoli, but even this the absurd Allies feared to let her use.

From Metternich she received a most courteous letter. (Did he still wear the bracelet with a lock of her hair?) Caroline's place of residence in the Emperor's dominions was to be entirely her own choice. The Emperor of Austria did not now think that she wished to go to France but, if she insisted, he would not stand in her way, although he did not quite see how the journey could be arranged; in the meantime she might stay at Trieste. The date of Metternich's letter was June 28th, when the battle of Waterloo had been fought and won, and there was no longer an Emperor but only somewhere in France a man wondering which way to turn.

Caroline's spirits were raised by Metternich's courtesy; she felt she had not been wrong in trusting to the old tenderness. In spite of Murat's *volte face* against the Austrians she was being treated with the kindness and generosity she had expected; it was a phase which did not last long.

She was allowed to remain in Trieste only for three months. Trieste was a seaport from which it would be all too easy, in spite of Baron Spiegelfeld's vigilance, for her to escape so, with exquisite Austrian politeness, the Emperor Francis invited her to move nearer Vienna.

On August 11th the Comtesse de Lipona, her children and her much reduced suite, left Trieste and the baron notified his government that 'la Lipona' had gone to Graz, but Graz was only a stage. On August 24th she arrived at the dreary Schloss Hainburg, near Vienna, which the Austrians capriciously decided was now too near the capital. She was informed that she must regard her stay there as purely temporary.

PART THREE

CHAPTER FOURTEEN

THE EXILES

When, in August, 1815, H.M.S. *Northumberland* sailed down Channel from Torbay in rainy weather, backed by fresh winds, she carried with her not only General Napoleon Bonaparte to exile on the rocky island of St. Helena in the South Pacific, but also an invisible cargo of all the hopes and illusions of his family.

The Empire had vanished almost overnight; they knew its disappearance to be irrevocable. As '*Napoléon retomba en Bonaparte*' even those Bonapartes who, like Lucien and Louis, had for long dissociated themselves from the Emperor's fortunes, found themselves at a loss. In or out of his orbit his magnetism was so strong and his dynamism so great that now, without his support and decisions on which, whatever their show of independence, they had come to rely, they were like lost children, facing a future both dark and uncertain, alone.

Almost resentfully some of those left behind thought that in adversity their brother was more fortunate than they. His future, even if he had only the hopeless security of a captive, was assured while they, who had themselves been sovereigns, courted and adulated, cousins and brothers to the monarchs of Europe, found themselves hunted along the roads of Europe and proscribed from France.

Until almost the last moment before he surrendered to the British at Rochefort it had been Napoleon's hope to escape to America.

Lucien wrote to Pauline: 'He is going to the United States of America where we shall all join him.' But it was only Joseph who managed to make good his escape.

With a sizeable fortune he settled down on large estates in

America where he lived for many years, leaving his family to fend for themselves in Europe. Happily for her his wife, Julie, was in a privileged position. As Princess Royal of Sweden her sister, Désirée, was able to exercise her influence on Julie's behalf so that she was allowed to come and go freely, the only Bonaparte to do so. Her self-effacement and complete abstraction from politics ensured her freedom from molestation even by the most suspicious of the Powers.

Madame Mère and Cardinal Fesch were fortunate in finding asylum in the Papal States where the Pope, forgetting his years as the Emperor's prisoner, remembered only that it was he who had brought France back to the Church and that Rome had always been the refuge of the disinherited. Brother and sister took up their residence in Rome, Fesch absorbed in the care of his increasing collection of pictures, Madame Letizia concerned only with her family and above all with the fortunes of Napoleon.

For the remainder of the family the problem was less simple. They had first of all to forget that they had been kings and queens, that once they had walked in palaces as masters. They had to learn that the great gilded grilles were now forever closed to them, that no longer at their approach would guards leap to attention or sabres rattle to a royal salute. While they were painfully dwindling into private individuals they had still more urgent preoccupations; to find homes and obtain enough money to keep themselves in at least something of their former style.

These aims were continually frustrated by the exaggerated persecution to which the Bonapartes were subjected by the triumphant Allies, always haunted by the possibility of a second escape from captivity by Napoleon, although they knew full well that escape from St. Helena was virtually impossible. The English even began to construct in Cape Colony a corvette (there was no yard at Simonstown, the naval base, and it had to be built up-country) to sail perpetually round the island to prevent any such attempt, an absurdity which in the end came to nothing.

In Europe, too, the Allies went to absurd lengths in malevolence, if there can ever be anything other than despicable in hounding the fallen. The Bonapartes were outlawed, deprived of their rights as citizens, forbidden the protection of the embassies, legations and consulates of France abroad, nor allowed to have any act notarised in any French chancellery. No Bonaparte was permitted to go anywhere whatsoever until he had requested the permission and obtained the authorisation of an inter-allied conference, assembled in Paris to determine each case.

If he lived in Rome, as both Lucien and Louis had done for some years, then he had to address himself first to the Cardinal Secretary of State, who transmitted the request to the Apostolic Nuncio in Paris, who referred it to the French Minister of Foreign Affairs, who would then call the inter-allied conference to discuss this important question. Whatever their decision it would be transmitted back wearily through the same channels.

The interdiction on the Bonapartes residing in France was at least understandable; there was strong Bonapartist feeling remaining among the discontented half-pay officers, and enough abortive Bonapartist plots to justify the Bourbons in rejecting a potential fifth column within their fortress. What they did not realise was that, in general, the Bonapartes were anxious only to settle themselves and showed small concern for their brother. If he had brought them to high estate and fortune it was through him that they had lost both. He dropped out of their calculations, as he seems to have done from their affections, so quickly that it poses the question whether he had ever been loved truly by any of them, excepting his mother and Pauline. In their extenuation it must be said that they were fighting in Europe for their lives and livelihoods while in St. Helena Napoleon was fighting only for his legend, the great rearguard action of his life.

Throughout what turned out to be the Hundred Days Pauline lived quiety at Bagni di Lucca, but Wercklein, intoxicated by having one Bonaparte in his power, seized her very innocent correspondence and tormented her with threats to send her as a prisoner to Brünn or Graz.

An even more exquisite pleasure was in store for him; he

was able brutally to announce to her with no preliminary warning that her brother had abdicated for the second time on June 22nd, 1815, and was in flight somewhere in France.

Pauline was prostrated when she heard the bitter news. She cared less for the disappearance of the Empire than for her brother's well-being. For a moment her anxiety was allayed when she received Lucien's letter, written from her old home at Neuilly, telling her that the family would follow Napoleon to America. She was again buoyed up with hope that, if he were successful in his plea to the Prince Regent to be allowed to settle in England, she might join him there. When this hope, too, was dashed, she began fearfully to apprehend that her premonition at Elba that she would never see her brother again was correct, unless the Allies would permit her to join him at St. Helena. She thought that Metternich might perhaps second her application to the Allies but there had never been any attachment between them to influence him in her favour; her plea was rejected.

To grief and ill-health was added anxiety about money. Little remained of what Pauline's fortune had been so that she was lucky still to have her inheritance from Leclerc. Louis XVIII had no intention of parting with any money to the Bonapartes in spite of the Treaty of Fontainebleau, which carried Talleyrand's signature on his behalf as well as those of Metternich for Austria, Nesselrode for Russia and Hardenberg for Prussia. The clauses of the treaty were categorical.

The mother, brothers, sisters, nephews and nieces of the Emperor were to retain, wherever they were, the titles of princes of his family. An annual revenue was to be reserved to the Emperor from the National Debt in consideration of the income and domains he was renouncing. This annual revenue, amounting to some 2,500,000 francs, would belong absolutely to the princes and princesses of his family and would be divided proportionately, the share of Elisa and Pauline being 300,000 francs each. Since the treaty was signed in 1814 when Caroline was still Queen of Naples she did not figure in it.

In addition to this annual income the princes and princesses of the Emperor's family were to retain and preserve all their goods, property and furniture of whatever nature whatsoever that they held as individuals, notably the incomes they enjoyed as individuals from the National Debt of France and the Monte Napoleone of Milan.

As far as Louis XVIII was concerned this Treaty was dead and buried. He had in his pocket, which for so many years had been empty, the Bonapartes' confiscated estates and property. If they begged their bread or lived on charity it was what he had done for twenty-three years; it was a matter of satisfaction to him if they were obliged to do the same.

For some months Pauline lingered in Tuscany although the Pope, wiser than the Austrians, fearing nothing from this delicate and fading beauty, authorised her coming to Rome, but it took her some time to resolve herself to re-entering Camillo's world.

To Elisa she wrote that she could not do otherwise since she must settle her affairs with her husband. Perhaps afterwards she would go to Elisa. Meanwhile, in October, 1815, she went to Rome.

Here she found half her family, her mother, her uncle, Cardinal Fesch, and Louis. Shortly afterwards they were joined by Lucien who, on his way back from Paris after the Emperor's abdication, had been kept a prisoner for some months in Turin. In Rome Pius VII made no difficulties for the Bonapartes, but they were still all subject to the strictest surveillance by the Powers, for whom the French Ambassador was chief watch-dog.

When they first arrived this office was held by an amiable cleric, Courtois de Pressigny, whose sympathies were more Papal than French. He left them in comparative peace but his successor was the implacable Duc de Blacas, whose embassy unfortunately was a long one.

Blacas made the sole object of his mission the rendering of the Bonapartes' lives as untenable as possible, having long forgotten his grandiloquent *pronunciamiento* 'that anyone who served Bonaparte in the interests of France served the King '. The Duc was an embittered and disappointed man, a royalist ' ultra ', who had learned nothing during his long years of emigration nor shed any of his outworn ideas and prejudices. The iron of exile had bitten deep into his soul although, as the favourite of Louis XVIII in exile, he might confidently have looked forward at the Restoration to a radiant future. Even the staunchest royalists could not, however, stomach his reactionary ideas so that, when opposition grew too strong, he was obliged to accept the honourable disgrace of the embassy in Rome.

If Louis XVIII's intention was to harry the Bonapartes his choice could not have been improved on. Blacas' methods of petty persecution were paltry. He spied constantly on the Bonapartes, exerting himself to grit the wheels of their lives. In his confidential reports he could not bring himself to spell out the hated name of Bonaparte, refusing even to recognise their incogniti ; he would refer to ' Monsieur Louis ' or ' Monsieur Lucien ', never to the Comte de St. Leu or the Prince of Canino, although this was a Papal not a French title. At his most vindictive he used the denigratory prefix of ' Sieur ' Lucien or ' Sieur ' Louis.

When he had to report that Pauline was suffering from some grave internal illness he cooed happily to the French Foreign Minister, and was patently gleeful when he again wrote that she had been so ill that she had sent for her confessor. It was disappointing that she recovered but the doctors were sure that the dangerous malady from which she was suffering must bring about her speedy end.

Any evidence of disagreements among the family Blacas seized on with delight. He glowed with pleasure when he learned of their difficulties about money but any display of wealth was at once suspect because their funds would naturally be used to foment plots.

It was natural to Blacas to construe the most innocent Bonaparte action as an indication of conspiracy so that it was fortunate for Caroline that she was beyond his jurisdiction as, in any event, the Allies chose to regard her as potentially the most dangerous of the family.

Caroline would have liked to return to Trieste from Hainburg, since on her going to Rome the Emperor of Austria had imposed a definite veto. Metternich wrote suavely on his master's behalf:

> In spite of the real interest the Emperor takes in the Bonaparte family it is not in his power to set aside the engagements he has undertaken with his Allies in order to be of service to you. The consent of France would also be required and I leave you to judge for yourself, Madame, if this last-named Power would be disposed to allow you to do so. It would be encouraging an illusion for you to nourish any hope in this respect and, however painful the truth may be to you, I ought not to let you remain unaware of it.

Rome was too near to Naples, Trieste too easy to escape from by sea. Since Caroline had not the means, the possibility, nor perhaps even the wish to try to recover Naples without Murat the Allies' suspicion was an ironic flattery which she would easily have foregone. At Schloss Hainburg in Austria she was forced to remain.

For months she had no news of Murat which added to the anguish of her situation; she looked for him hourly to join her, but still he did not come. Instead rumours began to reach her which she could scarcely credit.

Murat had lingered in France, hoping in spite of all to be called on to fight alongside Napoleon, but the Emperor could not forgive his precipitation in rushing to meet the Austrians in Italy and persisted in regarding him as the architect of his misfortunes.

Murat's position in the south of France was so insecure that he was forced to take to the hills, hiding here and there as he could, becoming increasingly desperate as the royalists gained a stronger hold on the country. He might even yet have sailed to join Caroline as he had passports for Austria, but he could not forget his kingdom nor his aspirations to lead the Italians to unity.

When he learnt that the Calabrians were in full revolt and that the Austrians had been obliged to send their best troops thither, he was convinced that they would be unable to maintain themselves in Naples. What Napoleon had done in escaping from Elba with a tiny force and rallying the whole of France Murat thought that he could do. From France, therefore, he sailed to Corsica where, in that Bonapartist stronghold, he managed to gather together a handful of men. With this little band he sailed to Italy to regain his kingdom.

Caroline discounted the news which finally reached her that Murat had arrived in Corsica and was there seeking adherents to his enterprise; she thought he would be mad to do so. When Elisa in Brünn heard of his arrival in Calabria she hastened to pass the news on to Caroline but both sisters supposed that he had been driven there by contrary winds and that he would be given means to continue his journey to Austrian territory. Neither suspected his real intention.

As time went by and Murat failed to arrive Caroline became increasingly apprehensive. She wrote to Elisa,

> I am extremely anxious as to what can have happened to him and I shan't be at rest until I see him again. Ah ! my dear Elisa, the loss of fortune is nothing to me when compared with the anguish with which I am overwhelmed. I should be happier in the most complete destitution if that were the price to be paid to spare my husband and me the anxiety of the days which have passed, and must pass, until the moment when he arrives here and I shall know that he is safe.

It was already too late. Joachim Murat was not to the Calabrians what Napoleon Bonaparte had been to the French. On the very day in October, 1815, when H.M.S. *Northumberland* dropped anchor in Jamestown Bay at St. Helena, in the little town of Pizzo in wild Calabria a shabby and haggard man faced a firing squad; his attempt had failed.

Captured by the Austrians, Murat's summary trial was a farce; he did not even listen to his sentence, refusing to recognise the competence of the military commission sent to try him by Ferdinand of Naples.

To Caroline he wrote his last letter:

> Never forget me. My life was stained by no unjust act. Adieu, my Achille, adieu, my Letizia, adieu, my Lucien, adieu, my Louise. Show yourselves to the world as worthy of me. I leave you without a kingdom and without fortune in the midst of my numerous enemies. Show that you can rise above misfortune. Remember what you are, what you have been and God will bless you. Do not curse my memory. My greatest grief in these last days of my life is to die far from my children. I bestow on you my paternal blessing, my kisses and my tears. Remember always your unhappy father.

Into the letter he slipped a lock of his hair. Then the man who had so strangely asked the Church's blessing on his marriage confessed himself, perhaps with thoughts of the seminary in the Quercy and the life which might have been his had he chosen the soutane and not the sabretache. Fixing his wife's portrait to his breast he went out calmly to meet the firing squad. As the last rays of the autumnal sun glinted on the metal of the rifles pointed at his heart he himself gave the word of command as so often he had ordered his troopers to the charge.

'Soldiers, do your duty! Aim at the heart but spare the face! Fire!'

Was it a last access of vanity, or in that moment did Joachim Murat remember the unrecognisable face of the Duc d'Enghien? He fell hit by seven balls. In his pocket the blue enamel watch with its miniatures of himself and Caroline went on ticking after the heart had ceased to beat.

> Poor, dear Murat, wrote Byron to Tom Moore. What an end! You know, I suppose, that his white plume used to be a rallying point in battle, like Henri IV's. He refused a confessor and a bandage so would neither suffer his soul or body to be bandaged.

In this Byron was wrong, nor were the white plumes Murat wore indicative of his courage. Courage he had in plenty to fight and die; it requires a colder courage to live.

Those numerous enemies of his did rejoice at his end. One of them wrote: 'It is a fine sight to see all these gentlemen of the terrible family cutting their own throats.'

In Vienna where the Congress was still sitting a joke went the rounds. A theatrical poster announced:

Le trône ébranlé par un mur abattu
2ième Représentation de Napoléon Détrôné
MURAT BATTU
Bénéfice des Alliés
Places en haut: Un LOUIS
Parterre: Un NAPOLEON

The despicable Ferdinand of Naples had a medal struck to commemorate Murat's execution, inscribed, 'For the rare fidelity of the town of Pizzo to the King'. In 1860 Garibaldi, recognising in Murat one, who in spite of all, could be regarded as a precursor of Italian unity, had the mould destroyed.

Today opinion has changed about Joachim Murat. The little town of Tolentino, where he met defeat at the hands of the Austrians, has requested that it be 'twinned' with his birthplace of La Bastide-Murat. If to the French Tolentino was a defeat which precipitated their own defeat at Waterloo, to the Italians it was the first blow struck for their freedom. To the citizens of Tolentino the Austrians were the usurpers, not Joachim Murat, on whose heart they believe the word 'Italy' was engraved.

There is a portrait by Gros of Murat which shows him almost as a demi-god on a rearing white horse, striking at an affrighted mob of Osmanlis with his scimitar. It is thus that he should be remembered in the pride of his youth and strength before his marriage to Caroline Bonaparte brought him the fatal dowry of a crown. Only great actions or great characters can justify to men sudden elevation to great powers. Murat did not have the quality of greatness but within his limits he followed a vision. In himself he was a man of good nature, kindly, to the last a devoted father if not always a good husband. Now his wife, and particularly his children, were deprived of his love and care What were their lives to be without him?

It was not until January, 1816, that news of Murat's execution reached Napoleon.

'It was in his destiny to do us harm,' he exclaimed. 'By deserting us he caused our first downfall, and then by his too impetuous support he caused the final disaster. He had lost all judgment, attacking the Austrians without a sensible plan, with insufficient forces and he failed without striking a blow.

'I would have had him at Waterloo but the French army was so patriotic, so imbued with moral sense, that it is doubtful if they would have stomached the disgust and horror inspired by the man whom they considered to have betrayed France and brought about her defeat. I did not think myself sufficiently strong to insist and yet his presence might have brought us victory—never was any one at the head of cavalry more determined, more courageous or more brilliant.'

To Joseph in America Madame Letizia wrote: 'You have heard of Murat's unhappy end. I have no news of your family, of Caroline or of Elisa.'

Caroline's entourage tried to conceal the news of Murat's end from her, but they had in the end to bring her a newspaper with its account of the last days at Pizzo; the news was already old. All night long she was attacked by violent outbursts which lasted until morning.

Here in enemy territory, a prisoner of war, although she was ironically called a guest, ex-Queen Caroline of Naples, known as the Comtesse de Lipona, looked back into the past and forward into the future. The past was Murat's and perhaps all the love she had once truly had for him welled up in her again. The future was hers to make, but what did it hold? She had lost the throne which she had been at such pains to get and such penalties to keep. She was only thirty-three, a young and beautiful woman still; much of her life lay before her.

Caroline's situation was considerably worse than Elisa's or Pauline's; she had fallen from a greater height than either of them. Although Napoleon thought it unpardonable that she was without sufficient means she was in truth very poor, with four children to bring up.

She had written to Elisa:

> I have neither governor nor governess for my children. The only ones I have with me are General Macdonald and Madame Courval. My means do not allow me the smallest expenditure.

Murat's death brought Elisa and Caroline closer together. Elisa would have gone to her younger sister to console her but that the passport she requested was naturally refused. Since all the letters the Bonapartes wrote to one another were intercepted and read by the Austrian secret police the Allies had no doubt that Elisa's request was dictated by sisterly feeling, but 'the terrible family' could not be allowed the indulgence of normal affections.

'Write to me often, my dear Elisa,' said Caroline. Letters were all she could hope for but later, when they were both allowed a little more freedom, the sisters did meet, in greater sympathy in their common misfortune than they had been during the years when Caroline was Queen of Naples and Elisa Grand Duchess of Tuscany. This renaissance of affection was important to Caroline; in spite of her poverty her greatest problem was a moral one. Up till now her whole life had been governed by the compulsive pursuit of power. She had to find and cultivate some other guiding principle by which to live, as well as to resign herself to the fact that she was no longer a queen.

In a curious way the Allies' singling her out for their fiercest persecution restored to her some of the importance she had lost.

At this moment in November, 1815, her most pressing preoccupation was money. There is ample evidence to show that the Murats took little away from Naples, a large part of their personal fortune having been spent for the good of their kingdom. The annual income they had been assured by the Treaty of Bayonne was a dead letter, but its recovery occupied a great deal of Caroline's life henceforward since her persistent demands, claims and protestations met with a continued blank wall of resistance.

First of all there were her obligations to Murat to be met. He had to be mourned suitably in black dresses ordered from Leroy, although his prices were now beyond her means. For whom did she wear the elaborate weeds he made for her? She no longer had her suite of secretary, doctor, ladies, fourteen servants, two female chief cooks, two second cooks, a superintendent of the kitchens, seven waiting women and six grooms who had left Naples with her. There was only General Francesco Macdonald, a kinsman of Marshal Macdonald and a descendant of one of the Scottish Jacobite families who had followed the Stuarts to France. A most faithful friend of the Murats, it was he who, with infinite respect, gave Caroline the consolation she needed, although the rumour of their morganatic marriage which so disgusted Napoleon when it reached him never had any official confirmation. Throughout his life Macdonald remained, with or without benefit of clergy, the perfect, faithful, devoted servant and lover, but he never overstepped the limits laid down for him by etiquette.

To etiquette Caroline still clung; it gave stability to her unstable existence. Although her household was reduced to virtually nothing, and for a time she had to look after her children herself, she still insisted on the outward forms of deference due to a rank she no longer possessed. It must have been humiliating for her, when Miss Davies's health forced her to leave the

Murat family, that she was able to give her only forty pounds, a gift far removed from the royal munificence so lately hers.

As if it were not burden enough to maintain her children and her household, Murat had left her an unwelcome heritage. From France, from Corsica and from Italy demands for money poured in to his widow for expenses incurred during his flight and brief attempt to regain his kingdom. Caroline never stopped to ask if they were genuine but with a royal gesture strained her resources to pay them all, determined to show the world that she honoured her husband's memory.

Caroline would have liked Pauline to live with her since her income would be a welcome addition to the upkeep of the household but, even if she had been able to obtain permission to do so, Pauline preferred to stay in Rome and keep her independence. Fond though she was of her sister she may have feared that, with no Murat to dominate, Caroline might try and control her.

As the unhappy year of 1815 drew to its close the Bonaparte sisters found themselves faced with the task of making new lives for themselves with what courage they could muster. Pauline had to reconcile herself to the loss of a beloved brother's presence, to forgoing much of the gaiety and luxury to which she had become accustomed, Caroline and Elisa to reigning only over their families and their households, their kingdoms and provinces in limbo.

It was Elisa who fared best.

CHAPTER FIFTEEN

COMTESSE DE COMPIGNANO

In character and circumstance Elisa was better prepared than Caroline for adversity, which she met with the fortitude her brother predicted. The tone of her mind, naturally serious, became more so as she grew older. Now, as she began her life of exile, she was nearly thirty-eight and able to call to her aid, to reconcile herself to the loss of rank and status, the philosophy acquired at St. Cyr, which had been enriched by her frequentation of men of letters.

Her passionate absorption in the arts had developed greater resources within herself, of more practical and enduring value than the corrupting ambition which had influenced and marred Caroline's life or the frivolity which consumed Pauline's. An advantage even greater than her education and personal qualities which Elisa possessed over her sisters was the stability of her marriage.

In spite of infidelities on either side her marriage was a real marriage; unlike most of her contemporaries, whose husbands were constantly absent from their homes, Baciocchi had always been at Elisa's side, giving the ménage time and opportunity to develop a harmonious existence. Too often, in Imperial society, the husband, with his brief and infrequent appearances in the home, assumed the rôle of lover, so that it was the lover, the man on the spot, who usurped his place. When the husband finally returned to home and hearth he not unseldom met his wife as a stranger.

This had not been the case with the Baciocchis. Moreover, as the husband who had gained most from his marriage to a Bonaparte, he always gave at least the appearance of gratitude for having been lifted out of his rut; he had done all that was required of him. Perhaps his chief virtue in Elisa's eyes was not so much his placid temperament but that, while admiring her attainments, he had not sought to emulate them nor compete with her in any way.

If, now, Felix's fancy strayed towards the children's governess, Elisa shrugged her shoulders; in the absence of regiments to review he had to occupy his time somehow. His flirtations were an easier cross to bear than the shame and sorrow of an end like Murat's. She herself was now content to be a faithful wife. It is probable that her extra-marital adventures were undertaken in imitation of her sisters', or because she thought her position required the moral indulgence usually accorded to itself by royalty, or because her amatory excursions during the years of her dominion of arrogance were part of the febrility of Imperial society.

Now that this society had disintegrated, and her period of power was over, Elisa settled down to an existence very similar to what might have been hers had she remained in Corsica as Madame Baciocchi and her brother had never become Emperor of the French. It is possible that, apart from the memories of former greatness which mocked her present obscurity, the Comtesse de Compignano was happier than had been the Grand Duchess of Tuscany.

Elisa had not yet reached this state while she was held a prisoner at Brünn. There she behaved as unpleasantly as she knew how, the more furious at her incarceration because Pauline was allowed to live in Rome and Caroline in Austria had some semblance of freedom. Her health, always delicate, suffered as a result of her imprisonment and her exacerbation at being so far from her baby son. In October, 1815, she wrote to Jerome that she had had a mortal illness but this seemed of less importance than that she had heard little Fritz now had four teeth. Her thoughts were constantly with the child, her anxiety about him the greater because of the three sons whom she had already lost in infancy. Her absence from Felix troubled her considerably less.

Her demands to be taken to a more salubrious climate than

that of Brünn were countered by offers of residence either in Carlsbad or Töplitz but, almost inconceivably, she still thought she would be allowed to return to Bologna, to see her son and re-establish her health. She even wrote to Jerome that she would be delighted if her mother would come and live with her at Ravenna. It is strange that a woman of Elisa's intelligence refused to accept the fact that neither she nor Caroline, who had been rulers in Italy, would ever be allowed to make their homes there. Since Italian residence was denied her she haughtily refused the alternatives and elected to remain at Brünn.

Soon shortage of money added to her mounting rage and despair, necessitating the sale of much of her jewellery and the reduction of her staff. She felt she was at last making some headway in her struggle with the Allies when Murat attempted his invasion of Naples.

If the Bonapartes now, in exile, considered themselves at last not as a clan but as individuals, in the eyes of the Allies they were still one family; whatever action was taken by one of them reacted on the others, however innocent of complicity they might be. Since Murat had tried to reconquer his throne might not Elisa attempt a foray into Tuscany? The Allies did not stop to ask themselves how the delicate Elisa, closely guarded, was going to make so bold an essay nor how or why Baciocchi, who to date had shown initiative only in his pusillanimous declaration of adhesion to the Bourbons, should suddenly manifest the courage, dash and ingenuity necessary to undertake so mad an enterprise. Their wisest course was to keep Elisa a prisoner.

By the early spring of 1816 the Allies suddenly changed their minds. Metternich had now come to the conclusion that Elisa's political importance was nil and she herself insignificant, a final insult made bearable only by her release. She was even permitted to have her wish and live in Trieste which, if not Italy, was at least in sight of it.

Once reunited with her family at Trieste Elisa immediately set to the task of finding a home and the funds to maintain them all. With her habitual energy she bent herself to extracting from the

Austrians some compensation for those goods and chattels she had left behind in Tuscany, claiming that they had been purchased with her own funds and were her personal property.

When she heard that the new governor of Tuscany, General Starhemberg, had sold all her liveries, harness, carriages and horses, she wrote furiously to Metternich,

> I should like to believe that the Emperor of Austria is informed about this, not from a feeling of vengeance, which is beneath me, because one may desire to avenge oneself on what one hates, but not on what one despises . . .

In misfortune Elisa had lost none of the grandiloquence of the splendid century; she still expressed herself in the accents of Corneille, as when she wrote to Jerome's wife, Catherine, 'Man is made to suffer; when he suffers, and has nothing with which to reproach himself, he may be proud'.

Proud Elisa still was but she was also prudent. She had always, as in her dealings with her brother when she was Grand Duchess of Tuscany, known the advantages of prudence. Although determined to regain her property she was equally resolved not 'to go on her travels again'; while remaining firm in her claims she scrupulously avoided any action which would bring her into conflict with the authorities.

In the end, by dint of persistence and eloquence, she reached a compromise with the Austrians, ultimately retrieving a substantial part of her fortune, amounting to an annual income of 300,000 francs, which made her one of the wealthiest members of her family in exile. She was able not only to buy a house on the Campo Marzio at Trieste but in addition a little later the seaside villa on which she had set her heart, the Villa Vicentina.

To the furnishing and improvement of her houses and grounds Elisa brought the same habits to order and method which had made her so able an administrator in a larger sphere. She kept herself in the state of busyness which she found most congenial. The Villa Vicentina was turned into a reasonable imitation of one of the Bonapartes' country houses in France but, in spite of considerable alterations, neither of her homes in Trieste ever had the charm and beauty of her residences in Lucca or Marlia.

As grudgingly as they had conceded to Caroline the incognito of Comtesse de Lipona, so the Allies allowed Elisa to use the title of Comtesse de Compignano, on the understanding that she use no other name. They had little to complain of in her behaviour but, when the Emperor Francis of Austria passed through Trieste in 1818, she and the rest of the French colony were severely enjoined that they were not to seek an audience. In addition they kept Elisa under strict surveillance, watching her movements and correspondence closely, although she was careful not to show even the modicum of independence which might provoke an expulsion order.

Life in Trieste was, nevertheless, monotonous. Four months of the year the Baciocchis spent at the Villa Vicentina, the remainder of the time at the villa on the Campo Marzio, except for the short breaks when Elisa went to a spa where occasionally she met Caroline or Jerome and Catherine, known now as the Prince and Princesse de Montfort.

Jerome was the member of her family on whom Elisa concentrated the affection once reserved for Lucien; it therefore gave her great pleasure when he, too, came to live in Trieste in 1819 with his family. Her opportunities of seeing members of the family were envied by Madame Letizia, unable to leave the Papal States just as those outside were unable to enter them.

> When shall I be able to embrace you and see you all together? My confidence in God reassures me, and I do not doubt that it will happen.

It did not happen. Madame Letizia had not seen Elisa since 1810 nor did she ever see her again. Since her mother complained that she received little news from her Elisa had evidently abandoned her habit of writing letters on every possible occasion; it must for a long time have been clear to her that her earlier belief that she was her mother's favourite daughter was unfounded.

When Madame Letizia wrote again it was to say that she did not doubt that Elisa would do everything she could for her unhappy brother. Napoleon's mother was busy collecting from her children an annual allocation for his maintenance and support. The final contribution arrived at was of 15,000 francs a years from each of the brothers and sisters, her own contribution being considerably more.

It could not have been often that Elisa thought of Napoleon. Perhaps, when she had leisure to think, the old resentments welled up and she remembered that, not only had he never favoured her as a sister but that, during her years in Tuscany, he had kept her on a tight rein, was critical of her achievements and constantly pressed her for money to the detriment of her own budget. Nor did Caroline, preoccupied with her own problems, seem to have much pity to spare for her brother. From Rome Madame Letizia wrote to her tartly:

> It is not for me to fix the amount my children should furnish to supply their brother's needs. My children have a sense of honour, feelings and hearts, and they will all have greater merit in giving if the necessity is less. I have started a fund by sending 30,000 francs to Monsieur de Las Cases. Everyone should get in touch with him. So far as I am concerned I am ready to give the Emperor my last penny. Nevertheless, the feelings you display in your letter have given me a great deal of pleasure. I expected no less from you. Believe in my affection, etc.

But the letter was signed 'Madame', the signature she habitually used to strangers, while to her daughter-in-law, Julie, her letters were infinitely warmer and were signed 'Your affectionate mother'.

It is said that Madame Letizia could not forgive Caroline for her defection in 1814, which she is held to have excused to her mother by saying that she had no control over her husband. Madame Letizia's scornful reply, quoted by Napoleon, was,

'If you could not control him you should have opposed him, but what battles did you fight with him, what blood flowed? It was only over your dead body that your husband should have pierced your brother, your benefactor, your master.'

Yet, when Madame Letizia was in Naples in 1815, the relations between her and Caroline were perfectly friendly. As she must then have heard Caroline's justification this perhaps is not the explanation of the coolness between them. It may be that Madame Letizia, brooding in Rome over her son's sufferings, was lashing out on every side. Certainly there was a marked absence of cordiality in her feelings towards Caroline for again that year she wrote to Elisa complaining: 'Since no one writes to me any more let me have news of Queen Catherine, of Caroline and all the family.'

There was little to tell. Always egocentric, Elisa, as she grew older, concentrated all her energies on her own small family and developing her estates for their benefit. She had transferred her ambitions to her children, realising, as Caroline had done, that her real happiness lay in them. To Pauline she wrote: 'The whole household seems to be one family; these are the riches which neither jealousy nor hate can steal and it is solely to my character and my philosophy that I owe them.'

The annual distraction of visiting a spa over, the Baciocchis returned to Trieste and to their accustomed routine. Much of the day Elisa spent at the work of administering her estates, still finding in work her greatest pleasure. The balance of the day was given up to such distractions as Trieste had to offer, which were not very great. There was a daily outing in the carriage and evenings at the theatre, for which Elisa had not lost her love, insisting in this case, in spite of Austrian disapproval, on having her box. At other times there was a little music at home. They played billiards and other games; occasionally they danced. Even more rarely there were amateur theatricals but now there was no admiring Court, only their small entourage, to applaud Elisa's declamation of the classics. It was all very quiet and domestic, a life more suited to well-to-do country gentry than to a woman who had been a reigning Grand Duchess and 'the Semiramis of the Serchio'.

Society in Trieste was limited; the Triestinos were neither particularly welcoming nor were they of much interest in themselves, being mainly merchant families with nothing of the great world in their manners or habits. From time to time there came to Trieste to relieve the monotony a few proscribed French men and women who had once been prominent members of the Imperial Court—Maret, Duc de Bassano, whose Duchesse had been one of the most elegant women at the Tuileries, Arrighi, Duc de Padoue, a cousin of the Bonapartes, and Savary, Duc de Rovigo, who at one time had replaced Fouché as Minister of Police.

In 1819 there was an unexpected addition to the small Bonapartist circle, Fouché, Duc d'Otrante, himself, whom Louis XVIII had spewed out of his government when his usefulness came to an end, unable any longer to tolerate for expediency's sake the ex-seminarist and regicide.

Fouché's presence was the more welcome because in 1820 the other Imperial dukes were amnestied and returned to France. Elisa knew that the Bonapartes would never, in her lifetime, be amnestied; perhaps, too, she was so firmly ensconced at Trieste that she did not want to leave. She had lived little in France since her schooldays; there was nothing there for her now. Trieste was her home, here were her family, her interests, prominent among them the archaeological diggings which, with her Bonaparte passion for excavations, she had initiated at the neighbouring Roman site of Aquileia.

Fouché's arrival in Trieste brought to Elisa's restricted circle a man of ability and intelligence, with whom she could discuss any subject at her own level. He restored to her the atmosphere which she had missed and which Felix had never been able to supply. Together she and Fouché could talk over the stirring days of the Empire and analyse its achievements and errors. Over their own mistakes they cast a veil, Fouché's defection and Elisa's own. She remembered only that it was his persuasion which caused the Emperor to confer on her the sovereignty of

Lucca and Piombino, Fouché that Elisa had intervened on his behalf with her brother when, in 1810, he fell into disgrace and took refuge in Tuscany.

Before Fouché arrived in Trieste Elisa warned him that he would not find her changed.

> I am the same as I was when you knew me at a time when I was concerned with matters of importance. My circumstances and those of my family are such that I may surely be allowed to have a few peculiarities.*

The peculiarities were not very serious, resolving themselves mainly into a habit of abstraction from the activities around her. If she absented herself from the company there was always Felix, not Fouché's chosen companion, but exiles have no choice. Happily the two men had one common quality and interest; both were devoted parents. The Triestinos were thus able to enjoy the sight of the man who had once terrorised Europe promenading peaceably by the shores of the Adriatic side by side with the harmless fly, Felix Baciocchi, both watching their children with indulgent eyes. No Golden Fleece or Grand Eagle of the Legion of Honour now adorned Felix's dress—his appearance was indistinguishable from that of any other wealthy bourgeois strolling with his children.

It was Elisa's interest in archaeology which put an end to this quiet existence. In July, 1820, she caught a putrid fever at the site of her diggings in the unhealthy marshland round Trieste; her delicate constitution was unable to withstand the infection. Jerome rushed to her bedside but his sister was already *in extremis*; she rallied only long enough to whisper an injunction to her brother that he should look after Baciocchi and to tell him that she had left all her affairs in order—as if Elisa would have left them otherwise!

On August 7th, 1820, Elisa Maria-Anna Bonaparte Baciocchi, sometime Her Imperial Highness the Grand Duchess of Tuscany,

* Quoted by Fleuriot de Langle in *Elisa.*

died in exile. The Bonapartes were all much affected by her death for she was only forty-three; most particularly Napoleon as, by the time the news reached him, it was already clear that he himself had not long to live.

None of her family except Jerome could be present at her funeral. To little Napoleone, overwhelmed with grief, her grandmother wrote assuring her that her mother would pray for her, by means of prayer procuring for her the grace which would console her affliction. Madame Letizia seems to have had some apprehensions about the kind of life Napoleone would henceforward lead with her father as she added: 'I wish I could be near you, to direct you in the world with the counsel of my experience and above all with the principles which ought to govern the children of my family. . . .'

Perhaps she was right about Baciocchi. Left with a sizeable fortune he soon deserted Trieste and hurried back to Bologna where he set himself up in great state. What he did was a matter of indifference to the Allies; they raised no objection when he dropped the incognito of Comte de Compignano and once again became Prince Baciocchi. They even graciously allowed no obstacle to be put in the way of the transport of Elisa's corpse from the Villa Vicentina to the Campo Marzio nor to Baciocchi's desire that she should be buried finally in the cathedral at Bologna where he erected a handsome monument in her memory.

Nothing of Elisa's work was left. Tuscany forgot her as the world forgot her. She had loved grandeur, magnificence, power, a throne, but she had shown the world that she could live without them; perhaps most of all one remembers of Elisa that she met with courage her sunset years.

To Caroline Elisa bequeathed her villa on the Campo Marzio but it was several years before she was allowed to take possession of it. Not for Caroline the calm of Elisa's last years; she was always harried by the Austrians in spite of the tenderness Metternich still had for her, which was part of the common gossip of Vienna.

She remained at Hainburg for several years, where at first she was very friendly with Jerome and Catherine until they quarrelled about money and were never reconciled. Before the quarrel she and Jerome had a moving experience which awakened many memories of the past.

Outside Vienna they one day caught a glimpse of their little nephew, Napoleon's son the King of Rome, whom they had now learnt to call the Duc de Reichstadt. His guardians were at pains to protect him from the contamination of his Bonaparte aunt and uncle; they were not allowed to speak to him.

Caroline had no further opportunity of seeing the boy for she moved away from Hainburg to Schloss Frohsdorf where she was allowed to remain for some years. Her means had become increasingly straitened so that she was obliged, in order to raise some ready money, to sell the gold lace from Murat's uniforms and then some of the best of her works of art; this sale to the Marquess of Londonderry raised the sum of 250,000 francs. The pictures, which had been given to Murat in Spain by the Prince of Peace, included two Correggios, 'The Education of Love' and an 'Ecce Homo' which now hang in the National Gallery in London. Nevertheless, by 1821 she was almost at the end of her financial resources as her continued reclamations in the French courts for the right to re-take possession of her properties in France, the Élysée, her houses at Neuilly and La-Motte-Sainte-Hérave, remained without effect.

Caroline's sons were now as much a problem to her as money and security. Her eldest son, Achille, was extremely difficult, taking after his father in the tempestuousness of his character. He, too, was an ardent Italian nationalist, who repudiated with scorn his French affiliations. Achille saw no future for himself in Europe and in 1822 he succeeded in getting permission to go to the United States where he joined his uncle, Joseph, living at Bordentown, New Jersey, as the Comte de Survilliers. In the following year his younger brother, Lucien, also left for the United States.

If the departure of her sons relieved Caroline of a certain

amount of anxiety, because Achille's political beliefs rendered him extremely suspect to the Austrians, it left her isolated in Austria from her family. In 1823 the lovely Letizia married the Marchese Pepoli, of an old and noble Bolognese family, and went to live in Bologna; it was a respectable alliance but not to be compared with the marriage a daughter of the King of Naples might have made.

Caroline was left alone with her younger daughter, Louise. These were dreary years for her.

'She must be suffering a great deal now,' Napoleon told Las Cases at St. Helena, 'the more so because one might say that she was born a queen. She never knew as we did what it was like to be simply a private person. She, Pauline and Jerome were still children when I became the first man in France so they never knew any status other than what they enjoyed during my period of power.'

Napoleon was right. This was the hardest part Caroline had ever had to learn but gradually, just as a gambler develops a profound revulsion against his senseless pursuit of gain, so did she little by little lose the desire to rule the lives of men and women, substituting for love of power a longing to be loved. Although she never shed the habits of royalty, which were almost innate in her, she did in time revert in character to what she had been as a young girl, amiable, peaceable, anxious to make and keep friends, resigning herself ultimately to the privations of a modest existence.

That existence she was now able at last, after a bitter struggle with the Allies, to transfer to the villa left her by Elisa in Trieste, finding there the consolation her sister had found of being at least in sight of Italy.

CHAPTER SIXTEEN

THE AUTUMNAL FACE

In Rome Pauline led two lives. Physically she was in the Eternal City but her heart and thoughts were with her brother in St. Helena; while he lived her chief concern was to alleviate his lot so far as lay within her power. There was little enough that she could do for him. She wrote to him and sent him packages, although communications were painfully slow, letters taking five to six months to reach him. When his *maître d'hôtel* died she sent out to him her own chef, but whatever came from Princess Borghese was suspect to Napoleon's jailer, Sir Hudson Lowe. On his desk he kept a copy of Lewis Goldsmith's scurrilous work and her solicitude must have been to him clear indication of the unnatural nature of her affection, serving rather to intensify than soften his inflexible attitude to a prisoner of such outrageous morals.

Pauline constituted herself her brother's champion but within the family it was originally only from her mother that she met sympathy because neither Lucien nor Louis manifested the same anxiety about Napoleon's well-being. Lucien had made his grand gesture in 1815; Louis was by now completely given over to hypochondria and neurasthenia and absorbed in his running battle with his wife, Hortense.

Later, when the Comte de Las Cases returned from St. Helena and the family learned exactly what Napoleon was enduring, Lucien did suffer a change of heart. He offered to go out to St. Helena for two years 'being no longer able to endure the idea of seeing his brother languish and die in exile'.

Time, however, brought no softening to the mutual antipathy between Pauline and Camillo; the early years of her Roman residence were clouded by disputes between them, disputes about money, about where she was to live and about their marriage itself which Camillo attempted, although unsuccessfully, to have annulled.

Finally, with the aid of Pius VII, who had a fatherly affection for this wayward daughter, Camillo was obliged to allow Pauline the use of the Palazzo Borghese and pay her the allowance due to her under their marriage settlement. She, however, preferred to build herself another home, the Villa Paolina, at the Porta Pia in Rome, a villa which is now the French Embassy. The décor of the ground floor is as Pauline left it, frescoes of Egyptian temples and scenes of the Nile, recalling her brother's campaigns in the East.

Pauline also built for herself another Villa Paolina at Viareggio for her use when she went to Tuscany to take the waters. In spite of Blacas' persecution of the Bonapartes she was by marriage a Roman princess, under the special protection of the Pope. It was difficult for him to put a ban on her movements within Italy, and soon he even gave up trying to do so. Although she went frequently to Bagni di Lucca to take the waters, of Borghese, now living happily in Florence with the beautiful Duchessa, Pauline saw nothing.

Pauline's income had never kept pace with her expenditure but she did now make some effort to curb her extravagance in dress at least. She decided that it would be more economical to limit herself to three colours only, white, pearl grey and rose; all her clothes were to be very simple, no crêpe, no tulle, no satin, no trimmings, no ribbons. But she laid down no limits for herself in building and decorating her houses nor in her frequent journeys out of Rome.

This expenditure alarmed her family so that Madame Letizia wrote apprehensively to Joseph in America:

> In spite of her daily expenses and in spite of the fact that every day she sells more of her jewellery (but her diamonds she had given to Napoleon), she has an income of 120,000 francs and from her dowry and investments an additional

> 40,000 francs a year. Besides she is claiming several millions from the French government and the company which is exploiting the German salt mines. But that is all in the air and, even if these hopes are realised, I don't think she has anything to give the others. She amuses herself with drawing up budgets but she never keeps to them for more than a month.

In the end the family found her an intendant to look after her finances as she was obviously incapable of doing so herself.

Since the French government showed no more disposition to allow Pauline's claims than Caroline's she was fortunate that the British paid in full for the Hôtel Borghese in Paris, when so many other people were defaulting. Although she stoutly averred that she did not regret Paris, because the French had behaved so abominably to Napoleon, it must have given her a pang to think that Lord Castlereagh was now occupying her beautiful salons and later that the arch-enemy, the Duke of Wellington, should there entertain her brother's former mistress, the diva, Grassini.

From 1815 Pauline's Paris home has been the British Embassy. Of late years great pains have been taken to restore the State rooms to what they were when she lived there, although the beautiful garden elevation was spoiled by the addition of a throne-room and a dining-room built during the reign of Queen Victoria.

Little of Pauline's presence pervades the house, too long overlaid with British officialdom. Furniture and hangings alone do not recreate an atmosphere; the miniature of Canova's statue of Pauline looks out coldly over the yellow salon.

It is said that some British ambassadresses do not care to share her bedroom with Pauline's ghost, that their sleep is sometimes troubled by the ghosts of her nocturnal visitors. No one should fear Pauline for hers is a benign spirit, nor should they grudge her haunting the rooms where she spent some of her happiest hours since, in spite of all her beauty and her many loves, her life was chequered by much grief.

Behind her superficial gaiety and the social façade she maintained, grief dwelt with Pauline. Neither the ravages made by ill-health and age on her incomparable beauty weighed with her as much as the omnipresent shadows of her brother's suffering at St. Helena. About the slow decline of her beauty there was little she could do except to employ artifice, although nothing could successfully conceal the inroads made on it by the ill-health which was aggravated by her sorrow.

She was very conscious of this erosion of what had been her glory and begged Borghese to shut up her statue by Canova so that people should not be able to make comparisons between what she was and what she had been. This is why Madame de Staël, visiting Italy, said that special permission had to be sought to view the statue.

> Beauty vanishes, beauty passes,
> However rare, rare it be . . .

The poet's eye of Lamartine caught the autumnal tints which now coloured Pauline's beauty when, as a young man, he visited Rome. He did not meet her, but several times he caught sight of her as she drove through the Borghese gardens under the umbrella pines. He thought that the many statues which ornamented the grounds were still less beautiful than she.

> It was during the last years of her short life; she was still resplendent with the reflections of her setting sun, like the head of a Greek Venus in a museum, on which the last ray of evening rests gently.
>
> I do not know by what whim, in a woman who was all caprice until the day of her death, that she ordinarily had by her side a poor monk in her carriage. The contrast between his brown coarse cowl, between that head of Christian asceticism, beside her head covered in flowers, and that face of beauty dying now after so much brilliance, made one either smile or brought tears to one's eyes. Charming creature who died still a child!

There was still enough of Pauline's beauty and grace left to attract many admirers, many of them foreign visitors, since she cared no more for Roman society now than when she first came to Rome in 1803. Their eagerness to make the acquaintance of Princess Borghese was a source of great annoyance to Blacas, who regretted his inability to put an interdiction on her receiving foreign guests.

It was the English Pauline cultivated most, with the pathetic hope that she could persuade the most influential among them to alleviate her brother's lot. It gave her great satisfaction to subjugate representatives of the people who had him under their yoke as well as to use in her nonchalant way the blue blood of England as her literal footstool. She made the Marquis of Douglas her lap dog while others in her circle included the Duke of Devonshire, Lord Kensington, Lady Morgan and Lord and Lady Holland, who earned her real esteem and gratitude for the devotion they both showed to Napoleon.

When his suite, with some trepidation, told Napoleon of Pauline's preference for English society, he merely laughed.

'Good! Then I will have so many enemies the less!'

Time, which had brought him so many disillusions, had brought him none about Pauline. She remained to him the loving sister of supreme beauty and charm as for her he was always the revered elder brother whom she still loved more than anyone else in the world.

Pauline's opportunities for loving and being loved were narrowing. For a moment she had hoped that Colonel Duchand, for whom she had great tenderness, would come to Rome, but he was arrested by the authorities on his way and no further opportunity came to him to join her.

In this era of the Holy Alliance, of peace on earth if not goodwill to all men, there were no longer any brilliant young officers to attract and be attracted, but there remained that other world which had always drawn her, the world of music. When Pauline rallied from the serious illness which had given Blacas so much pleasure to report, a new interest came into her life, the young composer, Giovanni Pacini, who at one time seemed to be a possible rival to Rossini. He was a prolific composer, writing over seventy operas, but his was a small talent and his work is not remembered.

It was as well that Pauline found Pacini for she was sorely tried when her mother and Cardinal Fesch fell under the influence of a mystic, whom they credulously believed when she assured them that the Emperor had made good his escape and was no longer at St. Helena.

However ardently Pauline would have liked to share their belief that this was so she was too shrewd to be taken in. For a time her relations with her mother reached a point of coldness which was almost a quarrel until finally Madame Letizia abandoned the mystic, awaking to the bitter reality that her son was still and would, in spite of all her pleas to the Allies, remain a captive.

Although she longed to join her brother illness had always prevented Pauline from doing so, but when letters came from the Emperor's suite, telling her that he had not long to live, that his agony was terrible and that he asked her to intervene with the influential English of her acquaintance to have him moved to a kinder climate, there could be no delay.

On July 11th, 1821, she wrote to Lord Liverpool, the Prime Minister:

> The illness from which the Emperor is suffering is mortal at St. Helena and it is in the name of every member of his family that I now demand from the British government a change of climate. If a request so just is refused then it will be his death warrant which is signed and then I ask permission to leave for St. Helena to go and join the Emperor to witness his last moments. . . . I know that the sands are running out for the Emperor and I should reproach myself eternally if I had not used all the means in my power to soften his last moments and to prove my devoted attachment to his august person.

Love gave Pauline's pen an unwonted eloquence. She did not

confine herself to writing to Lord Liverpool alone. Letters from her reached all the sovereigns, all the ministers of Europe, all the individuals who might still have bowels of pity for her brother's agony. To these letters there was no reply. Even if Pauline's intervention had moved the implacable Allies it was too late.

Only five days after she had written to Lord Liverpool the news reached Rome that on May 5th, 1821, the erstwhile Emperor of the French, Pauline's *fratello caro*, Napoleon, had died. To Pauline the shock was all the greater because she had cherished the hope that she would at least reach him before he drew his last breath.

For days she would see no one, not even her mother or her uncle. She could not bring herself to realise the horrible truth that she would never again in this world see her beloved brother.

Neither Caroline nor her remaining brothers felt Napoleon's death with the same intensity. Madame Letizia's letter to Caroline, in answer to her letter of condolence, must have shown her yet again that there was still some resentment in the old woman's heart, still some nagging doubt as to whether Caroline had justly appreciated her brother. It seemed almost as if she arrogated to herself alone the right to grieve for Napoleon's death.

> If you only ask news of me to soothe your own affliction, I can tell you that everything that has been suggested to assuage an inexpressible grief has not allowed me to shed a single tear.
>
> All that remains of such a son is an inanimate corpse at St. Helena! Alas, what can I say to you? Leave me alone to drag out my days in sorrow. Conserve yourself for your children and put an end to your grief.

To Caroline's children she wrote with more warmth and affection. Perhaps it was her mother's coldness and the realisation that in Rome she would, so long as her mother was alive, be constrained to live in the shadow of St. Helena which finally influenced Caroline to abandon any idea of seeking permission to go to Rome.

For Pauline it was different. After 1821 it is probable that life no longer meant very much to her. She was over forty, her youth gone, her beauty waning fast. Tired, sick and unhappy, all she had to cling to was a capricious musician. She tried to find in the younger generation of her family an outlet for the love she had to lavish on someone. If only it could have been her brother's son, the Duc de Reichstadt, so that she might trace in his face her brother's features, perhaps recapture in him some of her brother's ways ! But Reichstadt was quarantined in Vienna from his father's family.

Pauline turned to Jerome's son by his first marriage to Elizabeth Patterson, who was now in Rome, but her interest in the boy infuriated Jerome. Pauline was again frustrated, so it was to Pacini and the furthering of his career that she devoted herself.

When Pacini obtained the appointment as *maestro di cappella* to the Princess of Lucca who sat in Elisa's place Pauline followed him to Tuscany, obliged for once to subordinate her own caprices to his, poignantly aware that he was a young man while she was an ageing woman, that Princess Pauline Borghese did not have as much to offer as Her Imperial Highness the Princess Pauline, sister of the Emperor Napoleon.

The lovers were together at Viareggio on that day in 1822 when Shelley's body was burnt on the seashore, although Pauline's presence went unremarked by Byron and Trelawney. From Viareggio they went together to Pisa, to the Palazzo Lanfranchi which Shelley had called ' one of those marble piles which seem built for eternity '. Here Byron had lived in what he described as a palace ' large enough for a garrison, with dungeons below and cells in the walls, and so full of ghosts ', a setting both too sinister and too solemn for Pauline.

She seems, however, to have been unaffected by its gloom since she was in good spirits when Henry Fox, afterwards Lord Holland, visited her there. On arrival in Pisa he sent Pauline his card because of his parents' friendship with her, but it was with some nervousness that he called on her at the time she had appointed. She was, he found, about to give a concert yet he had to wait for a full hour and a half before she appeared.

> Her manner and reception could not have been more royal if Napoleon was still upon the throne he once made illustrious by possessing. She has been very ill. Her face is very beautiful but angular. The expression of her countenance is very *vif*, and full of talent; her voice oppressed as she was afflicted by a cold but very harmonious, and I was far from disappointed.
>
> Her manner is very royal, and that well-bred indifference which persons in such exalted stations must assume, and which makes them, while engaged in one conversation, say a civil word in another, prevents any *suivi entretien.* She was amazingly civil to me and talked a good deal. Now and then her conversation bordered on what was *leste.*

To the son of the Hollands who had earned her gratitude by their kindness to her brother Pauline could not be other than welcoming. Moreover he was a young man and the deference and admiration he showed might impress Pacini, increasingly temperamental and impatient of being tied to a woman no longer young.

Never yet had Pauline been constrained to hold an unwilling lover but it required all her resolution and dignity as a woman to let him go. Even if she kept him against his will she began to apprehend that it would not be for long. Perhaps, too, to reinforce her courage she called to mind her brother's words, written so long ago, 'Everything earthly is evanescent except the impression we make on history'.

For the first time in her life Pauline Borghese began to think of what history would say of her; it seemed that in the interests of her good name and reputation that she must somehow be reconciled with her husband and with the Church. Through the good offices of Pius VII's successor, Leo XII, husband and wife were brought together again, unwelcome to Camillo though the reconciliation was. It is to his credit that early in 1825 he consented to keep house again with Pauline, dismissing happiness with the Duchessa Lante delle Rovere.

Camillo's self-sacrifice was not long required of him. A few months of the old social round then Pauline fell seriously ill with symptoms apparently of pulmonary tuberculosis, her illness aggravated by the denial of her wish to have her brother's body brought back to Europe. Fearful of the Emperor in death as in life, the churlish Allies refused this consolation to those of his family who had, and still, held him dear.

Some echoes of her brother's voice came to Pauline when the *Mémorial de Ste. Hélène* was published, the collection of random thoughts dictated at St. Helena to the faithful Las Cases. She was delighted to hear that he thought of her, and that he thought of her so well.

> Pauline was always probably the most beautiful woman of her time and will, to her end, be the best creature in the world.

Even the familiar tone of reproof must have been welcome since it came from him.

> Pauline was too prodigal, too wild. She should have been enormously wealthy with all that I gave her, but she gave it all away although her mother often lectured her, warning her that she would die in the workhouse.

The smile came back to her lips when she had read to her,

> It was agreed without contradiction that Pauline was the prettiest woman in Paris; artists were unanimous in considering her another Vénus de Médicis.

She had need of comfort. To her brother, Louis, in Rome, she wrote her last letter on May 13th:

> I do nothing but vomit and suffer; I am reduced to a shadow. They are repairing the street and I can't stand the awful noise. The Prince is going to take a villa in the suburbs here where we shall spend the month of May. It is impossible

in the state in which I am to think of going to the villa in Lucca. . . . Embrace Mamma and I send a thousand good wishes to the family.

In her own hand Pauline added a postscript: 'I am ill, ill, but I embrace you.'

To escape from the insupportable noise Pauline made the last of her painful journeys, to the Villa Strozzi, where on June 9th, 1825, Camillo Borghese closed her eyes.

One last vanity she allowed herself; there was to be no *chapelle ardente*, her body was not to be exposed for the world to see how ravaged was that face on which she had lavished so much worship.

Her will was less the disposal of her possessions than a tribute to her brother's glory. She forgot no one. Everyone had some souvenir of Pauline Bonaparte; her nephew, Napoleon-Louis, eldest son of her brother, Louis, and his wife, Charlotte, daughter of Joseph, her Villa Paolina in Rome; her nephew, Napoleon—she disdained to name him the Duc de Reichstadt—the Villa San Martino at Elba and the little golden jewel left to her by the Emperor. To him also she bequeathed the porcelain service used at the Coronation, 'which will remind his son of a glorious epoch in his father's story'. The Villa Paolina at Lucca was for Camillo, 'for the sincere and real interest that he has shown me in my long last illness', and 'because he always behaved towards the Emperor, my brother, with the greatest loyalty and fidelity'. Her little house and garden with its furniture at Viareggio she left to her sister, Caroline Murat.

For all the English friends there were mementoes; to the Duke of Hamilton she left her silver-gilt dressing case, to the Duke of Devonshire the little medal-case of forged iron left her by the Emperor, to the Duchess of Hamilton two Sèvres vases from her Villa Paolina in Rome, to Lord Gower her Sèvres porcelain tea service and to Lord Holland the library in her villa at Rome.

Pauline asked to be buried in the Borghese chapel in the church of Santa-Maria-Maggiore in Rome. There, between the Borghese Popes, Clement VIII and Paul V, now lies the body of Pauline Bonaparte, 'amusedly, among the ancient dead'.

Pauline had all the defects of women spoiled from their earliest years by the adulation of men, although she might not have been so wayward if she had not known that her caprices would always be forgiven. Her greatest quality was hidden except from those who knew her best; lovable herself, she was capable of the greatest devotion.

Superficially hers was a futile life, given over to frivolity, blighted by her unending quest for the perfect love which, after the *affaire Fréron*, eluded her. Yet, perhaps unknowingly, she had her perfect love, not the passion she pursued, not the perverted passion assumed by those who sought only to vilify her family, but a love, deep, sincere and disinterested, the love between her brother and herself. Not as Queen of Hearts, not as a woman given over to frivolity, narcissism and promiscuity should Pauline Bonaparte be remembered, but as a perfect example of a devoted and loving sister.

CHAPTER SEVENTEEN

CAROLINE ALONE

Pauline's death closed a chapter in the Bonapartes' lives. No one would scandalise and charm them in the same way again. Oddly, too, because of her devotion she had kept Napoleon alive for them. Now, with her death the French Empire was becoming even more a tale that was told.

Although they had not met since 1814 Pauline's death was one more factor underlining Caroline's isolation. Since Jerome moved away from Trieste, first to Rome and then to Florence, she was cut off from her family. In her solitude it was a pleasant shock to receive a letter from Madame Récamier, travelling in Italy.

Caroline answered her at once, telling her that her letter had arrived on her birthday, giving her greater pleasure than any bouquet.

> I trembled when I saw the date on your letter; for ten years that name has never come to me and I avoided remembering it, not from indifference but for fear of compromising people who had shown me devotion and who were dear to me.

How much of bitterness and disillusion was in that phrase, what recollection of rebuffs and insults! How she had been belittled and humiliated!

Her letter went on:

> I should like to find the same pleasure again. It can only be when I see you that I can tell you about the persecution I have to endure, in the name of the French government, and which is too long to tell you about in a letter.

She was allowed to live neither in Italy, the Low Countries nor Switzerland although she might go to Germany or America.

> Through unparalleled injustice I am condemned to travel, constantly to change the country in which I live, while at the same time my private means are sequestered in France and Naples. You can imagine how wretched are my finances in Trieste and you see that I can tell you nothing about my future. I am sure that if I could see you and speak to you, you could, when you go back to Paris, take up my rightful claims with success.

Caroline could no longer be disinterested, although it must have been galling to her to ask rather than to bestow. She had become a suppliant, seeking help from any friend of the old days who could possibly be of service to her; Juliette Récamier was a very old friend, deeply attached, moreover, to Chateaubriand, now Minister of Foreign Affairs.

To her Caroline opened her heart about her loneliness but most of all she dwelt on her bitterness at being singled out for persecution.

> My isolation ought to quieten any anxieties and allow me to enjoy the rest to which I have been looking forward for so long and that I cannot get. If anyone could read my heart he would see that my most secret ambition is for peace, and why am I refused what my family has obtained so easily? They are left in peace at Rome, they can travel, they don't suffer any disabilities—I am the only one who is persecuted.

Early in the following year Madame Récamier made a détour through Trieste to see Caroline. The old friends talked far into the night; next day Caroline took Juliette out to the Villa Vicentina where she lived during the summer months through the kindness of her niece, Elisa's daughter, Napoleone, now married to Count Camerata.

Madame Récamier observed that Caroline was still pretty, with all her old powers of charming. To her daughter, Louise, lately married to Count Rasponi, she was most tender while to General Macdonald she showed affection, tinged with a nuance of domination. For Juliette herself she was all enthusiasm. Already when she reached Paris there was a letter awaiting her from Caroline, who excused herself for writing so promptly, but she saw so few friends from the old days; she would never forget the touching proofs of Juliette's friendship. But there was nothing Madame Récamier could now do to help Caroline in her claims, for Chateaubriand had, during her absence, ceased to be Foreign Minister.

Loneliness settled back over Caroline so that, when Countess Potocka spent six weeks in Trieste in 1826, she was warmly welcomed. The Countess confessed a certain awkwardness at meeting her again; she had last seen her in Paris in 1812 at the height of her glory and she was uncertain how to go about seeing an ex-queen.

> When I saw her again I found that her face was still as pleasing as it had been. One felt that she needed to be loved by everyone who came near her. She had a rare strength of character, a serious turn of mind, kindliness and an equable temperament.

As Caroline saw her every day the Countess had ample opportunity to judge how time had worked its changes on her. She was much impressed with the exquisite taste of her home, known now as the Villa Murat; one large salon was given over to souvenirs of the family and dominated by a magnificent equestrian portrait of Murat. It was left to General Macdonald to do the honours of this room; Caroline herself never showed it to vistors, the memories it evoked were perhaps too poignant.

Countess Potocka was aware of the rumours that Caroline and the General were married but she saw nothing in their behaviour to give credence to the story; in public he always treated her with profound respect.

Caroline now talked a great deal about her brother, averring that for a long time she had been his favourite sister, that he had even several times taken her advice. For her sister-in-law, Marie Louise, she had only contempt, naughtily imitating her and mimicking her Austrian accent. She expressed herself forcibly in favour of energetic measures, saying she preferred definite decisions to temporary expedients, no doubt an oblique justification of her action in 1814, but she added sadly,

'Unhappily I am now convinced that too much intelligence is often a deterrent to happiness.'

As she travelled onwards through Italy Countess Potocka continually came upon memories of the Bonapartes. In Rome Pauline's Villa Paolina was deserted, the grounds overrun with weeds; at Caroline's villa at Portici she was surprised by the austerity of her bedroom.

From the towns where she stayed the Countess wrote to Caroline, who replied eagerly to her letters. It was a sad winter for her, she said. In the following summer she would go and spend a few days with her brother-in-law, Prince Baciocchi, living at Bologna with his son, Frédéric: 'The change is necessary and a short trip will do me good'.

Gradually, however, Caroline was settling down to life at Trieste and Lady Holland wrote that she had heard that Madame Murat's society there was delightful. Although she was still strictly watched it seemed to Caroline that the Allies were at last leaving her to the peace she craved. She soon learnt her error.

In May, 1830, Madame Letizia, now eighty and very frail, broke her hip; it seemed unlikely that she would survive the accident. Caroline wrote at once to Metternich, asking permission to go to Rome; 'I do not wish to believe that I shall be refused permission to go and embrace my dying mother.'

The permission was grudgingly accorded, for a period of ten days.

After an interval of fifteen years the meeting between mother and daughter could not have been without awkwardness. Certainly Caroline must have been censured for her approaches to the French government. Her mother's opinion on the subject was categorical.

> I have never allowed myself to entertain any illusions, she wrote to Hortense. Besides, I have always thought that it was the duty of our family not to demand the execution of the Treaty of Fontainebleau. I would disavow the slightest step taken in my name and, even if my children thought differently, I was resolved to solicit nothing from a Bourbon.
>
> Honour should take precedence of money and I would never outrage the Emperor's memory by taking steps which show that I appeared to recognise that everything which was done in 1815 is null and void. Let us husband what we have and if we cannot live royally let us live with honour as private citizens and not expose ourselves to the humiliations and to the reproaches of our conscience. . . . If I had been attended to the shame of having solicited in vain would have been avoided.

In Rome Caroline met Henry Fox, now Lord Holland, to whom she had once written seeking his help with her claims. When he called on her he found her in a room full of half-packed trunks, boxes, waste paper and perfect disorder. She was extremely agitated; the ten days she had been allowed in Rome had been reduced to eight. Since she had been in the city no less than twelve meetings of the Corps Diplomatique had been held about her and several reams of paper filled. Lord Stuart de Rothesay, the British Ambassador in Paris, signed a protest against her being permitted to remain at Rome.

'How completely,' sighed Lord Holland, 'we are become the instruments of these rotten old dynasties.'

Caroline herself he found very graceful and dignified in her movements although she was now stout, thick and stumpy. She had great remains of beauty. 'Her mouth has a very peculiar expression of firmness and decision which, when it relaxes with a smile, is uncommonly pretty and playful. Her voice is very sweet. She speaks French with a very strong Italian accent.'

It was so long since Caroline had been in France.

Caroline invited him to come with her to the Colosseum,

'if he did not fear being seen in her carriage'. Lord Holland did fear it, apprehensive lest he be refused a passport for Naples, most persistent in its persecution of the unhappy Caroline. An English nobleman could not show the white feather abroad; in spite of his fears, he went with her.

> She speaks with much agitation of the persecution of the Allies towards her and said she almost regrets having come as now, when she is torn away from her mother, she must make up her mind never meeting her again on this side of the grave.
>
> However, her vanity is considerably flattered by the importance all the foreign courts seem to attach to her movements, and the persecuting distinction they shew her in contrast to the other members of the Bonaparte family.
>
> All ideas of being still an object of admiration to men she has not relinquished . . . she has much dignity and nothing repulsive in her manner or the least etiquettical.

While she was with Lord Holland Caroline received the information that she would be allowed to stay in Rome the next day but on the day following she *must* leave. 'She turned very pale, her voice quivered from agitation. "Very well, I will go when they come and throw me out. An insult more or an insult less won't cost them anything."'

It was ironic that the distasteful task of pursuing a woman who asked only to be left in peace should fall to the one man above all others who had such a sensitive appreciation of the anguish of exiles. The implementation of this heartless order, inspired by the vindictiveness of the Court of Naples, devolved on Comte Auguste de La Ferronays.

Blacas had been briefly succeeded in the Rome Embassy by Chateaubriand who, although now an ultra-royalist, never forgot that it was Elisa's intervention which secured his removal from the list of émigrés, nor that it was through Napoleon that he had been appointed to his first diplomatic post. He remembered his obligations and left the Bonapartes in peace, behaving to them all, particularly to Fesch, with great courtesy.

Chateaubriand was replaced by La Ferronays, a man of even stouter royalist principles, but which in him were allied to liberal and humanitarian ideas. Unlike Blacas, who was his brother-in-law, he was not embittered by his twenty-five years as an émigré; on the contrary his character had broadened and deepened in exile and he himself knew too well its humiliations and sorrows not to have pity for any exile, Bourbon or Bonaparte. It was this man, who had once queried his own future, asking:

> 'What will happen to us then, miserable creatures, expunged from the numbers of the living, without a country, without a home, rejected and cast out everywhere?'

who was forced to order Caroline Bonaparte from the bedside of her eighty-year-old mother. Perhaps he was relieved when, so shortly afterwards, the July Revolution terminated his embassy and with it the necessity for such distasteful action.

Madame Letizia's old bones were more solid that those of her children; she survived her accident for another six years, but Caroline never did see her mother again.

With the disappearance of the Bourbon régime there was an official change of heart towards the Bonapartes. Louis-Philippe, the new King of the French, stood greatly in need of popularity, which could be cheaply bought by making concessions to the strong Bonapartist feeling remaining in France.

At his persuasion the Neapolitans relented so far as to put no obstacles in the way of Caroline's returning to Italy, not to Rome or Naples, but to Florence where she settled in January, 1831, in a house which is now the Hôtel Excelsior in the Borgo Ognissanti on the Lung 'Arno.

It was thirty years since Caroline had lived in Florence when Achille was a baby; the city had kept kindly memories of her and gave her a warm welcome. After so many vicissitudes it seemed to Caroline that she had come home.

For six years she lived quietly at Florence, able at last to take possession of the villa at Viareggio left her by Pauline. In Florence now were her brothers, Louis and Jerome, but the quarrel with Jerome had never healed and carried on to the next generation.

Her niece, Mathilde de Montfort, clearly did not care for her aunt.

> It happened more than once that, when I met her in the Cascines, we had to turn back and look the other way, so that we need not greet her. I must say we did not feel very friendly towards her. She treated us without any consideration, and never failed to make some unkind remarks to us. She made fun of my clothes, which was humiliating for me. Sometimes she would say: 'Mathilde is growing too fat', or 'Napoleon has not grown an inch'. In short she was never nice to us.

On her friends Caroline made a different impression. Joseph Méry, the writer, spoke warmly of her hospitality. He was invited to visit her one day after hearing Catalani sing the litanies of the Virgin with her daughter, a superb contralto, in a village church near Florence.

> In her house no one asks the political opinions of the guests. On the threshold one says, 'I am French' and the doors open and one is given a cordial welcome. The whole universe is represented in the salon of the Comtesse de Lipona—kingdom, empire or republic does not matter; each state sends its ambassadors and courtiers to see Queen Caroline with no ulterior motive. There are no titles or offices to be sought from the Emperor's sister.

Méry's report is corroborated by Horatio Greenough, one of the earliest of American sculptors, who was travelling in Italy. Americans were particularly welcome in Caroline's house because her two sons were still in the United States. Both were married, Achille to Catherine Dudley, a great-niece of George Washington, Lucien to Carolina Fraser, who was an heiress. Achille obtained a high administrative position in the postal department of the United States, subsequently going to Florida where he owned a large plantation called Lipona. Lucien suffered reverses of fortune and, with his wife, was obliged to open an academy for young ladies. Neither returned to Italy during his mother's lifetime.

Greenough was very pleased with his reception.

> I was at Madame Murat's the other evening, and saw a fine bust of the King, her husband. She receives every evening in a way which I think agreeable. There are commonly four or five rooms open: in one are card tables; in another billiards; in a third tea is served throughout the evening. She has only the trouble of recognizing her friends as they enter, after which she leaves her maids of honor to entertain, and goes about looking on, or sits down to cards, or listens to music. It is very pleasant.

It was a slight exaggeration to speak of Caroline's maids of honour. By the time she reached Florence her household was reduced to a *dame de compagnie*, three servants and, of course, General Macdonald. But Greenough was quite correct that it was a pleasant house; Méry was full of enthusiasm.

> One goes to her house to see her, admire her, listen to her, and above all to be touched because never did any woman have more grace or seduction in what she said. . . . Sorrow and years have passed over her without the brilliant éclat of her youth being dimmed by the tears she has shed. If a stranger went for the first time into the salon filled with the most beautiful women in Florence he would not hesitate in picking out the one who today calls herself the Comtesse de Lipona.

In the salon where Murat's portrait hung, painted against a background of Vesuvius—two volcanoes, one extinct, the other dormant—the guests drank tea and ate biscuits, biscuits moulded with the arms of the Queen of Naples; the Comtesse de Lipona never forgot Queen Caroline. Early in the evening they listened to music which had become Caroline's passion; all the new music and the new singers were heard at the Palazzo Murat and Catalani was a frequent guest.

After the music was over—it was most often Bellini's music which was played and sung—towards midnight the guests sat talking, music scattered on the piano, cards on the whist tables, while Caroline led the conversation which went on until the small hours. With charming grace, part French, part Italian, she would say, 'Three hours of sleep are enough for me; it's a good habit I owe to my brother, the Emperor.'

Napoleon now loomed much larger in Caroline's consciousness and conversation, whether because as she grew older she returned in thought to the days of her youth or from opportunism, to enhance her own importance by stressing his.

When she read an impromptu poem which Méry wrote in her album Caroline said to him,

'I have two names of which I am proud; I am the sister of Napoleon and the wife of Murat. Write me an ode on these two names, "Bonaparte and Murat".'

Méry obediently produced an heroic piece of eighteen verses on the spot. As she read them Caroline wept, thinking perhaps of the first time she had heard those two names linked when Murat's messenger thundered on Madame Campan's door to announce:

'Bonaparte and Murat have saved France!'

In February, 1836, Madame Letizia died in Rome. With her died the clan Bonaparte. No one of them had sufficient authority to hold it together; it was now each for himself. Almost immediately this became manifest in trouble over her will. Caroline was dissatisfied with her share, making herself so unpleasant that she aroused the anger of Joseph, now returned from the United States and living in London.

At this late date Joseph could not re-assume the authority of an elder brother but, when Caroline was at last allowed to go to Paris, he wrote scathingly to his friend Menéval, in whose house she was staying, that he would not think of living in Paris with *permission*. He understood that his sister would do everything in her power to improve her children's lot, that her presence in Paris was dictated by her mother's heart, but it was less excusable in the Emperor's sister.

For a long time the Murats' faithful friend, the Comte de Mosbourg, had been working quietly on her behalf; it was through his good offices that the climate in the Chamber of Deputies, to which he had been elected as deputy for Cahors, had changed sufficiently to enable Caroline to come to Paris in September, 1836, to pursue in person her claims to her forfeited estates. Once Caroline had journeyed from Italy in royal state, received everywhere with honours. Now she travelled very modestly, to find a Paris changed almost beyond recognition from the city she had last seen in 1812.

The panoply and gorgeousness which had distinguished her brother's Imperial reign had vanished; Louis-Philippe walked through the Paris streets in simple, civilian dress, protected by his bourgeois umbrella. The court was a bourgeois court, lacking entirely the brilliant *mise en scène* of the Empire; the Parisians themselves jeered at the tailors, drapers and bootmakers who now frequented the Tuileries, scorned alike by the old aristocracy of the Faubourg St. Germain and the *noblesse de l'Empire*. The gilded youth, the new young exquisites, the Mussets, the Vignys, the Hugos, with their narrow shepherd's plaid trousers, frock coats and beaver hats could not rival the magnificence of the Flahauts, the Balincourts the Canouvilles, in their frogged and braided dolmans and pelisses, their tall shakos, colbacks and shapskas, their luxuriant feathers, aigrettes and horse-manes. The citizen-king ignored the Parisian's craving for pomp and display; a mousy respectability hung like a pall over Paris.

Although fast becoming unwieldy with fat, Mademoiselle George, once Napoleon's mistress, was still acting, not in the classic pieces so beloved of the Emperor but in the new romantic melodramas. At the Opera the names were all new; Rubini, Tamburini, Lablache and Grisi trilled their notes where once Grassini, Catalani and Crescentini sang. Fanny Elssler, whose name had been linked with Reichstadt's, dead now for four years, was the rage of Paris.

Unconsciously Caroline had chosen her moment well. Bonapartism was resurgent in France. Once again the Emperor looked out over Paris from his column in the Place Vendôme. Horace Vernet's great canvases of the battles of Jena, Friedland and Wagram were drawing the crowd; Béranger's poems were on everyone's lips, rekindling the Emperor's flame.

Il avait petit chapeau
Avec redingote grise . . .
Il vous a parlé, grand'mère !
Il vous a parlé !

Caroline trembled when her nephew, Louis-Napoleon, since his cousin's death heir to the Empire, thought this an opportune moment to attempt at Strasbourg to overset the régime; she feared with some justification that his precipitance might prejudice the authorities against her. The French government did, indeed, try to go back on its word, desiring her to leave France but, with her old determination, Caroline was set on staying to see her cause through to the end.

While waiting for her case to be debated in the Chamber—and the delays were prolonged—Caroline saw something of her old friends. Juliette Récamier had retired now to the Abbaye-aux-Bois, still with Chateaubriand in her train.

From Menéval's house Caroline moved to an apartment she rented in the Rue Ville l'Evêque, the street in which Pauline lived when she first came to Paris as a young woman, almost opposite the Elysée, but what worlds away the quiet little Comtesse de Lipona, unhappy and desperately poor, from the Grand Duchess of Cleves and Berg who, at the Elysée, had flaunted her love affair with Junot, Duc d'Abrantès. Did Caroline see Laure? The Restoration had dealt with her no more kindly than it had with the Bonapartes; her situation had gone from bad to worse. With the help of Balzac she wrote her memoirs, but receipts could never keep pace with debits; creditors and bailiffs mingled with her guests, still numbering some of the paladins of her heyday, Forbin, Balincourt, even at times Chateaubriand. Paris eagerly devoured her memoirs but, like her mentor, Balzac, Laure d'Abrantès could not write fast enough to keep pace with her expenditure.

When Caroline read the memoirs her daughter said that she wept at the unkind passages concerning her. It was so long ago that she and Junot had humiliated Laure that perhaps she had forgotten and was surprised that Laure should have nourished such enmity against her.

But Caroline was not in Paris to re-live the past; she was there to ensure her future and that of her children. In August, 1837, *The Times* reported that her claim was to be considered by the Chambers in the autumn, remarking that 'Madame Murat is very poor and she did not inherit from her mother as much as she expected'. Still the Chambers dallied, but Caroline was full of hope. To little Miss Davies she wrote:

My dear Davies,

It gave me great pleasure to receive your letter. The evidence of your affection and your remembrance touched me but I was sorry to learn that you are nearly always ill. I myself have been ill for a long time but my journey here has done me good. My stomach troubles are far less here than in Florence.

I hope to go to London next year and meet my sons and their families, whom I do not know. When we are there I shall write to you to come and see us. I often hear from them. They are well and so are my daughters. Laetizia has four superb children, Louise three, Lucien two and Achille none.

I was very pleased to see the lady who brought your letter and I asked her a lot of questions about you. I gave her a small package for you and I regret very much, knowing your position, that I cannot do anything else but it is absolutely impossible.

Au revoir, my dear Davies, until next year, if nothing prevents my carrying out my plan.

One sad duty Caroline performed during her stay. Her old friend and sister-in-law, Hortense de Beauharnais, died in Switzerland in the winter of 1837; her son obtained permission to bring her body back to Paris to be buried in the parish church of Malmaison at Rueil.

On a wintry morning in January, 1838, in the absence of Louis-Napoleon, who had sought refuge in America, Caroline Murat led the mourners at Hortense's funeral. She must have shivered with more than the cold because by now she knew the nature of the illness from which she had so long been suffering.

Valerie Masuyer, Hortense's faithful companion, thought her 'very well preserved, especially in the nobility of her bearing, but very much changed from what she was because of the stomach malady from which she is suffering, the same from which her brother died'.

Another death that year affected Caroline more nearly. During her stay in Paris General Macdonald died in Florence.

At last the law that was to accord Caroline not the restitution of her property but an income was considered by the Chamber of Deputies. It had been for many months on the agenda but came up for discussion only in June, 1838. The project did not have a smooth passage. There were angry scenes and scuffles in the Chamber; harsh words were spoken about Murat which deeply distressed Caroline and her daughters. Las Cases spoke up in Caroline's favour:

'The project before you is one of sentiment. There are times when a great nation should have bowels.'

Finally it was agreed by 213 for and 137 against that Caroline should receive a pension of 100,000 francs a year, but, 'This is an act of national munificence, not in favour of the widow of Murat, but of the sister of Napoleon.'

The Chamber made it quite clear that there was no recognition for the widow of the man who signed the treaty of 1814 with the Austrians.

When, at the end of June, 1838, the law was published officially Caroline returned to Florence, her mission accomplished; she had spent nearly two years in Paris, long enough to know that henceforward it held no place for her. Her friends were dying out—in that year alone Laure had died, in a room emptied by her creditors of all its furniture except the bed on which she lay, La Vauguyon, who had been Caroline's lover when she was Queen of Naples, and Bassano, once her brother's Minister of Foreign Affairs. Perhaps thankfully Caroline returned to Florence, to her home and to her children. Her twenty-years-long struggle to have her claims recognised had ended in her victory.

There was little else left to do; the task of clearing her husband's name must be left to others. During her stay in Paris she had talked much about the past to Mosbourg; when he once again retired to his high hill-top of Mercuès near Cahors Caroline wrote to him, for he held many of the papers which justified Murat's actions.

> Tell the whole truth. The truth alone can win lasting confidence. Happily for the man who will tell his story the character of the King is rich enough not to make it necessary to try and hide his faults. Like all passionate beings the King had his weaknesses, but, as you say, they were always weaknesses inspired by generous feelings.

Once again Caroline was waging a battle with her brother, only now it was a battle of the printed word. At St. Helena Napoleon seemed haunted by Murat; he returned to the subject again and again. Certainly he always praised his courage, his boldnesss, his supremacy as a cavalry leader but he was brainless, a buffoon in dress and manners. The pinpricks did not hurt; Caroline had heard them many times already, but there were graver charges which could not go unchallenged.

Murat was responsible for the disasters of 1814. Yet the

original fault was mine. I made several of them too great, raising them above their capacity.

A few days ago I read for the first time his proclamation when he dissociated himself from the Viceroy. It is difficult to conceive greater turpitude; he said that the time had come to choose between two standards, that of crime and that of virtue. It was my standard he called that of crime! And it was Murat, whom I made, my sister's husband, the man who owed me everything, who would have been nothing, who lived and is known only because of me, who wrote that! It would have been difficult to separate oneself from misfortune with greater brutality, to run more shamelessly after brighter opportunity. . . .

Murat was very courageous and very stupid. The great divergence between these two qualities explains the man. It would have been difficult, even impossible, to be braver than Murat and Lannes. Murat was never more than brave.

But Mosbourg was never able to write Murat's story; the papers in which it was told lay scattered about Europe. Perhaps 'the whole truth' is not yet known.

Only in Florence did Caroline realise the empty place left by Macdonald. Like Elisa and Pauline she could not live alone, but in the end they had both been supported by their husbands. Caroline fell into the hands of an adventurer named Clavel, who exploited the need for affection of an ageing woman, attacked by a mortal illness for affection.

'The hussy!' Napoleon had exclaimed when told of her supposed marriage to Macdonald. 'She has always been led by the nose in love!'

The *affaire Clavel* was only the spurt of dying embers before the fire went out.

On May 13th, 1839, Caroline Murat died. With her at the end were her brother Jerome, reconciled at last, and her daughter, Louise; Letizia was too ill in Bologna to be with her mother in her last moments. They did not have far to carry her coffin because she is buried in the church of Ognissanti, not much more than a stone's throw away from her last home.

Her death passed almost unnoticed, *The Times* kinder than the French papers, reporting on May 30th,

> The ex-Queen sank under the same disease as destroyed her brother, the Emperor Napoleon and their father, a cancer in the stomach. She was delirious with occasional lucid intervals. The absence of her sons in the United States is said to have greatly increased the bitterness of her last moments.

In Paris only *La Quotidienne* gave her a brief notice, far less space that was accorded to her uncle, Fesch, who had died five days before her.

> She had taken an active part in the administration confided to Murat and her regency at Naples was not without distinction. After the fall of the Empire she was able to keep many friends.

A meagre tribute and a final humiliation to a woman who had sought to be a leader of peoples.

Two years after Caroline's death Baciocchi died just before his eightieth birthday after a tranquil old age. He had survived Elisa by twenty-one years, living at Bologna in great state on the fortune her determination had wrested from the Austrians. His marriage into the Bonaparte family had served him better than Borghese's, who outlived Pauline by only seven years, in the end grown so fat that ' he looked as if he had been sewn into an eiderdown '.

Elisa's descendants were cut off by premature death and suicide but Caroline's children lived into normal old age. Her daughters were absorbed into the Italian aristocracy, her son, Achille, remained in the United States where he died at the ranch in Florida he called Lipona. Lucien Murat, her younger son, finally returned to France, where today his family alone represents the female branch of the Bonapartes.

AFTERMATH

Measured in miles the distance from Corsica to the mainland of Europe is not great, yet to Elisa, Pauline and Caroline Bonaparte the passage was that from one world to another, from the modesty of life at Ajaccio to the brilliance of the fairy-tale world their brother made of France, but a world which saw them as mechanical toys, to be wound up or left inert at Napoleon's will. When his motive force was removed they fell back into obscurity and are mainly remembered for their relationship to him. Only occasionally does some ray of light illuminate the darkness which now cloaks them.

It is on Pauline that the light shines most brightly as her legend and her beauty continue to fascinate, in death as they did in life. Men still linger beside her statue at the Villa Borghese in Rome to admire the perfection of her classic features, the languorous port of her head and the voluptuous beauty of her body. They may know little of her story but in cold marble she represents for ever the disturbing power of beauty in men's lives.

After the fall of the Empire there was little apparent change in Pauline's life; she continued the peripatetic existence which was now confined to Italy alone. In character she remained what she had always been, frivolous and *volage*, the only visible alterations those of fading beauty and the toll of perpetual illness. There was, however, a difference. In her years of decline Pauline's virtues stood out more boldly than in her years of prosperity. Through all she said and did, through all that was still meretricious in her life, ran the golden thread of her complete devotion to Napoleon, gleaming more brightly because any element of self-interest had now vanished.

Elisa, Pauline and Caroline were only fortuitously French; temperamentally and by ancestry they were Italian which was why, in the end, they felt themselves more at home in Italy.

Elisa's innate moral fibre was much stronger than that of her sisters and her strength of character had been reinforced by her education. During her years at St. Cyr she learned greater self-discipline as well as the devotion to the arts which was her ruling passion. She was, in her own way, as ambitious as Caroline, but her ambition was constructive, the will to create some lasting contribution to art and letters in the territories she ruled. Her tragedy was that little of her real achievement is credited to her.

Neither Pauline nor Caroline was to blame for the errors of her upbringing nor for the fact that lack of guiding principles led in Pauline's case to promiscuity and in Caroline's to nothing but the desire for self-aggrandizement.

Caroline's ambition was wholly subjective; her desire for power was for its own sake, not for the opportunities it offered for beneficent action. Her aim, as she had confided to Murat, was to keep the kingdom of Naples for themselves and to keep it within the French satellite system. There is no evidence that she shared Murat's Revolutionary ideas about the rights of man and of peoples. Because she allowed herself to be corroded by power Caroline's reputation now suffers from the stigma of treachery, harsh and not wholly justified though it may be.

Caroline's last act showed that the Comtesse de Lipona, so affable to all and sundry and not in the least 'etiquettical', wore a mask. Her will opened,

> I, Caroline, widow of King Joachim Murat, sister of the Emperor Napoleon, at present known by the title of Comtesse de Lipona . . .

Not Elisa, not Pauline, not Madame Letizia, not Napoleon himself in their wills had used so arrogant a preamble. To the last Caroline stood by her queenship but she, who had so greatly desired her independence, who had gone to such lengths to shake off her brother's mastery, could not in the end establish her place in posterity without acknowledging that she owed it to her relationship to the Emperor Napoleon.

It is by their sombre years of exile that the real merits of the Bonaparte sisters must be judged, although their opportunities for developing their gifts and talents were then circumscribed by restrictions and the constant surveillance of a malevolent police. Yet neither Elisa nor Caroline, who had both plumed themselves on their capacity, showed any inclination to be more than the private citizens into which they had dwindled.

At Trieste it might have been expected that Elisa, even within the narrow limits imposed on her activity, would have spent some of the time lying heavy on her hands in that dull city in promoting greater recognition of art and letters, but she was content with passivity. Too wounded, perhaps, by the indifference of her former Tuscan subjects to pursue these interests, or do more than give an example of classical stoicism, she preferred to remain arrogantly obscure since she could no longer dominate.

After the ignominy of 1815 Caroline's life was burdened with a young family to bring up and educate, and a constant struggle against poverty; in no other direction than seeking money did she expend the ferocious energy she once displayed. She believed that the story of her reign and Murat's should be told and their actions justified. She could have done this herself but she did not. Was Madame de Cavaignac's judgment of her correct? Was she in the last analysis no more than a pretty and charming woman who arrogated to herself more capacity than she, in fact, possessed?

It is interesting to speculate what Caroline's life would have been had Murat indeed joined her in Austria. Certainly the couple would have been even more suspect than Caroline alone, hedged about with even more galling restrictions, objects of even greater anxiety to the Powers. With him Caroline's life would have retained the electric quality and glamour it had lost. In losing him she lost the clash of personalities which provided the friction to generate much of her force. While she rated her capabilities above Murat's the greatest proof that she overestimated them is that, without him to kindle her flame, she attempted nothing of note by herself.

Together the three sisters had qualities which would have made one perfect woman—Elisa's strength of character and intelligence, Caroline's energy and force of will, Pauline's beauty and talent for affection. Perfection can be cold and lifeless. It is their human weaknesses which give their interest to Elisa, Pauline and Caroline Bonaparte.

St. Marylebone, 1963

BIBLIOGRAPHY

NOTE: Since it is impossible to list a lifetime's reading on Napoleon and his family, I note below those books which have been specially consulted.

Abrantès, Mémoires de la Duchesse d', Paris, Chez L'advocat, 1831–35

Alger, J. G., *Napoleon's British Visitors and Captives, 1801–1815*, Archibald Constable & Co., Ltd., 1904

Alméras, Henri d', *Une Amoureuse—Pauline Bonaparte*, Paris, Albin Michel

Archeografo Triestino, Trieste, Tipografia del Lloyd Triestino, 1924–28

Beaufond, Emmanuel de, *Elisa Bonaparte, Princesse de Lucques et de Piombino*, Paris, Au Journal de l'Univers, 1895

Bersanetti, Alda, *Donne Napoleoniche*, Bologna, Editore L. Cappelli, 1931

Bertaut, Jules, *Le Ménage Murat*, Paris, Le Livre Contemporain, 1958

Bertrand, Général, *Cahiers de Sainte-Hélène*, déchiffrés et annotés by Paul Fleuriot de Langle, Paris, Editions Albin Michel, 1949–59

Blangini, *Souvenirs de Félix*, pub. par Maxime de Villemarest, Paris, Charles Allardin, 1835

Boigne, Mémoires de la Comtesse de, Paris, Librairie Plon, 1907

Bonaparte, Joseph, *Lettres d'exil inédites*, publiées avec une introduction par Hector Fleischmann, Paris, Lib. Charpentier, 1912

Bonaparte, Joseph, *Mémoires du Roi Joseph et Correspondance Politique et Militaire*, ed. A. Du Casse, Paris, Perrotin, 1855

Bonaventura, Arnaldo, *I Bagni di Lucca, Coreglio e Barga*, Istituto Italiano d'Arti Grafiche, 1914

Borghezio, Gino, *I Borghese*, Roma, 1954

Bouchot, H., *La Toilette à la Cour de Napoléon*, Paris, A la Librairie Illustrée, 1895

Le Luxe Français, La Restauration, ibid., 1893

Bourrienne, M. de, *Memoirs of Napoleon Bonaparte*, Richard Bentley, 1836

Cavaignac, Madame de, *Les Mémoires d'une Inconnue*, Paris, Librairie Plon, 1894

Chantemesse, Robert, *Le Roman Inconnu de la Duchesse d'Abrantès*, Paris, Librairie Plon, 1927

Charles-Roux, F., *Rome Asile des Bonapartes*, Paris, Hachette, 1952

Corsini, Andrea, *I Bonaparte a Firenze*, Firenze, Leo, S. Olschki, 1961

Davies, Catherine, *Eleven Years' Residence in the Family of Murat, King of Naples*, London, How and Parsons, 1841

Davois, Gustave, *Les Bonaparte Littérateurs*, Paris, l'Edition Bibliographique, 1909

Dupont, Marcel, *Caroline Bonaparte, La Soeur Préférée de Napoléon*, Paris, Librairie, Hachette, 1937

Durand, Madame la Générale, *Napoleon and Marie-Louise, 1810–1814, A Memoir*, Sampson Low, 1886

Fleuriot de Langle, P., *Elisa, Soeur de Napoléon I*, Paris, Les Editions Denoël, 1947

La Paolina, Soeur de Napoléon, Paris, Editions Colbert, 1946

Fouché, Les Mémoires de, Introduction et Notes de Louis Madelin, Paris, Flammarion, 1945

Foville, Jean de, *Pise et Lucques*, Paris, Librairie Renouard, H. Laurens, 1914

Fox, Henry, Journal of the Hon., (*afterwards Lord Holland*), edited by the Earl of Ilchester, Thornton Butterworth, 1923

Garros, Louis: *Quel Roman que Ma Vie, Itinéraire de Napoléon Bonaparte, 1769–1821*, Paris, Les Editions de l'Encyclopédie Francaise 1947

Goldsmith, Lewis, *The Secret History of the Cabinet of Bonaparte*, J. M. Richardson & J. Hatchard, 1810

Greatheed, Bertie, *An Englishman in Paris, 1803*, ed. J. P. T. Bury & J. C. Barry, Geoffrey Bles, 1953

Greenough, *Letters of Horatio Greenough to his brother Henry Greenough*, Boston, Ticknor & Company, 1887

Guedalla, Philip, *Napoleon and Palestine*, George Allen and Unwin, 1925

Guerrini, Teresa Luzzato, *Paolina*, Firenze, Casa Editrice 'Nemi', 1932

Iung, Th., *Lucien Bonaparte et ses Mémoires*, Paris, G. Charpentier, 1882

Journal des Débats, 1800, 1837
Kühn, Joachim, *Pauline Bonaparte*, Paris, Librairie Plon, 1937
Lacour-Gayet, G., *Les Merveilles de l'Epopée Napoléonienne*, Paris, Hachette, 1921
Lamartine, A. de, *Souvenirs et Portraits*, Paris, Hachette et Cie, 1872
La Quotidienne, 1836, 1837
Las Cases, Comte de, *Mémorial de Sainte-Hélène*, Paris, Garnier Frères
Lavallée, Théophile, *Histoire de la Maison Royale de St. Cyr*, Paris, Furne et Cie, 1856
Lazzareschi, Eugenio, *Lucca*, *Bergamo*, Istituto Italiano d'Arti Grafiche 1931
Leclerc, *Lettres du Général*, publiées avec une Introduction par Paul Roussier, Paris, Librairie Ernest Leroux, 1937
Lucas-Dubreton, J., *Le Culte de Napoléon*, Paris, Editions Albin Michel, 1960
Lumbroso, Alberto *Napoleone*, *La sua Corte e la sua Famiglia*, P. de Fornari et C., 1935
Marmottan, Paul, *Les Arts en Toscane sous Napoléon*, *La Princesse Elisa*, *etc.*
Elisa Bonaparte, Paris, Honoré Champion, 1898
Madame de Genlis et la Grande Duchesse Elisa, *1811–13*, Lettres inédites, suivies de l'ouvrage sur les Mœurs de l'Ancienne Cour
Lettres de Madame de Laplace à Elisa Napoléon, *Princesse de Lucques et de Piombino*, Paris, A. Charles, 1897
Masson, Frédéric, *Napoléon et sa Famille* (13 volumes), Paris, Librairie Paul Ollendorff, 1897–1918
Les Quadrilles à la Cour de Napoléon, Paris, H. Daragon, 1904
Masuyer, *Mémoires*, *Lettres et Papiers de Valérie*, Paris, Librairie Plon, 1937
Mathilde, *Mémoires de la Princesse*, edités par le Comte J. Primoli, Souvenirs des Années d'Exil, *Revue des Deux Mondes*, December, 1927, January, 1928
Melegari, D., *Une Reine en Exil*, Paris, *Le Correspondant*, December, 1898
Méry Joseph, *Les Nuits Italiennes*, Paris, Michel Lévy Frères, 1868
Misciatelli, Piero, *Lettere di Letizia Buonaparte*, Milan, Ulrico Hoepli Editore, 1936
Monvel, Roger Boutet de, *Les Anglais à Paris 1800–1850*, Paris, Librairie Plon, 1911

Murat, Lettres et documents pour servir à l'histoire de, publiés par le Prince Murat, Paris, Librairie Plon, 1908–14 (8 volumes)
Murat, La Princesse Louise, Comtesse Rasponi, *Souvenirs d'Enfance d'une fille de Joachim Murat*, publiés par son arriére-petit-fils le Comte Jean-Baptiste Spalletti, Paris, Librairie Perrin, 1929
Murat, Correspondance de Joachim, edited by Albert Lumbroso, Turin, Roux, Frascati et Co., 1899
Letters from Joachim Murat to his daughter, Letizia, 1893
Nabonne, Bernard, *Pauline Bonaparte*, Librairie Hachette, 1948
Nicolson, Harold, *The Congress of Vienna*, Methuen, University Paperbacks, 1961
Noel-Williams, H., *The Women Bonapartes*, Methuen & Co., 1908
Parlange, H., ' Une " Grande Malade " : Pauline Bonaparte, Princesse Borghese,' *Aesculape*, 1938
Plitek, V., *I Napoleonidi a Trieste : Caroline Murat, Contessa di Lipona 6 giugno-15 agosto 1815, Archeografo Triestino* ser. 3, Vol. 13, 1924
Plumptre, Anne, *A Narrative of a Three Years Residence in France from the Year 1802–05*, London, 1810
Potocka, Countess Anna, *Voyage d'Italie 1826–27*, Paris, Librairie Plon, 1899
Mémoires de la Comtesse Potocka, Paris, Librairie Plon, 1897
Raguse, Mémoires du Duc de, Maréchal Marmont, Paris, Perrotin, 1857
Récamier, Souvenirs et Correspondance de Madame, Paris, Michel Lévy Frères, 1859
Revolutionary Plutarch, The, John Murray, 1805, 3 volumes
Rodocanachi, E., *Elisa Napoléon en Italie*, Paris, Ernest Flammarion, 1900
Sancholle-Henraux, *Le Chevalier Angiolini Correspondance*, Paris, 1913
Ségur, Comte de, *La Campagne de Russie*, Paris, Nelson
Stenger, G., *La Société française pendant le Consulat*, Paris, Perrin et Cie, 1905
Stirling, Monica, *A Pride of Lions*, Collins, 1961
Talma, *Lettres d'Amour Inédites de Talma à la Princesse Pauline Bonaparte*, Fleischmann et Pierre Bart, Paris, Librairie Charpentier et Fasquelle, 1911
Trotter, John Bernard, *Memoirs of the latter Years of Charles James Fox*, Richard Phillips, 1811

Turquan, Joseph, translated by W. R. H. Trowbridge, *The Sisters of Napoleon, Elisa, Pauline and Caroline Bonaparte*, T. Fisher Unwin, 1908

Vandal, Albert, *Le Roi et la Reine de Naples*, 1808–12, *Revue des Deux Mondes*, Paris, February, March, 1910

Vialles, Pierre, *L'Archichancelier Cambacérès*, Paris, Perrin et Cie, 1908

Vitrac, Maurice, *Journal du Comte P-L. Roederer*, Paris, H. Daragon, 1909

Weil, Commandant, *Les Dessous du Congrès de Vienne*, Payot, 1917 (2 volumes)

Yorke, Henry Redhead, *France in 1802*, William Heinemann, 1906

INDEX